Secrets Of The Untold Spirits

Secrets Of The Untold Spirits

Part One
The Soul Seeker

CHRISTOPHER J. CALHOUN

To order additional copies of this book, contact:
Xlibris Corporation
1-888-795-4274
include: www.christophercalhoun.com
www.Xlibris.com
Orders@Xlibris.com
77533

CONTENTS

To my mother ChaJuana L. Hannah, her mother Mary E. Anderson, her mother Lula Bell Wilson, and her late mother Mary Ella Tucker. Thank you for the love upon your hearts.

And the Lord God formed man *of* the dust of the ground, and breathed into his nostrils the breath of life; and man became a living soul. (Genesis 2:7)

ACKNOWLEDGMENTS

To Jesus Christ and God the Father, my Savior.

Ms. Cynthia Simone, eighth-grade English teacher, who understands the meaning of a true spirit.

Coach William Stephens, great coach, truly talented mind.

My Pastor Dr. William S. Winston, and his wife Dr. Veronica Winston. They are an inspiration to Me.

To Mrs. Theresa Byrd-Smith, Principal of Living Word Christian Academy. Thank you for all of your support.

And to all who made this dream become real.

Prologue

Before you start reading, there is something I ought to tell you: You are going to die. One day, you *will* die. I hate to tell you something so unpleasing like that, but the truth is—the truth. You're probably wondering who I am. I'm sorry to tell you this, but I cannot tell you who I really am. You will have to guess that throughout the story. Enough about me. What you are about to read is a story so controversial, so keening, you may want to turn off every distraction or diversion around you. Clear your mind. Catch a glimpse of immorality. Here's the first question I pose to you: Have you ever had a place of your own? A place where you could relax. A place where you could call your own. Everyone has one, believe it or not. If that includes the playground down the street, the backyard where the little playhouse was, a cardboard box in the basement, or just your room, that was the specific place you called your own. That place was filled with happy and sad thoughts. That place is or was your own life. You'd be crushed to see that place of your own leave or disappear. That place holds memories of your lifetime; secrets of your own. Never doubt anyone or anything; you could be the "doubted." If you've never had a place of your own, or if you cannot recall that place (whatever or where it may be), then that place of your own is hidden inside of you. You may not know it yet, but once you start reading all of these things: the good, the bad, and even the ugly, will come out of you, and everything will be fresh again. If you have a place you call home, try to bring memories of it. Never forget who you are in this world. The next question I would like to ask is have you ever had something or someone in your life that you know you couldn't live without? (And don't say your parents!). It could be your teddy bear you'd talk to when you were little. It could be that journal you found yourself writing in every single day. It may even be a pet, a necklace, or your friend's special bracelet. We all need a foundation in our life sometimes. It tells us the tales of what we know, what we don't know, and how we as people could improve society. Let me reassure you, if you are saying yes to all of the questions I am asking you, you will gain knowledge. If you are saying no, you will gain more knowledge, because the principle of the situation is limitless, and you will HAVE to take in more knowledge (which is a very good thing). I'm asking these questions so that you can get familiarized with not only the story, but with me as well. You've probably figured it out by now, but I am a tough person to comprehend. The last question I would like to ask is what is your identity? What that means is who are you as a person? I bet most of you reading this went to go frantically search for your social security number.

Others are probably wondering who I am before they tell me who they are. And that's okay! Once you start reading, you will get used to understanding who you are and what the Lord has in store for you. Don't take this as a punishment. The point of this is to get away from the world's system. To tackle the system of your own. The world cannot define identity. Why can't they do that? Because everyone's identity is different from each other's. If it wasn't, everyone would be exactly the same. Having good character about yourself is looking in the mirror every day and saying, "I'm going to be something great today." Some people don't believe it, nor do they want to try it out because they've lost their job, or they can't pay bills, or they can't have a happy family, or they don't have enough to plan a funeral, or they are oblivious to the obvious (which means they won't look at the cards that are being dealt to them). Usually, all of that stuff is in the past. If bad news happened to you a decade ago, a year ago, or a second ago, you have to know that it was the past and try to move on. You could move on easily if you have good character. For those of you who do not keep reading, and believing for the best, I am certain that your life will never be the same again. Our story takes place in the present day, as a girl who never had hope takes on the world. Try to see if she answers those three questions I had you answer. It may be throughout the story, it may not be. She is finding love in a new way, like most of us are. If you are still guessing who I am, I'd stop guessing by now. What I want you to do is take a glimpse of your past and future, think to yourself, and testify. You will probably be happy to know that you will not see me throughout the story, or maybe you will not see me at all. I just want you to know that I'm everywhere, and I'm nowhere. Now clear your mind, take a deep breath, and more importantly, have some fun! What I want you to do now is to turn to the next page.

<<<IMAGE>>>

CHAPTER 1

A Dreadful Yet Dreamful Dream

So there, there lies the place where everything is heaven. Well, not heaven, but you might as well say that it was Heaven. Flowers roamed throughout the area. The birds were singing, and you can see the sun brighter than ever. This truly was called paradise. It was just gorgeous. The trees rose high and tall, and nature blossomed here. Mother Nature was in her spring outfit, and the outfit was beautiful than all of the outfits in the land. A glorious waterfall just dazzled this Paradise City, as the glimmering waters opened up the city. Whoosh! Whoosh! Whoosh! That is the sound of the waters that the waterfall would make. A cool breeze cooled the warm waters, which made the sound of the waterfall even more majestic. It appears as if the sun was just rising above the city. Bunnies were watering their flowers in their garden. (This place is not reality; it is a place of its own kind. Reality is no match for a place like this). Bunnies were also heard mowing their lawns, trimming their hedges, and creating magic from this beloved place. But the real story is this: Ginger McFraidee. Ginger McFraidee is an average teenage girl. Her blond hair bristled through the land, as she gracefully hopped through the grass of this land, her pink dress following her. Her blue eyes were shining in the midst of dawn. Her purple glittered shoes were dazzling, making the grass flow along with her. The cool and calm breeze was making her hair wave in the center of the city. The birds were singing even more then ever. The bunnies were staring at her, wondering why she was so happy. Even though it's impossible to not be sad, the bunnies were a little puzzled. Dorothy Gale has arrived in the Land of Munchkins. They are not munchkins; they are cute little bunnies that roamed the land of paradise. The bunnies were wondering: What could she be doing here? They have never seen her here. As she wandered through the blissful grass, they wondered if *she* herself was Mother Nature! Mother Nature would be wearing a yellow and white dress, and the flowers would be rising, waiting for summer to come, so Mother Nature can change into a new and improved dress, a cool and summer blue one, with many flowers painted on it. Ginger was wearing an elegant pink dress, one that matched the flowers and the bunnies' ears. She skipped through the grass, her purple glittering shoes sparkling, causing a bright yellow glow. The bunnies knew that she WAS Mother Nature. But she wasn't. The power of this paradise land gleamed on her. A chorus of bunnies (children bunnies) was singing as the sun started to beam on the land. All you can hear was beautiful and domestic singing (from the birds and the children bunnies).

"La-la-la! La-la-la-la! La-la-la-la-la!" This is what Ginger could only hear. All of a sudden, Ginger stopped hopping and skipping. She just seemed to be lost in this world when she really wasn't. All of the mother bunnies watering the plants and the male bunnies mowing the lawn or trimming the hedges just stopped and stared at her. All of the attention was on Ginger. Ginger seemed to not notice anything at all. She just stood plain and tall. The only noise was coming from the waterfall. It was most beautiful, because the sun was raying at the gorgeous waterfall. The light was shining on the water, which was a great view of nature at its own work. So there Ginger was, standing in front of the sun. It was morning now. The lawn mowers were rumbling the grass, and the water sprinkles were on, as bunnies watered their plants and their grass. A large yellow glow was right in front of Ginger, waiting for her presence. A few seconds later, a chubby bunny with glasses on and some sort of equipment in his hands appeared beside her. The bunny was much clumsy. The equipment he was holding fell out of his hands, and he was rambling to pick up the equipment. "Oh dear! Oh dear! Oh dear!" the bunny said, scrambling to get everything. Ginger just chuckled. "That's okay, Mr. Chippers. I'm just glad we can have tea time now. I have been awaiting this moment," Ginger responded to him. They were having a tea party. Seems fun and and much sophisticated. To Ginger, anyway. Ginger helped Mr. Chippers set up the table, which was the size of people playing a good game of cards, or even a game of poker. Ginger gathered the teapot and some saucers. The pot was filled with tea. "Good thing the tea didn't spill!" Ginger teased him. Mr.

Chippers set up the chairs and the saucers (which were decorated with pink flowers on it) for four people. Who were the other two bunnies and or people? Ginger had a good clue of who it was, or who they could be. Ginger and Mr. Chippers took their seats on the marble chairs. "So, Ginger, how have you been?" Mr. Chippers said, pouring a cup of tea for both him and Ginger. "It's been fine, I guess. Pappy slipped and fell on his booty yesterday while attempting to fill the bathtub with soap and water," Ginger responded, as both Ginger and Mr. Chippers laughed. "Your family is funny, Ginger. Very funny indeed."

"Oh thank you so much," Ginger replied, taking a sip of the hot tea. Mr. Chippers cooled the tea with his mouth, and drank or sipped. "So how is Miss Lanely Tildon doing?" Mr. Chippers asked. "She is doing well. I sometimes worry about her. She seems so swell and exasperated. Something must be on her mind. Her antique shop is going well, I must say. Many of the gifts have been sold. She just hasn't been the same since her mother disappeared and moved to England. I try to call her and visit her as much as I can." Ginger sighed a little, for once a dust of sadness paved through her veins. "Aww, it's okay, Ginger. As long as things are getting better," Mr. Chippers said, pouring himself some more tea. "So, how have you been?" Ginger asked, moving her long yellow hair away from her eyes. "Pretty good, I must admit. My sister is a very good singer and is working on an album that will be number one on the charts. But me myself am doing fine. My elegant suit at home makes me the star at my job," Mr. Chippers boasted. "That's great, and the best of luck to your sister," Ginger told him, giving him a small smile. "Oh I almost forgot!" Mr. Chippers was rumbling through some bags, searching for an item. "Oh here we are! One-of-a-kind crackers!" he said, getting the crackers and setting them down on the table. Ginger tried one, and boy, were they delicious! Mr. Chippers nibbled on a cracker or two, and then pushed his glasses up to his face. His chippy teeth made some small noises as he ate the crackers. Ginger sighed, just to remember the benefits of her life. Mr. Chippers seemed to be engorged in the tea. This was his fourth cup, and Ginger was only on the middle of her second cup. Other bunnies didn't too much care about the tea party, or about "Mother Nature." It was nearly afternoon already (or as it seemed). The sun was gleaming in on them two, and the empty chairs, as the water's sparkles were seen more clearly. More bunnies were out at this time. Bunnies with flowers on their hats were carrying baskets and collecting some flowers to give to others. Many others were surrounding to set up a picnic to enjoy this wonderful day in paradise land. "This day is oh so lovely!" Ginger said joyfully, as if she were a girl in the 1930s. "I must say it is. The birds are still singing, and we are enjoying this peaceful day," Mr. Chippers agreed. "Time for the sandwiches! Pastrami with turkey meat on a panini rye bread. Yum!" Mr. Chippers said, grabbing a plateful of sandwiches from the bag. They were sealed in a plastic wrap. Ginger helped Mr. Chippers unwrap the sandwiches. The sandwiches triggered an aroma that was very tasty. Ginger and Mr. Chippers chewed on the sandwiches. Ginger was most hungry from the crackers, and from the tea. "Thank you for inviting me here today for this wonderful tea party!" Ginger told Mr. Chippers. "Anytime, Ginger. I'm just glad we caught up with things. It seems like forever since I've seen you," he responded, eating another cracker after he gobbled down a sandwich. Ginger gazed around the area. She could see many bunnies still picking flowers and watering the grass. Everywhere she looked, the bunnies were skipping, like she was doing before the tea party began. She saw many of them smile, and they were all happy. It was their happiness that made her feel sad. Over and over she would think of her late parents, and how much fun they would have together. Mr. Chippers saw a teardrop in Ginger's eye. The tear sparkled as it trickled down her face. "Mr. Chippers, do you ever feel like there is something or someone missing in your life, and you can't get it back?" Ginger asked, sneezing a little. "Well, a little. It's just I have to tell myself to move on, and that every day is a special day, and I have to cherish that," Mr. Chippers told her. "But what if it was something or someone really special that has impacted your life? The people to show you and to lead you through life. The people to tell you what life really means!!" Ginger expressed herself. Mr. Chippers handed her a handkerchief to clean her pale face. "Is this about your parents?" Mr. Chippers asked her. "Yes, Mr. Chippers. And now I will never see them again. When they left, they took my soul away." Ginger said, wiping tears off her face. "I feel like I'm an outsider, sometimes. No one wants to listen to me. No one even cares. Not even my own grandparents." "I care about you, Ginger," Mr. Chippers told her, trying to make her feel happy in this land of goodness. "Life is hard. Life is tough.

But we have to look at the positive side of things. You're a great girl Ginger, and you may be sad, but happiness is in the wisdom of your sadness." Mr. Chippers gulped down some more tea. "Thank you, Mr. Chippers. I do have some good friends and a great home," Ginger replied, chewing on leftover bits of crackers. Just when Ginger had dried up her tears, a chorus of small little children bunnies passed by, as they danced and sang. Light was literally visible through the roaring waters of the fall. The sun was at its brightest in this land. The bunnies were celebrating. Mr. Chippers pecked at two of them, and the two small bunnies (brown and fluffy), no taller than a bush, approached him. "Yes, sir?" the bunny with the ribbon on its head asked. Mr. Chippers cleared his throat. "Please braid this young lady's golden hair. I'm sure she'd much appreciate it." "Okay!" the bunny with no ribbon responded, as both of the bunnies started to twirl Ginger's golden hair. Ginger was in her own place right now. She considered herself an outsider, because she cannot understand the world quite clearly. You might as well call her a fool. She can relate to the world, she has friends and is popular, but she just doesn't understand her life. This is only because no one can take the time to teach her this. Only her parents could. Although she may consider herself this way, the world accepts her for who she is. Everyone can see her soul, but she can't; which is peculiar because she is the source of her soul! The bunnies were la-la ing as they braided Ginger's hair. Mr. Chippers, Ginger, and the bunnies talked and had a delectable good time. When the bunnies were done with her hair, they showed her a mirror, and did her hair ever look so beautiful! She was very amazed at how well the bunnies did, and stunned at her own two braids. "Thank you so much!" Ginger told them. "You're welcome!" the bunnies replied, as they strutted into the wonderful world of paradise and nature. "Mr. Chippers, you didn't have to do this," Ginger told him. "I wanted to. I only wanted to make you happy, and to make your hair look most delightful," Mr. Chippers told her, gulping down another sandwich, as if he hadn't eaten enough already. This made Ginger smile; the first time since they started the tea party. "I wish I could see my parents just one more time," Ginger cried. Mr. Chippers had a curious look on his face. "Hmm," he pondered. It took him a while. "So can you, Mr. Chippers? Can I see my parents for one last time?" Ginger asked him. "Yes! I can bring them back by magic! That's what I will do!" Mr. Chippers finally came to a conclusion. Anything is possible in this paradise land, although some things will seem impossible or just plain weird. Mr. Chippers stood up, standing away from the table, the tea, and the food. "Oh the Great and Wise from the Book that has been Read, bring forth Ginger McFraiddee's parents from the dead!" Mr. Chippers performed a spell. Ginger was amazed, and she stood up. Within seconds, a huge yellow glow awoke the entire land. Soon, the glow had stopped. There, stood a middle-aged man and woman who were next to each other. The woman had brown hair, which was in a ponytail. The man had wavy black hair with glasses. They were Ginger's parents. "Oh my goodness! Mom! Dad! I missed you so much!" Ginger screamed. Her parents were real. It was as if they had never left the earth. "Ginger!" both of them yelled in unison. They all sprinted toward each other. Ginger gave her parents a great big hug. "Ginger, it is so glad to see you again!" her mother told her daughter. "We love you so much, and we oh so miss you very much!" her father cried. "I'm glad to see you too! Gosh, it has been so long!" Ginger replied, as they were still hugging like one big family. "Oh, I just miss the hot chocolate and the Christmas dinners and especially Grammy and Pappy!" her father mentioned. Ginger and her mother couldn't stop hugging each other. They were continuing the love that had stopped between them (physically anyway). "Wow! Such wonders of this place!" her mother commented. Ginger gave her father another big hug, for she hadn't seen him longer than her mother. "I must say so myself, this place is filled with wonders and dreams!" Mr. Chippers cried. Ginger's parents were astonished. "Did that bunny just talk?" her father asked, a little puzzled. "Yes. This place is where literally anything can happen," Ginger explained. After Ginger's parents took a look at the glorious world of Nature around them, the four of them sat down where Mr. Chippers and Ginger were having tea. "Help yourself to some tea and other goodies," Mr. Chippers told them. "Thank you," they responded, as Mr. Chippers poured some tea into the empty two saucers (before, it was set up for four people for tea). While her parents were admiring the place they were in and eating cookies and sandwiches, Ginger was most happy of all. She was glad to be reunited with her parents, whom she hadn't seen in years. She was also glad to know that she would be going home with her parents for the very first time in years. "So, Mother and Father, we have so much stuff to catch up on!" Ginger told them. "We certainly do. How have your volleyball skills been coming, sweetheart?" Ginger's mother asked her. Ginger's mother played volleyball, track, soccer, and some other sports that she herself taught her own daughter. "Pretty good, if I say so myself. My running speed is getting a lot better, now. In fact I can run two miles in about or under ten minutes," Ginger responded. "That's good. I would love to see Grammy and Pappy, again. It was fun when we would play card games and Pappy would complain that he would lose, and that your uncle would cheat," her father laughed, as Ginger and her mother chuckled, agreeing with him. "Those were the days. In fact, I think I still remember how to cook Grammy's famous Hungarian stew! Yummy!" Ginger's mother said. Ginger can indeed taste the stew herself. It would be nice and hot and cooked to perfection. Grammy is indeed a good cook (from what her parents, her husband, her son, and her granddaughter). The stew she would cook is just mouthwatering, and Ginger would be in love with the stew. It was food for her pure soul. The sound of the waterfall roared louder. The sun was lowering and would soon disappear into the clouds. Children bunnies were out at this time. Most were near the waterfall, getting soaked by the waters, or drinking some to avoid dehydration. Many farmers and gardeners were outside, picking their flowers and enjoying the wonderful day. It has been a wonderful day for Ginger. Although she felt some pain in her heart earlier, she is glad that it is all gone. She can now start a life with her parents in this magnificent place she calls home. She can live life to the fullest. Here, she won't have to worry about being whom she thinks of herself as an "outsider," when only she herself thinks this. This struck her very mind because she could understand and comprehend her mind, but it seems she hasn't the confidence nor the diligence to see her own soul in a better way than she does. "Mother, thank you for this wonderful locket you have given me," Ginger told her. On her neck was a golden heart that looked like a necklace. Ginger will never put it in an unsafe place, as the locket tells stories from the past; stories that may have not been uncovered yet. It shares secrets as well. Ginger doesn't know this, and maybe it is just her destiny that will allow her to see better things. "You're very welcome, Ginger," her mother responded, taking a sip of tea. "In fact, Ginger, that locket was worn by your great-great-great grandfather who lived in Poland and was born from Poland. It is very delicate to the family," her father explained. "Yes, and we value that and our family treasures so much," her mother agreed. Family values. What did her mother mean by family values? Were there other secrets that were hidden and unknown to Ginger? That is what Ginger wanted to find out for herself, but she wanted to act as if she was a spy. "I can tell you that I just adore this great day, and the good time we're having," Mr. Chippers said. It seems as if he was silent the entire time. Well, Ginger couldn't blame him. After all, he figured she wanted to communicate with her parents, whom she thought she'd never see again. "I am glad too, Mr. Chippers, and if I must agree, this tea party was ever so delightful," Ginger replied. Ginger's parents nodded in agreement. Ginger was already planning out her future life with her parents. Her father can bake cookies with her, which they use to do all the time together. Ginger and her mother can learn more sports and just do more activities they couldn't do before. They could sew more (even though it sounds boring), read a little more often (her mother just treasured books), and do more things together as a big happy family. Ginger just wants to see enchantment come upon her life once more. She can already feel the magic within her spirit. "Oh, we're going to have tremendous fun like we used to have!" Ginger was excited all over again. "It sure will. I think we should all go to Australia for a family vacation!" her father suggested. "In due time," her mother reminded him. Most of the food was gone, and there were few amounts of tea left. Their tea party was starting to come to an end. "I was feeling so detrimental without you two in my life. Now, we can live a happy life together! We can live here in this wonderful, wonderful place!" Ginger shouted out loud. "Yes. We can even have our weekly ice cream social and our family game night!" her father cried. Just thinking about all of this made Ginger want to cheer and dance and have a good ole time with her folks like before. "Oh, yes! Oh, Ginger, how I missed you so much!" her mother told her, as them three hugged. Mr. Chippers put all of the equipment, saucers, plates, and food away. "I will be going, now. Your new home is two blocks north from here. You won't miss it! Bye-bye!" Mr. Chippers told her. "Bye, Mr. Chippers! Thank you very much!" Ginger waved. Her parents waved as well as Mr. Chippers teleported away with the equipment, table, and chairs that were set up. "Well, what are we waiting for?!" Ginger's father said, "Our house is waiting for us! We can be together again!" "Yes! On we go to our new home!" her mother was excited. They were running north right to where the home would be. When they arrived to their new home, they were amazed. "I'm finally home!" Ginger announced. "Ginger, Ginger, Ginger, Ginger, Ginger," her mother kept saying. "Yes?" she asked. "Ginger, Ginger, Ginger, Ginger, Ginger, Ginger." Ginger was having a dream.

Chapter 2

The Enchantment: Part 1—Identity

It was Ginger's grandmother who tried to awake her. "Ginger, Ginger, Ginger, Ginger," her grandmother kept saying. Ginger nonchalantly yawned in her bed and stretched. Her blond hair was all over the place, and she smelled like a pig covered in murky mud. "Yes, Grammy?" Ginger asked, still yawning from here and there. Her grandmother sat on the edge of the bed. She was starting to wake up, and she could see her grandmother in a white flowered dress. Grammy has a noisily voice (the one most grandmothers do), and she usually never takes her brown apron off in the house. Her curly gray hair was seen from Ginger's eyes, and she could also see that Grammy didn't clean her glasses. Grammy's glasses were bigger than her own eyes (you can call them reading glasses, because that is what they look like). "Ginger, it's Saturday morning, and you know what that means, right?" Grammy told her. "Oh yes, oh yes, oh yes! Today we get to see Madame Lanely

Tildon! Oh my gosh, I completely forgot today was Saturday!" "I hear she has some new antiques that were shipped in a couple of days ago. I must see what they are!" Grammy cried. "I will be ready soon," Ginger said, happily jumping out of her bed and starting to fix her bed. "Okay, I will be waiting downstairs," Grammy responded, walking out of the room and closing the door behind her. After Ginger fixed her bed, she went to the bathroom, took a shower, and got dressed. Her blonde hair and blue eyes were sparkling in the window now. Every Saturday morning, Ginger and her grandmother go to an antique store owned by Madame Lanely Tildon. Sometimes her grandfather and uncle join and go to the antique shop themselves. It is extremely rare when her grandfather (Pappy) and her uncle go to the antique store. Lanely Tildon has known her late mother for over fifteen years. They were very good friends, and Ginger's mother would buy all kinds of antiques from there, including a genuine diary that her mother bought for Ginger when she was just a baby. Ginger always wears the locket, for it symbolizes all of her mother's destinies and characterizes her creditability. The locket traces back to her ancestors. Ginger put on her locket, darted on her shoes, and quickly trotted down the stairs. She went to the kitchen, and there she spotted Pappy and her uncle. Pappy is a very old man. He is a veteran of the Vietnam War, and served in the U.S. Navy soon after. Like Grammy, Pappy had gray hair, and he too has a raspy voice, similar to a normal grandparent's voice. Although he is old, he has many Medicare, medical bills, and pensions. He's still strong and mighty, and that's the best part Ginger loves about her grandfather. Ginger's uncle is a middle-aged man that is still in good shape. He has brown hair and is a little taller then Grammy. Ginger's uncle has the same traits Pappy has himself, but one thing separates the two: her uncle understands Ginger's broken soul. Ginger's uncle is her mother's brother. Shortly after her mother's death, Ginger had to move in with her grandparents. Knowing the sacrifices of Ginger's old home, and now having both her parents dead really had an impact on the family. Her uncle then decided to move in with his mother and father to not only take care of them, but to also help Ginger in her time of need and to take care of her too. He can relate to the problems Ginger is facing and can try to give her loving and kind support. He knows how hard it must be for her to pick up her own two feet when her parents both died when Ginger was still very young and really knew no better. Ginger is glad that she can talk to her uncle about the problems she faces in regular life. Ginger heard the television on in her grandparents' room when she went in the kitchen. Pappy and Uncle were sitting at the table, having some morning coffee her Grammy made. They were also eating toast, and Pappy was reading the morning paper. "Morning!" Ginger announced, grabbing some jam toast from the napkin on the stove. "Good morning, Ginger!" her uncle and Pappy replied. While Pappy took a bite of his toast and slowly drank some coffee, his fist hit the table, splashing some of the coffee inside of the mug. "Gosh! Gas prices have went up yet again!" he complained in his angry, raspy voice. Pappy's voice is deep, but from some complications and old age, his voice sounds wretched and creaked from time to time. "How do they think we can live if prices keep going up? Everyone would soon be dead!" Pappy's voice was rising. "Calm down, Pappy, you don't want your medications to wear off," Uncle responded. "So, Uncle, how's work and stuff coming along?" Ginger asked. "It's coming along great, Ginger. I will ask for a raise," he replied, as he, Pappy, and even Ginger gave a small chuckle. "Good, very, very good," Ginger cried. "How is school? A lot of homework these days?" Pappy asked her. "Good; in fact great! We haven't been getting that much homework, which is a really good thing." Ginger took a bite into the toast. "I'm glad to hear that," Pappy said, taking a sip of more coffee. A couple of seconds later, Grammy came into the kitchen. "Pappy, what are you wearing? Why are you still in your pajamas? Are you coming to see Miss Lanely Tildon?" Grammy wondered. "I can come like this! She won't mind, anyway," Pappy responded. "Well, publicity matters. Please put on a jacket at least," Uncle suggested. Pappy grunted and slowly walked to get his jacket. "Ginger, go to the car. I'll help Pappy out," Grammy told her, as she and Uncle walked outside to the car. When Uncle walked to the car and opened the door, he got in the driver's seat. Ginger sat in one of the back seats. "So how is life treating you?" Uncle asked. "Good, I must say. Gosh, it's hard to not grieve," she said. "I know. It is hard to get over that, but as long as you are still happy and sustaining your heart, things will be fine. Your father and I started to have a relationship together. After the car accident he was in, I was devastated. I felt the pain you were in, and that was when you were six. That relationship was just tearing apart, and now I will never see him again on this earth. I just have to move on now, and remember the memories and the good times." Some tears started to flood down his face. He was even in the same pain as she was. His sister and brother-in-law have left this earth. He had a great relationship with them, and he has known his sister all his life. Sure, they would fight, bite, and kick each other, but they were still in the best relationship they could be in. He loved his sister dearly, and now he must look at the past and recognize the good. "It's okay, Uncle, as long as we can get along as a family, that's all that matters. Sure we can grieve for a while, but when I look at our family, I can see the progression in our lives," she responded. At that point, Grammy was struggling to put Pappy in the seat next to Ginger. Grammy got in the front seat. "Are you okay, Pappy?" Ginger asked him. "Of course I am."

"Okay, off to see Lanely Tildon!" Grammy cried. Uncle turned on the car, and they drove off to see Lanely Tildon. The antique store was not far from their house at all. The car ride was uncomfortable however. The car was too small to hold all four of them, nonetheless two people anyway. Pappy kept coughing while on the car ride (his medications were wearing off already). "Lanely Tildon ought to be here today. Although sometimes she is not here," Ginger cried. "She should be. I told her Thursday that Pappy and your uncle would be joining to possibly buy some soaps and candles," Grammy replied. After what had seemed forever, Uncle found a park, and they were outside of the antique store. Grammy was right: there were more new antiques in the store. Last week there were no signs telling them that. The sun was just about at its highest peak as they all hopped out of the car. They strutted to the stairs, which lead to the antique store. Ginger has told Miss Tildon numerous times to fix those wretched wooden stairs. Someone could fall and severely hurt themselves. They carefully walked up the noisy stairs. "Yikes! Miss Tildon or her daughter ought to fix these stairs!" Grammy cried. They finally approached the door. The bells on the door came louder as the winds blew more. Ginger cautiously opened the door. There were many boxes and shelves and appliances inside. There was barely any space for a customer to maneuver. Many smokes and spices were coming out from another room. Lanely Tildon thought of herself as a "gypsy." Part of the reason that Ginger can talk to Lanely is that she herself considers herself an "outsider" when she really is not. Miss Tildon does have habits of self-respect, but she can still be a human being. This may make no sense, but if you consider yourself an "outsider" when you are "normal," you perfectly understand life in your natural perspective. But then again, you ask yourself "What is normal?" and then the whole theory will be crushed, then reasoning will come into play. It is good to question the earth, but it is also good to learn from not questioning yourself or the earth. The cash register was empty (no one was standing there), so Ginger and Grammy went into the spare room, the room that Lanely Tildon was in. Pappy and Uncle were wandering around the store, possibly wanting to buy some soaps, sanitizers, and some antiques with plate sets. Ginger and Grammy walked into a room where bells and some covers covered the door. "Um . . . Lanely Tildon. Are you here?" Ginger asked. "Come in," a mysterious voice said. That voice was the voice of Lanely Tildon. Ginger and Grammy stepped inside and sat down in the two chairs available. A huge "cauldron" was on the table, and bubbles and acid came out. A very weird green and pinkish color came from the huge bowl. Spices, herbs, weeds, and potions surrounded the bowl and even Lanely Tildon. Around her were many books and shelves of ingredients she needed. It was as if she was making some sort of potion or soap for the store. Lanely Tildon has gold skin and wears many necklaces and earrings. She is an older woman, but not as old as Grammy or Pappy. Lanely threw in some spices into whatever she was making, bubbling it more. "Hello, Ginger and Marybeth," Lanely greeted. "Hi, Miss Tildon. How are ya?" Ginger asked. Grammy just spoke as well. "Well, very, very well, I must say. We are selling more items in the shop, which is very, very good!" Lanely responded, coughing from the acid of the potion. "What are you making?" Grammy asked. "A new formula for the soaps and antibacterias. I need a new scent," Lanely responded. "Maybe an idea will just pop in your head," Grammy replied. "Very true," Lanely agreed, being very keen. "Things are going well for me as well. I'm maintaining all A's, and I'm on the school's volleyball team. We won last week's game, and I have many more practices to go," Ginger told Lanely. "Good, good, good. Are you gaining some confidence in yourself?" Lanely wondered. "What do you mean?" Ginger pondered. "Remember last week when you were here and I asked you about your own self?" "Well, yes, it's just . . . ," Ginger paused. "I really didn't have the chance to consider thinking about that. I guess my mind was just somewhere else." Ginger put her head down. "That is okay. Sometimes it takes awhile to answer a question. If it's really personal, it could take years. Now let me ask you this: When you look in the mirror, what do you see?" Lanely asked her. It took Ginger awhile to answer. "Um . . . I see myself." "Yes, but what else do you see?" "I don't know." "Beauty. Beauty is what you see," Lanely answered for her, "When you look in the mirror, you see a beautiful girl with charming looks, a very smart, kind, and most of all; a very nice girl. Mirrors are closer than they appear. You are more than whom you appear of, Ginger. You are going to be someone special. I can see it, your grandparents can see it, your uncle can, the children at your school can, and even your own parents can see the beauty and talent in you. Although they are not here, they know it. They know what they have instilled into their daughter. They have instilled greatness in you, Ginger. You just don't know it. When you finally see the destiny of yourself, you will go a long way in your life. The path you're taking will be greater than the world's path, because the world doesn't care. Remember that, Ginger. Always remember that. It will carry you a long way for the rest of your life. I promise you, it will. You will be someone special, Ginger McFraiddee. Now it's time you see the greatness within you." Once again, Lanely's words of wisdom have come across Ginger's heart. She knows her blessing, but she feels a disturbance; that something or someone is missing in her life. Of course that someone is her own parents. "I know all of those things. Its just it's so hard to pick up my own two feet nowadays. When my parents died, I could barely walk. I saw my father get in that car crash, and I saw him die at the hospital with you, Grammy, Pappy and some family relatives beside him. I was just a small girl at the time, and my mother was crying as well. I saw my mother suffer. I knew we were in tons of debt. My mother couldn't survive without him. Two years later when I was seven or eight, she gets breast cancer. She was really hurt, and so was I. She left this Earth, and she didn't bother to take me with her. It's hard for me to live when grace was taken away from me. Now I have to go into this world *alone*," Ginger cried. "You're not alone, Ginger. Lanely Tildon is here, I'm here, Uncle and Pappy are here as well. We feel the same pain as you do. My own daughter and son-in-law have left the earth in my own two eyes. Even so, that doesn't stop your path of greatness, Ginger. You finding yourself is the key to success, and all you need for that is motivation and endurance. You will find your way, Ginger," Grammy said. "It may not be easy, but it can be done," Lanely added, "it can take some time, but that is okay. Ginger, this world is nothing to play with. We all know this. But you can take on the world. Your parents have died, and they have left a message for you Ginger, and that message is to be successful in life and make them proud. It is your responsibility if you want to fulfill this message." "I will. Trust me, I will," Ginger responded. "I'm glad to hear that. I better check to see the new antiques, and to see what Pappy and Uncle are up to. Thank you once again, Lanely," Grammy said, as she got up from her seat. "You are most definitely welcome," Lanely responded. Grammy left the room as the bells sounded from behind. Lanely added more ingredients to the "scent potion." "I had that dream again," Ginger told Lanely. "Which dream?" "The one with the bunny. This time I was having a tea party with one of the bunnies and my parents, and I was home with my parents! My, it was wonderful. The land and the sky and everything!"

"Interesting. Dreams are very powerful indeed. They tell stories. You can actually see your mind and identify the world around yourself in dreams. That is what makes them so interesting and powerful."

"I wish dreams could come true," Ginger complained. "Ginger, there is a difference between the truth and plain words. The truth cannot make words true, only facts and knowledge can. When someone teases another person, it is not true. The person who is being teased must know who he/she really is, because those words could be true to them. Am I making any sense?"

"Yes, ma'am."

"Unfortunately, dreams can't really come true, depending on the dream anyway. But if you have enough faith, it can come true. The impossible of life is possible."

"I feel much, much better now. Thank you for your words of wisdom Lanely Tildon," Ginger said. "These are also words of encouragement. Like your grandmother said, you're on a path of greatness, Ginger. You are just temporarily oblivious to that path. That is okay, because we all need to start from somewhere. You have a long way to go, Ginger. Keep doing well in school or whatever you may want to pursue in, and you will eventually see your own blessing." A huge red glow came out of the cauldron, and it was in the shape of a heart. Destiny reigned on Ginger. "Time for the Enchantment. Ginger, please give me your hand," Lanely said. Ginger gave Lanely her hand. Lanely closed her eyes, and the potion scent inside the potion bubbled fiercely. "Close your eyes," Lanely said. Ginger did so. Lanely hummed and hummed, and then she said, "By the power of destiny, Lord of God! Enchant Ginger McFraiddee now with wisdom, faith, and most of all, confidence and strength!" The light from the potion started to beam, and the bright red light shined on Ginger. Her spirit has been enchanted. The light was shining up on her soul. Soon it had stopped, and Lanely and Ginger opened their eyes. "Wow. I only thought Enchantments could be done in movies," Ginger was amazed. "Once again, the impossible is possible. You just have to believe," Lanely told her. "I feel a lot better now. Thank you for the wisdom and enchantment, Lanely," Ginger cried. "No problem, Ginger. I am always here if you need me. You and your grandmother have my phone number right?" "Yes, we do. It's been a while since you first gave it to us," Ginger cried. "You're going to be fine. You have a great destiny waiting. Here's how you know you're ready: when you look in the mirror and see something great about yourself (besides beauty), then your path will start. Actually, the path has started now, but the end will require faith and respect." Lanely stirred some of the potion, and soon enough, the bubbling stopped. "It's finished, and it smells delightful!" Lanely boasted. "Indeed!" Ginger agreed. It smelled of a fruity aroma mixed with sanitizers and a dash of some fresheners, whatever it may be. Lanely and Ginger walked out of that room and back into the store where they spotted Uncle, Grammy, and Pappy in the bathroom/soaps aisle. Lanely waited by the cash register, and Ginger was curious about what they were going to buy. "Can't decide between Dial . . . or magic soaps . . . ," Pappy was clueless. Uncle had some items in his hands. Ginger knew that they were probably buying those items. "Pappy, just pick one!" Uncle moaned. "Okay, okay! Fine! Magic soaps sound dumb anyway. Dial it is!" he said, grabbing a pack of Dial soap and throwing it into Ginger's arms. Lanely rung up the items, while Pappy and Uncle paid for them. Grammy helped Lanely put the items into bags and carefully stacked up the new plates. "Well, that's all I need," Pappy cried, taking some bags and leaving the store. Grammy and Uncle took more bags, and walked out as well. "I will see you next Saturday, Lanely," Ginger said. "I'm looking forward to that. Remember, Ginger, your path will be more significant than ever before," Lanely responded. Ginger waved good-bye and walked out of the door.

CHAPTER 3

A Family's Way of Life

Grammy was just delighted of the elegant new antiques she bought while they were in the car driving home. Ginger saw some perfume in a bag and sniffed it. The aroma of the perfume fumed through the entire car, and the other smell in the car disappeared. "Aaaaah," they all said, relieved from the smell. Pappy kept sneezing unfortunately, which ruined the silent moment. The sun was still shining when they returned home. Pappy unloaded the bags with Uncle, when Grammy and Ginger went inside the house. "It was good to see Lanely again. She makes me feel less of an outsider."

"Ginger, you're not an outsider. What makes you say that?" Grammy wondered, "Is it because you feel like you have no knowledge of life?"

"Yes. That's exactly it. How did you know?"

"Because you yourself can't see the benefit, and you think you lack wisdom when you do not lack it at all," Grammy answered.

"That's exactly right. What will make it better?"

"My Hungarian stew!" Grammy laughed, as both of them went to the kitchen. The front door slammed. Pappy and Uncle stumbled inside the kitchen, setting the bags down. "You know, you could've helped!" Uncle complained. "Yer sure could've. I might get a hunched up back now," Pappy agreed. "I'll make you some tea, Pappy," Grammy suggested, as she helped her husband up to their room. Uncle was sorting out the bags to get organized, and Ginger went upstairs to her room. Ginger was proud of her grandfather. Although he may be feeling ill and is on tons of medications, he is still strong. He has come a long way in the family if you were to ask Ginger. Pappy is a veteran of the Vietnam War and served in the U.S. Navy for over a decade. When Ginger's father passed away, he supported Ginger's mother solemnly. Ginger's mother had many bills to pay and was in tons of debt. But Pappy came to save the day. He tried to use some of his social security money to help his daughter. He urged Grammy to help pay as well. (Grammy would just encourage her daughter). Unfortunately, Ginger's mother was diagnosed with breast cancer just two years later. Grammy and Pappy stayed at the hospital from day to night. When Grammy wanted to go home, Pappy would insist on staying, to see of what was possibly left of his own daughter. When Ginger's mother passed away, Ginger would've had to become an orphan. After her mother's items and home were sold, Pappy decided that he and Grammy could take care of Ginger, and that is exactly what they did. So it was Pappy who made Ginger avoid a cold and heartless orphanage. It is Pappy who is taking care of Ginger. Even though it may not seem like Pappy wants to help or even cares for the matter, he really does care and wants to see his granddaughter succeed in life. His heart and loyalty is hidden beneath the rudders of the human flesh. Ginger keeps a diary with her. Every girl should have a diary. A diary is a special place where they can say just about anything. In a diary, girls can release their minds and record it in a diary. Ginger even has an old diary, so old that it goes all the way back to when she was like ten years old. That's her oldest diary. To her, a diary is like communicating with her own parents, even though what she writes in the diary is about her, and that her parents aren't physically there to intoxicate the words. Ginger opened the diary and flipped to a new page. Ginger writes in her diary every day (if she gets the time), mainly just dialogue with herself. This may sound weird, but Ginger can't really talk to anyone about personal feelings, except to her parents and Lanely Tildon. Today, she wrote something like this:

> Dear Diary, Today, I visited Lanely Tildon, and Uncle and Pappy came with Grammy and me. Lanely Tildon enchanted me, which seemed a little strange, at first. She mixed potions and ingredients together, and then a giant light glowed on me. I do not know how else to

describe it, but you get the idea. Now, I can gain some strength back and encourage myself to see my character and have a vision for my future goals. Every day I grieve over my parents, when I should be celebrating the pleasant memories and ideals that were passed around. Lanely Tildon's advice is always right, and I know she was right from what she told me today. Well, Diary, that's just about it. I'm finally off my knees and on my own two feet.

With loving kindness, Ginger McFraiddee

PS
Pappy has bought more soap which he doesn't need . . . , again.

What is interesting about what she had just written is not the context but the connections. "I'm finally off my own knees and on my two feet" really makes Ginger wonder: Is this true? She always writes that sentence at the end of the diary (for all of the diary entries). If she herself cannot answer that question, she needn't write that in her diary at all. If she is still grieving about her parents and still looking and searching for an answer to her life, she is still crawling on her knees and not walking just yet. It is hard for her not to grieve, but if that statement is all the way false (and Ginger herself knows this), she shouldn't write that sentence, or at least not for all of her diary entries. She can say something like: "Even though I am still in grief, I am trying to move on with life and make every day a new day." Is this true for Ginger? Absolutely. She herself even knows that, but whatever is on her mind, or whatever she may need to write about, she can do so in her diary. It just amazed her when she noticed she writes that sentence in her diary every time, knowing that it's not true whatsoever. But it was on Ginger's mind, and it's out now, and that is all that really matters. For the rest of the day, Ginger was just on Facebook and MySpace. She was just chatting to some of her friends from school, and some on Aim and MSN. She was also texting some of her friends on her cell phone. She was just bored, and needed someone to talk to (about school stuff). Just when dawn arose, Ginger walked to the radio and turned it on. She put the volume on exceptionally high. The song that was playing was "Up Up Up" by Rose Falcon. Ginger just adored that song. That song always makes her happy and lighthearted. While the song was playing, she was even jumping on her bed and waved her hair about. Whenever she would feel sad (which is quite often), she would listen to that song to be happy again. Ginger was just glad she found some solution to her dilemma. While the song was still playing, Grammy went to Ginger's room. Ginger bounced off the bed and turned off the music. "Having fun, I can see," Grammy said. "Yep," Ginger agreed. "Well, it's dinnertime now. I made your favorite: Hungarian stew with Polish sausages and some crackers on the side."

"Yummy! What am I still doing here?! Let's go!" Ginger cried, as she and Grammy went downstairs. "We're having tiramisu for dessert," Grammy also said. When they went downstairs, Uncle and Pappy were already sitting down at the table. Ginger also sat down with the food in front of her, and so did Grammy. The aroma of the stew filled the room. *Grammy cooked the best Hungarian stew ever*, Ginger would think. "Well, let's start eating!" Pappy cried, and they all started to eat. Judging by the food they are eating, Ginger's family is not all-American. Grammy was born from a small city in Germany (Grammy doesn't have a German accent anymore), and Pappy himself was born from Ireland. Grammy's family moved to Hungary, around the same time during the Holocaust, and when Hitler wanted all Jews killed. She was raised in Hungary, and when she became an adult, she immigrated to the U.S. Pappy was raised in Italy, and when Grammy took a vacation for a year in Italy (job issues), they met, got married, and had a son, who is Ginger's uncle. When those three went back to the U.S., they gave birth to Ginger's mother. So Ginger was German, Irish, Italian, she was Hungarian (other family relatives were born there), and she was also Russian, Polish, Scandinavian (mostly Swedish, Dutch, and Turkish). But their family mainly had customs of Polish, Hungarian, and German. Ginger could speak German and a little Italian (her uncle taught her Italian), and that's all the languages she knew (besides English). It was silent as the family was chewing on bits and pieces of the Polish sausage and sipping on the chilled Hungarian soup. In fact, it was always silent when the family ate together. You couldn't blame them actually, because the food was so scrumptious; you had to enjoy and savor each bite. That's exactly what they do for every meal. This was a good thing because they would be full after dinner and wouldn't need to eat anything else. All of them finished what was on their plates. "That was delicious!" Ginger complimented. "Sure was! Thank you, Grammy," Uncle agreed. "Now let's bring on the dessert!" Pappy replied, as dessert was his favorite meal of the day. After they ate the yummy tiramisu, Grammy had started washing the dishes. Ginger helped her dry the dishes as she washed. Ginger loved to help wash the dishes with her mother. Her mother would wash, Ginger would dry, and they would talk to pass the time. "That was delicious, Grammy," Ginger told Grammy again. "I'm glad you liked it. I'm glad I still have the strength to cook and clean," Grammy responded. Ginger wiped the towel around and inside a cup and set it to where the other clean and dry dishes were. "You're going to help volunteer at the Red Cross this week?" Ginger asked. "Not this week. Last week, I already went to help. I decided to go every other week, to take a break," Grammy responded. That was Grammy's part-time job: volunteering. Surprisingly, she gets paid for helping out. "I have to remember to wash your volleyball uniform." "I have volleyball practice Monday after school and a game on Tuesday," Ginger said. "Okay, I will inform your uncle," Grammy responded, handing a wet but clean dish to her. Ginger was on the volleyball team, and when track and field starts, she will definitely get on that team. As a matter of fact, Ginger is captain of the volleyball team. Hopefully, she can lead her team to victory in the semi-playoffs? that are in a couple of weeks. To do so, their team has to win a majority of the games. Ginger is not worried; she is more concerned about teamwork. She herself cannot win, and the team will need to work together to win the glory. When the dishes were done, it was just about 8:00 p.m. Ginger's family loves to play board games with each other. Some Saturday nights when Ginger wasn't invited to her friends' house, or to just hang out on Main Street (which was often), she and the family would play board games. You are never too old to play board games with your family. "Time to play a good game of bingo and cards!" Pappy announced. Ginger helped Uncle gather the cards and some other board games. Grammy and Pappy waited as they sat at the dining room table. "Well, that's everything," Uncle cried, as he and Ginger set the board games down and sat at the dining room table. "So what game are we playing first?" Ginger wondered. "Let's play some cards first," Pappy answered, as Grammy took the cards and shuffled the deck. After playing cards for about an hour, Grammy got tired of the game. Pappy won the majority, Ginger won some games, Uncle barely won, and if you were watching them play cards, you'd assume that Grammy didn't have a clue of what she was doing. Grammy sighed. "Can we please play bingo, now?" she asked. "Sure," Uncle cried, getting the bingo game out. "Oh come on, Marybeth. Don't be a sore loser," Pappy told her. "I'm not. Are you sure you didn't cheat?" Whenever they do play games, Pappy wins an awful lot of time, which makes Grammy, Ginger, and Uncle wonder if he really is cheating, or if it's just some coincidence. "Pappy probably found some way, but luckily it's just a game," Ginger agreed. Pappy's eyes just dozed off into the air, pretending that he wasn't listening. Uncle set the bingo cards and the chips on the table. "Okay, pick two cards, and let the games begin!" Uncle announced, as they all took two bingo cards. Uncle was calling out the numbers as they were placing chips on the card. By the last call, Pappy had four chips in a row and only needed one more. Grammy had only three, Ginger and Uncle two. This definitely led them to believe that Pappy was indeed cheating. This wasn't the first time either. In other times they would play, he would win by a landslide. But sometimes, he would totally lose. Grammy, Uncle, and Ginger haven't a clue of what it may be, but people have their own strategies. Pappy has been playing these board games for a while now, and maybe that could be it, because when Uncle announced "B51," Pappy yelled "Bingo!" After making sure Pappy had Bingo, he started doing a little dance to celebrate. The others started laughing, as they were being entertained. "What can I say? I'm just good like that!" Pappy cried, as they all laughed and had a great time. It was getting a little late, so Ginger and Uncle put away the board games, and they all had ice cream and leftover tiramisu. "That was fun if I must say!" Uncle cried. "Sure was, even though Pappy kept winning," Grammy agreed. "I believe it just comes to a person," Pappy tried to be philosophical. "Right . . . ," Ginger was being sarcastic. "We ought to do this more often! It takes away the idea of work," Uncle said. "I'm on retirement," Pappy budded in. "It's just fun to play these games when the family is playing too," Ginger specified. "Yes, it is. Now, everyone off to bed," Grammy said, collecting the plates and throwing them into the sink. Ginger gave her uncle and grandparents a big hug, and then they all went up to bed. What Ginger enjoys about playing games with the family is not who wins or who the champion is, she enjoys seeing all of them laughing and having loads of fun. When Ginger would play Guess Who and Clue with her parents, they would have a wonderful time playing those games, and they would laugh and have fun. To Ginger, it doesn't matter who wins or loses, what matters is the fun of the game, and the family having a great time. Most of the time, people get mad at losing and end up having no fun at all, not realizing that it's just a game, and it won't kill you if you lose. Ginger can see this because she used to play these board games and cards with her parents, and she is fortunate enough to continue with her grandparents and her uncle. She is fortunate enough to have continued happiness, instead of cherishing, which only makes life more miserable and frustrating. Playing cards and board games lifts a heavy weight off Ginger's shoulder, because she is having fun and having a good time with her family, which is why they should play cards and games more often. Ginger crept into the bed and lay down, thinking of how much fun they had. Seeing this makes Ginger feel less of an outsider and more of a happy medium. Happy mediums are usually average people (per se), and they can give good advice. You can consider Madame Lanely Tildon a happy medium, even though she may not seem happy at all. If someone is called a happy medium, it is up to the person to see how well they will take it or to see what it actually means. But to Ginger, she can see it in herself, to sometimes be considered this, but it all depends on the specific time of day, and what is going on around the time period. Ginger wearily turned off the light, and then listened to her iPod before she fell asleep toward the middle of the night. Sunday was no different than Saturday, to be honest, except that they didn't see Lanely (her antique shop is closed on Sundays). Ginger did some leftover homework and helped Grammy clean the house a little. Uncle was out doing some errands or getting groceries, and Pappy stayed in the bed watching some television and eating jam toast. After Ginger was finished helping Grammy sweeping the kitchen, she was in the mood for coffee. "I want some Arabic coffee. Coffee soothes my throat, sometimes," Ginger said. "I'll brew some right now. Your mother use to love Arabic coffee. That's all she'd practically drink," Grammy responded, as she got the coffee brewer from the shelf. In about five to ten minutes, the coffee was nice and hot. Ginger loved her coffee with not too much cream and sugar, but just enough. She wanted it just perfect, to engage the taste of the coffee itself. Uncle returned just about an hour or so later, when Ginger was watching television. "Where were you?" she asked him. "Just taking care of some home things and bills," Uncle seemed worn out. "Is everything okay?"

"Of course. I'm just tired from running around, today," Uncle answered, as he walked to his room. It was mostly quiet throughout the whole house for the rest of the Sunday. God wants rest and peace for the Sabbath day. The family went out to a restaurant for a Sunday dinner, one that was not too elegant, or too sophisticated for that matter. Their food was off the chain, however (meaning that it was most delightful). The purpose of food was not just for eating and survival, but also for the comforting of the mind and soul, especially soul food. Food can be as sweet as an ice cream sundae with a cherry on top, or it could be as bitter as liver casserole. It just depends on your solitude of taste and your filling for desire. Do not have an overdose of food, because you will probably regurgitate it all back out. Another day, another dollar, another week, another $1,000. Ginger was tired after the week before, and even the weekend. The Enchantment Lanely Tildon has performed has made Ginger realize the sincerities of life and has maybe even opened her own heart. But then again, you cannot be so certain about things, especially things that can greatly impact your life. Life is like a bowl of cherries and must be nourished as well, because if there is no nourishment or plenty, they will just rot. This affects many people on this earth in great ways. Some disabilities or difficulties people suffer from make life tougher than it already is. Bills and taxes and jobs, oh my! Ginger's father would sometimes say that when she was a little girl, and didn't know what the heck he was talking about. But after seeing the *Wizard of Oz* and seeing the dangers of the world, Ginger now understands. Grammy came into Ginger's room with her volleyball outfit. Ginger gathered her backpack and her school ID to get ready for yet another school day . . . "The uniform is washed and ready to go," Grammy cried, setting the uniform on Ginger's backpack. Her clothes were set aside. "Remember, I have volleyball practice tomorrow and a game on Tuesday," Ginger reminded. "Okay as you know, Uncle will take you to school and pick you up these days." "Good night," Ginger cried. "Goodnight, Ginger. Your parents would be so proud of you, right now. In fact, they are. Sleep tight, Ginger," Grammy cried, as she left the room. Ginger turned off the light, and took a long and huge sigh of relief. She yawned and stretched a little, and then she soon went to sleep, wondering what the next day could be like.

CHAPTER 4

USMS

Ginger woke up the next morning and aimlessly wandered around the area. At least the sun was shining during this fall season. Ginger washed up and put on her clothes for school. Ginger is in eighth grade and is considered "popular" in her school. Her school started at 8:30 a.m. and ended at 3:00 p.m. To her, school was a place for learning and understanding and preparation for reality. For others, however, it was about popularity, getting the girls or the guys, and being a bully. You have to be good at something to survive at her school. You can't be a loser at this school, because if you are, you might as well transfer schools (it will benefit you, probably). Ginger slipped on her shoes and put her volleyball uniform in her backpack. Pappy and Grammy were staying home (they are retired). Her uncle worked as a construction worker, which was very dangerous. Despite this, he was making good money, enough money to hold the house together. "Ready for school?" Uncle wondered. "Yes." Ginger grabbed her backpack and ID. Her Uncle was wearing a Home Depot shirt. Today he was fixing a house and remodeling some of the inside. "Have a good day at school!" Grammy called from her and her husband's room. They were both in the bed watching TV. "Don't let any bullies hurt you!" Pappy added. "Bye!" Ginger and Uncle called back, as both of them left the house. Other kids were walking, but for today Uncle was taking her. She had on her locket, the one that was owned by her late mother. They got into the car and drove off. "So what did Lanely Tildon tell you on Saturday?" Uncle wondered. He forgot to ask her. "She enchanted me, and of course gave me words of wisdom," Ginger answered. "Hmm. That's good. Strange, but weird, well, here you are." They were approaching the school. Aha! Ginger's theory was right after all! Uncle didn't understand Lanely at all. When he heard the Enchantment, he was surprised. Only she knows what Lanely is talking about, but Ginger should really focus about the part of Ginger's her intellect. Several students were lined up and in their own groups talking. Many others were walking and getting dropped off. "Well, this is your stop, kiddo. Have a good day!" Uncle told her. "Thanks," Ginger cried, as she got her backpack from the backseat. Ginger got out, and Uncle took off. She walked to her circle of friends, Meredith, Sally, Jenny, and Summer. Some other girls were there as well. "Hi, Ginger!" Summer greeted her. Summer has braces and is a very happy girl. Summer is probably the nicest girl in the entire eighth grade. Meredith wears glasses and braces but has many friends, so she isn't considered a nerd.

Ginger has known Sally the longest. In fact, Sally has seen and known Ginger's mother and the locket on her neck. If anyone knows Ginger, it's Sally. Sally is on the volleyball team as well and is very good too. Jenny is also on the volleyball team and is friends with a lot of girls. She has her own unique style. "So how was the sleepover?" Ginger asked. Summer, Jenny, Sally, and two other girls had a sleepover. "It was okay, we had some fun," Jenny responded. "You should've came," Sally cried. "It's okay. I had to stay home to take care of my grandma," Meredith said. "Yea, and Pappy is sick, so I had to make sure he didn't tear down the house," Ginger responded, as the girls were laughing when kids were going into Upton Sinclair Middle School. Many kids were chattering and screaming. One kid was pushing some of the sixth and seventh graders. Ginger's classes were all the way on the fourth floor. In fact, the fourth floor was where the eighth-grade classes were. She and her friends went their separate ways and went to their lockers. As Ginger was going to the locker bay, a boy squeezed the side of her belly, which greatly startled her. It was Bailey, her boyfriend. "Hey, cutie," he told her. Bailey is the biggest bully in the school, and yet he thought Ginger was hot and attractive. Both of them came from different worlds. Ginger does her work, gets good grades, and is really nice. Bailey, on the other hand, gets D's, bullies other kids, and does no work whatsoever. But Ginger likes his creativity, and Bailey really likes her. That's why Ginger is going out with Bailey, though he is mean. He was wearing a hoodie that was black. He has black hair and was much taller than Ginger. Ginger smiled and gave him a smack on the face. "What was that for?" Bailey put out his hands. "You startled me. I nearly got a heart attack!" "Oh, I'm sorry. Lemme kiss you to make it better," Bailey offered. "Fine," Ginger smiled, as he kissed her cheek. "I gotta go to class. Cya later," Bailey told her as he walked off. Ginger went to her class. While Bailey walked to his class, his friend Billy walked with him. "Dude, you're going out with Ginger now?!" Billy didn't know nothin'. "Of course I am, dumbass. You didn't know?" Bailey wondered. "No. I thought you were just friends with her." "Ginger's hot. She has the nice body and the ass," Bailey responded. "True that. She's tough. She can fight," Billy cried. "I know, and she's hot. That's why I'm going out with her. She's also captain of the volleyball team." "Yea, I'd go out with her too," Billy agreed. The second bell rang, and kids were racing to get to their first period class. The eighth graders question Ginger about her going on with Bailey, especially her own friends. Why is such a kind girl going out with such a mean person? What does she see in him that no others see? Physically, Ginger cannot answer that question. Mentally, she certainly can. But when it comes with a relationship between two people, only they can answer. But the school has a pretty good idea of their relationship. Bailey thinks Ginger is hot and is captain of the volleyball team and that is why he asked her out, and Ginger accepted to get to know him better. This equals a failure in the relationship, but so far it has been going well. Ginger has language arts first with Mrs. Smith. Mrs. Smith is an African American and is probably the coolest teacher in the eighth grade. She even lets the students use their cell phones or iPods in school, which is strictly prohibited. There were a fair amount of kids in the class, including Todd, Malcolm, Jason, Hillary, Stacy, and Luna. Todd is the most popular and hottest guy in the school. He is captain of the basketball and football team, and he plays numerous sports. Malcolm is Todd's best friend. He too plays sports and is charming. Both Todd and Malcolm have brown hair, and Todd has blue eyes, Malcolm has green. Todd always wears a backward cap, Malcolm does sometimes. The girls just go crazy when they see Jason. They think he is the sexiest in the school (teenage love . . . you gotta love it). He sometimes sits with Todd's friends, but he has friends of his own. Hillary is just plain preppy. Everyday she dyes her hair a different color. Today it was a turquoise color. Why she does this, the whole school ponders about that. Stacy is Hillary's BFF for life. Both girls pretty much do everything together, and they've both known each other since elementary school. Those two are considered cool, but not as cool or popular as Todd and Malcolm. Luna is the most well-known girl in the entire school. She is black, but she is loved by the whole school. At lunch and after school some days, she has her own book club (which a lot of girls go to). She even hangs out with Stephanie and her friends, the most popular girl in the school. The students took their seats as the chattering stop, waiting for class to begin. "Okay, y'all, as you know your 'what makes you happy assignment' is due today and will be presented. Hillary, you may go first," Mrs. Smith said. The class gave a golf clap as Hillary went in front of the class with her paper and a radio in her hands. "The song 'Barbie Girl' always makes me happy. In fact, I sometimes dance to that song," Hillary talks like Karyn Parsons. "Let's hear the song!" Stacy yelled, as she and the girls in the class cheered. "All right! All right! Hillary, let's hear the song!" Mrs. Smith cried, as the girls shouted. The boys didn't care at all, so they just stayed silent. Hillary put on the song, and all of the girls (including Ginger) were singing along. How it made Hillary happy was mysterious, but only Mrs. Smith paid attention to that. When the song was over, Mrs. Smith said: "Thank you, Hillary, for a wonderful presentation."

"No problem," Hillary answered, handing Mrs. Smith her paper and sitting down at her desk, setting her radio under her desk on the floor. "Next up is Max Graganolf," Mrs. Smith announced. Max Graganolf. He is the biggest loser in the entire eighth grade. He has no friends, and nobody relatively likes him or his nerdy personality. Max barely made it to the front of the classroom. Kids were booing at him and calling him mean names. One kid even threw a paper ball at him. "Enough! Have some respect for your peers. Max, go ahead and read, honey," Mrs. Smith told him. Tears were in his eye. He could hardly get the words out, let alone saying a sentence. "What m—m—makes me h—happy is my f—f—f—family," he started, starting to sneeze. "I myself know w—who I am . . . ," he kept going. "Which is a loser!" Jason yelled out, and the entire class laughed. Even Ginger gave a small chuckle. "Jason . . . no . . . you know better," Mrs. Smith said. The class didn't even care for what Mrs. Smith said. Max darted to the door, crying even louder now. He truly was a loser. Before he got to the door, he stepped on his shoelace and fell right to the ground. This was quite a show to the class. The students laughed and giggled even more. Mrs. Smith gave out a few laughs from here and there. Soon enough, Max ran out of the room and into the bathroom. You could hear him crying in the bathroom. The class was still laughing. Malcolm, Todd, and some other people high-fived Jason, and gave him a pat on the back. Mrs. Smith went to the front of the class, still laughing. "That was not nice. But oh well, he will get over it soon. Cassie, you're next," Mrs. Smith cried, as Cassie went up to present. The class was silent now. When Max read the first part of his presentation before he started crying, this really amazed Ginger. How is that a kid with absolutely no friends or dignity sees himself? That answer, as Ginger took no time to realize it, is family. He most likely has a mother and father. Ginger will never have that again (not on the earth, anyway). But as Cassie was reading through her presentation, Ginger was just thinking to herself about that. When Cassie was done, the kids were clapping. Todd and Malcolm were texting girls, and Hillary and Luna were texting friends in other classes. Jason was also texting. Ginger was texting Bailey from time to time (he'd only send her, "I heart you" messages). Mrs. Smith wasn't even looking at the class, but at the person presenting, so she saw no one texting. (If you get caught with a phone in the school, you'd have to serve an after-school detention). It wasn't until the end of the period when Max returned. His face was bright red and wet on some parts. He was completely pale. Mrs. Smith too much didn't care about Max either. Jason should've gotten a detention for blurting that out and making Max cry, but Mrs. Smith didn't give him one; she just told him to stop. That is what makes Mrs. Smith a cool teacher, you won't get into that much trouble with her (only if you sneak cell phone texting when she gave no permission to do that). The bell rang, and students gathered their belongings and headed to the next class. Max left quick, fast, and in a hurry. While Ginger was leaving, she saw Malcolm, Todd, and Jason in a group near a water fountain. "Man, that was funny," Malcolm said. "I know. Max started crying and being a total nerd," Todd agreed. "Sure was. That kid has major problems," Jason replied, as them three headed to their next class, still laughing. Ginger spotted Bailey, and a few of his friends in the hall (one of them was Billy). "What happened? Why didn't you respond to my last text?" Bailey wondered. "I'm sorry. Max was crying, and you can hear him from the bathroom," Ginger said, as she and Bailey's friends were laughing. "That kid is a nerd anyway. He cries every other day, to be honest," Billy said. "What do you have next?" Ginger asked. "Spanish. You?" "Science," Ginger answered. "Oh, I have to go that way, I'll walk ya there," Bailey responded, as he wrapped his hands around her, and walked her to her next class. Bailey's friends went their separate ways. Ginger arrived to her next class, and then Bailey ran to his next class. Ginger started not to care what some kids were saying about their relationship. As long as they were happy, and Bailey treated her with respect, that is all that matters to Ginger. After what had already seemed like a long day, it was finally lunch. Ginger bought her lunch from home, which mainly consisted of soup or pasta made by her Grammy. Ginger was eating with Bailey and his group of friends. Although she and another girl sat at the all-boy table, she did not feel uncomfortable. The boys were just gossiping about other eighth graders, like normal bullies do. Ginger didn't say too much of anything. She never really does, as she has nothing to say, or she is in the incorrect genus. It was just Bailey of whom she knew. She relatively didn't know the rest of the kids, let alone their names. When Ginger was done eating, she told Bailey. "I'm going to go sit with my other friends. I will talk with you after school." They talk every day after school. "Okay, I'll walk ya to the gym later on today," Bailey agreed, as Ginger took her lunchbox, and sat with a group of girls. Many of Ginger's friends were sitting here. Some of the girls were Hillary, Stacy, Shandi, Brianna, Jenny, Sally, and Cindy. "Hey!" Ginger waved. "Hi, Ginger!" the rest of the girls responded. "Ginger, where were you? We saved you a seat!" Stacy cried. Stacy has black hair and is sort of mixed and accessorizes incredibly. "Sitting with Bailey. Thanks for saving the seat, though," Ginger replied. "Anytime," Brianna responded. Brianna is a chocolate-skinned girl and is very nice. She has known Hillary and Stacy and Shandi for years now. "Wow, your relationship is skyrocketing with him! Is he sweet?" Hillary wondered. Hillary always wants to get into people's business. "He may be a bully, but he is sweet. Cute too. You just have to get to know him."

"That's cool. I like Malcolm, Todd's friend, he is cute," Shandi said. Shandi is a blonde with curly hair. Some say she is Paris Hilton's little sister. She even acts like Paris Hilton sometimes.

"You should totally ask him out, then," Cindy cried. Cindy was a blonde with straight hair. "Yea, you should. He will totally say yes," Jenny agreed. Shandi is friends with Stephanie (the most popular girl in school), and sometimes even sits at their table, which means Shandi could have a chance with Malcolm. Todd and Stephanie were going out, but now they are friends. Both of their friends would be on Main Street to just hang out and talk, and some of Stephanie's friends would be hitting on Todd's friends. "He's very cute," Sally cried, "plus I hear he's single." Typical teenage girl talk. "I'll think about it. So what's new?" Shandi wondered. "Nothing much, just volleyball," Jenny said. "Same here," Ginger replied. "I know. The practices just go on and on," Sally said. "But our team is going to win this year!" Stacy cried, as the girls cheered a little. "We have nothing to worry about, really. With Ginger on the team we know we will win," Brianna cried, as all of the girls cheered for Ginger, which did cause attention. "Oh yeah, Ginger'll totally lead our team to victory!" Hillary added. "We haven't lost a game yet!" Cindy cried. "Thanks, you guys," Ginger said. Jason walked past the girls and sat with Todd's friends. Todd's friends were staring at the girls. It could've been because of the attention they attracted, or simply because they think those girls are hot. "Oh my God! I have a crush on Jason!" Hillary announced, as she and the girls were giving small screams. "I wouldn't blame ya. He's hot!" Stacy agreed. "It's too bad he's annoying . . . ," Brianna mentioned, which was only so true. Jason has smooth and scattered brown hair and was about ya tall. All of the girls thought he was sexy and wanted to go out with him.

The problem was that no girl sought the courage to even ask him, because they'd do something crazy or dumb. He was a little of a bother to some, but nonetheless, he was still attractive. Todd, Jason, and his friends were still looking at their direction. "What are they staring at?" Ginger whispered. "At us, probably," Shandi answered. "Why?" "Because they must like us, duh!" Hillary said. "I don't see how we can be attracted to them. They are such jerks," Ginger cried, which indeed was certain. "Bailey is a jerk, and you go out with him," Stacy made up a good point. "But they're all stuck up and sometimes mean to us."

"That's true. They'd come over here any time just to annoy us, usually once per week," Cindy cried. "Try once per day, actually," Brianna corrected her. "As long as they're not causing trouble, all is good," Jenny said. "Not really. In band class Andy, Malcolm, and Todd bothers me, Hillary, and even you, Brianna," Sally stated. "I try to ignore them. Joel the homo is enough to worry about," Hillary said, rolling her eyes. Joel is gay. He plays the flute (same as Hillary), and he is always bothering her in band class. He crosses his legs while he sits (wherever it may be), and he wears way too much makeup and lipstick. Kids call him gay, and he talks like a girl, which doesn't help his reputation at all. Joel has been stalking Hillary, and he keeps asking her to go out with him, and of course Hillary is going to say no. Although Joel is gay, he has friends that are straight, and he is not a nobody at the school. "Joel needs to get a life and get one quick. I cannot stand that kid," Shandi complained. "Me either, and I sit next to him in band class," Hillary agreed, not seeming too happy. "Tell me about it. And I'm sitting right in front of Todd and Malcolm. They are always throwing paper balls and even pencils at me," Brianna said. "Me too," Sally agreed. "Does the teacher ever see?" Jenny asked. "No. Mrs. Alvarez is too much of an airhead to see anything," Hillary answered. "Yea. She can't even see Joel messing with Hillary, and we are in the front row, right next to Mrs. Alvarez," Stacy added. "Typical teachers, not caring at all," Shandi responded, rolling her eyes. "Sure don't. That's why I try to stay silent when they ask me a question, because I know they will just criticize me," Brianna said, finishing her lunch and throwing it in the trash. The bell was about to ring, which means lunch was just about to end. "You know who the weirdest teachers in the school are?" Ginger asked the girls. "Who?" they all wondered. "Mrs. Robbin and Mrs. Duffy. They are always staring out of a window, looking at nothing. They are very mysterious."

"Oh yea, the psychology teachers, aka, the mysterious teachers," Jenny cried. "Oh, them. They are weird. What are they looking at, anyway?" Sally wondered. "Who knows . . . The whole school is concerned about both of them. Sometimes the principal criticizes them," Hillary responded. The bell rang, and the eighth graders piled out of the lunchroom, and they were going to their next class. Ginger said bye and gave hugs to them (like most girls do) and headed for her next class. Mrs. Robbin and Mrs. Duffy both taught junior psychology at Upton Sinclair Middle School. What Ginger said about them was right; except them being weird. They are always looking out of a window (both of them), and they never smile. How is it that both of them feel this way? What feelings do they share? What has made them who they are? The whole school questions those teachers, especially those three, but too hesitant to ask one of them those questions. In fact, these two teachers are just like Ginger in many ways. Ginger and the two teachers just don't know that they are on the same path, a path that leads to external destiny. It is bad for Ginger to judge these two teachers, when she knows nothing about them. In fact, Ginger does not have a class with the two teachers, nor does she see or talk to them. You cannot judge a book by its cover, unless you have read the story and can comprehend it very well. It would be wise if Ginger would take those words she said about the teacher, and throw them to dust, unless she knows Mrs. Robbin and Mrs. Duffy, which she does not. Her afternoon classes are much swifter than the morning classes are, which is a good thing. Seemingly, Ginger is always tired on Mondays. The first day of the week is always the worst. All through her afternoon classes and much of the weekend, Ginger was thinking about Lanely Tildon's question. Is she gaining more confidence? Is she answering her parents' message? What does she see when she looks in the mirror? Ginger still cannot answer these questions, but perhaps some help may help her. One day, Grammy and Pappy took Ginger all the way to Chicago to see the play *Wicked*. During the play, there was one song that touched her heart, and the song was "Change for the Better." Has Ginger really changed? Is life getting better for her? Maybe the death of her parents is a sign of the better change. This song has really inspired Ginger to see herself in another way, and to mostly see life in a better form, then looking at the negative aspects of life. Those two questions and the answer to the death of her parents is what Ginger will need to find out about and answer. So many questions and not even a single answer. But that is not a problem. If Ginger can answer these questions when she is dead, that is fine with her, because then she will realize her own life. During the afternoon classes, Ginger was also looking at the outside world around us. You only have once chance with life, and it is very important that you maintain it, because Lord knows where you're going when you leave. People are crazy and very cruel. But then some people are nice and courteous. It is just good to be aware of your own surrounding, wherever you may be. As scientists say, "The world is coming to an end." People are trying to make it one day at a time, if it means smashing the piggy banks for money, or providing food on the table, and working their butts off to pay bills. Ginger knows that life must be treated with TLC and with delicate compassion. Life only gets harder and a lot worse when you grow up. Unlike life, Life is not a game. This is really important that everyone in the world see what life really is, and how they can make a difference life by changing for the better. That is really what the song "Change for the Better" means, and it is up to you if you will take a step, and change your life for the better, because life must be treated with respect, and you only have one life to live with no second chances.

CHAPTER 5

Memories of the Past

Ginger met up with Bailey after school. "Do you have a lot of homework?" Ginger asked him. "Not really. Just language arts and social studies," he responded. "Well, I'm going now. See you later, cutie," Bailey told Ginger, as he left the school. Ginger only smiled, and then entered the gym. Many other girls were already there, warming up for volleyball practice. Ginger quickly went to the locker room and got changed into her uniform (which was optional because this was just practice). Whenever Ginger has a volleyball game or practice, her locket is on the inside of the shirt, that way no one can see its powers working, or make other kids curious about what she is wearing. It almost works as a good luck charm, but it is not luck at all. It is the work of her mother, at least that is what Ginger believes (her mother used to be a pro at volleyball, literally). She immediately spotted Jenny, Sally, and Meredith stretching in a group with themselves. "Hey, guys," she greeted, taking a seat on the dirty gym floor, stretching as well. "Hey, Ginger," the girls responded. "I think we're going to have to run today. The coach is going to be pushing us for the semifinals," Meredith sighed. The red-headed girl took a deep breath and stretched some more. "We shouldn't be worried. We won all of our games so far," Jenny said. "We just need to win these next couple of games and then . . . ," Sally started. "And when the playoffs come, we will win the championship!" Ginger finished, as the girls high-fived each other, and making some noise. "With us on the team, nobody can dare stop us," Meredith cried, as the girls cheered to that as well. "Girls, this is volleyball practice, not the gossip club. Less talking, more stretching. We have a lot of work to do," Coach Hector told the girls, as the girls gave a silent giggle. Coach Hector. He is a gym teacher (Mr. Hector is what they'd call him, even though that is his first name), and he was also the volleyball coach. All he wants to do is work, work, work. It is all about goals and accomplishments, and if you knew or even met Mr. Hector, you would know that he is like that. He was pushing these girls to the extreme, because he wanted to win. When it comes to winning, there also comes a price or even a consequence. You have to work to win, but after all of the work, it will pay off more than you expect. This is what Coach Hector wants. His volleyball team has never made it to the semifinals for ten years, and he has been working at USMS for fifteen years, and those teams in the first five years made it to the semifinals, but only two teams won the championship. But this year was much different. Coach Hector was even more aggressive than before. He wanted to see gold in his hands, which he hasn't seen in over a decade, now. These girls are aggressive and strong, but what will unlock his message to Coach Hector is the girls winning the championship. Coach Hector blew the whistle, and the girls all clumped in a group in the middle of the gym, surrounding the coach. "All right. The semiplayoffs are coming up in a couple of weeks, and we need to win!!" the coach announced, as the girls cheered. "Tomorrow you have a volleyball game, so make sure you get enough rest, because we came here to win!" the coach also announced, as the girls cheered some more. This was a major big deal for not only the girls or Coach Hector, but also for the school. The school has been waiting for this moment just as long as Coach Hector, and they too are anxious about winning the gold. But the team has won all of their games so far, and is number one in the division, but it is not over until the fat lady sings. "Okay! Time to get to work! Fifteen laps around the gym! Let's go!" the coach clapped, as the girls started jogging around the gym court. The girls ran at average speed to keep their oxygen and to not pass out. Ginger was going a little faster, probably because she was on the track team, and did tons of running. Coach Hector was just staring at all of the girls, making sure that they weren't slacking off. He wants all of these girls to succeed, and there should be no excuse of this, whatsoever. He was especially looking at Ginger, however. Remember, Ginger is the star player of the team. She is the reason why they won all of their games (mainly when they were behind). He was expecting more from her, because she has such a responsibility for the team.

He knows she has potential and can play, but it's about performance and quality. Whatever you do in practice, that is what you are going to do when you perform. You could be a star when you perform, but you could also embarrass yourself completely. The coach knows she has the potential; in fact, the whole school knows this, but is she ready to perform after a little more practice? Yes! But it is up to her if she is willing to take charge and win for her team, which she most likely is. From time to time, Coach Hector would give words of encouragement to the girls, because by the tenth lap, they were getting tired. "Keep going! You can do it! Never doubt yourself!" he would tell them. Those words sounds like something Ginger's parents would tell her when she maybe stuck in the rut. Ginger finds it very weird how what her coach is saying, her parents would tell her when she was little. It's that path connection of destiny that they share. In fact, he himself almost says words of wisdom like Lanely Tildon, only her words are more dynamic. Ginger will never forget Lanely's words, nor will she forget Miss Tildon's loving kindness. After running laps, Coach Hector gave the girls a ten-minute break. "Yikes! Fifteen laps! It was ten just last week!" Meredith complained, as her, Sally, Jenny, and Ginger got their water bottles and drank furiously. "I know. It's just crazy!" Sally responded. "He has to now. He wants us to win the championship, and he wants to win so bad," Jenny added. "Yea. Our school hasn't won in over a decade now. He thinks we have a good chance of winning this year," Ginger replied. "True, plus we haven't lost, and we won't lose!!" Meredith cried, as the four girls drank more water and were trying to control their breathing. "I'm just glad we made it this far," Jenny said, wiping off her face. "Me too, and we all worked as a team, and we will WIN as a team!" Sally declared, as the four girls had enough strength to cheer. Some of the other girls heard this, and they agreed. Well, of course they would agree, they helped pitch in to perform and win. But now it was time to step it up a notch, and that was exactly Coach Hector was doing. After the ten-minute break, the girls were up and ready. They were practicing their serves in small groups, and then practicing spikes and bumps, which was important in winning games. The girls also worked on defense and practiced on knowing the basics of defending when the opposing team serves the ball. Defense also wins games, no matter what sport or activity you are involved in. After practicing in small groups, the coach split up the girls into two teams to see what they have really been taught and what they need to improve. Ginger and Meredith were on one side of the net (they were on the same team), and Sally and Jenny on the other. The team was about equal, which was good. The coach blew the whistle, and a girl on Sally and Jenny's team served the ball, and started the game. The ball was going back and forth, but it changed when Ginger spiked the ball, and it hit the floor on the other side of the net (Ginger was in the front row). Her team cheered and high-fived her. The coach blew the whistle, and a girl on Ginger's team served the ball. Once again, the ball was going back and forth of the net, and no girl allowed it to touch the ground. Meredith bumped the ball, and it hit the ground on the opposing team, which scored their team a point. The girls gave Meredith a high five, and then the opposing team served the ball. When the game was finally over, the score was 21 to 15, Ginger's team had 21. "Okay, girls, huddle up! Huddle up! Good practice today. I was most impressed at how you girls didn't let the ball fall to the ground as often as before. If you do this during the game (which you do, anyway), you will be set. Teamwork is more important than winning, but winning is nice too!" Coach Hector announced, as the girls cheered and wooed. "Now get some rest tonight, because you have a big game tomorrow! Good practice today, girls! We're going to win the championship this year!" Coach Hector emphasized, as the girls cheered even more. "Get some rest, and I will see you tomorrow after school. The game starts at four! Have a good evening!" Coach Hector said as the girls huddled and then cheered. The girls were getting their bags, and starting to leave the gymnasium. "Ginger, could you come here for a sec?" Coach Hector asked her. She walked up to him with her bags in her hands. "Yes, Coach Hector?" "Ginger, I just want to thank you for leading our team this far. Without you and a couple of other girls on the team (Jenny is one of them), we wouldn't be this far, so thank you very much."

"You're welcome, Coach. I am just playing the best I can," Ginger told him. "I know. You have a lot of potential, Ms. McFraiddee. You will lead our team during the playoffs, and we will win the championships. I believe in you and the whole team. We will win! Okay, Ginger, you can go, now. But thank you so much," he said. "You're welcome! Bye!" Ginger told the coach, as she grabbed her bags and left the gymnasium. She caught up with Meredith, Sally, and Jenny. "What did Coach Hector want?" Sally wondered. "Nothing, really. He just wanted to tell me how well I'm doing," Ginger answered. "Oh, okay," Meredith added, as the girls walked outside. The sun was almost at dusk when the girls were leaving the school to go home. Ginger spotted the car and approached it. Inside was her uncle (he would pick her up today). She set her backpack down on the backseat and got in the front seat. "So how was volleyball practice?" Uncle asked her, as he pulled off. "It was good. We had to run a lot," she replied, gazing out of the window, "What about you?" "Mine was fine. We finally finished that house. It took nearly two months," her uncle said with relief. He must've been proud. Tired but proud. "We have a game tomorrow after school." "I will try to come, and hopefully Pappy and Grammy will feel like coming," Uncle cried. Ginger was all of a sudden sensing a flashback. "Higher, Daddy, push me higher!" Ginger told her father. This was when she was little, and her father was still alive. "Okay, Ginny!" he would say, pushing her even higher on the swing. "Is this high enough?" he would ask her. "Yes, Daddy! Yes, it is! I can see the whole world from here! I'm queen of the world!" Ginger would say, as her father would laugh. Her mother came, and took a picture of the two. "Aww, how sweet!" her mother commented. "Mommy, Mommy! Let's get some ice cream!" Ginger cheered. "Should we?" her mother asked. "Of course! I'd do anything for my special little girl!" her father would say. "Yay!" Ginger cheered. "Let's take a family photo. One . . . two . . . three!" her mother would say, and she held the camera out, enough to where it saw three people. Ginger's mind was now roaming all over the place. In fact, those pictures her mother took are framed at her grandparents' house. Ginger had another flashback. This one was her father's last hours. She was just six at the time, and it was dark outside. "Honey, I'm getting some more snacks," he said that night. "Okay," her mother cried. Ginger came racing down the hallway. "Can I come?" she asked. "No, honey. But on the way back, I will bring you back a candy bar. I promise!" her father promised. "Okay!" That was the last time her father was in that home. When her father was driving back home, he was hit by another vehicle. The police immediately called Ginger's mother. "Hello?" she said that night. Ginger was right beside her on that very night. After a few seconds on the phone, Ginger's mother burst into tears. When her mother and Ginger arrived at the hospital, Lanely, Grammy, and Pappy were there. His last words were, "Ginger . . . , I love you, sweetie, and I will . . . , I will be back . . ." That is when the beeping noise came, which meant it was time. He was motionless and didn't move. Ginger's mother and Grammy were crying the most. Ginger was still little but knew what happened and cried several days later. By now, Ginger was crying in the car. Uncle didn't want to ask what she was crying for, because he knew it was most likely about her parents. "Come on, Ginger, stop crying. It's gonna be okay," Uncle told her. "No, it's not. My parents aren't here, and now nothing will ever be the same, again!" Ginger cried even more. Just those last words of her father would make Ginger cry. It was so special to her, because he knew he was being separated by his own loving daughter. Ginger can only remember her father up to those words, because she knows nothing her father has said, wherever he may be (most likely heaven). But he is now watching over his own daughter and making sure that she is being protected. Ginger wishes that what her father said can come true, and that he can see his own daughter, again. But nevertheless, this won't stop Ginger from glory, as Lanely Tildon told her before. Finally, they were back at the house, still decent outside. Ginger's face was dry, now. She was sobbing in the car instead of crying. Uncle opened the door, and they were inside the house. "We're home!" Uncle announced. "Hello!" Pappy and Grammy greeted them. "Hi!" Ginger said, walking up the stairs precariously. Pappy and Grammy were in the same spot since Uncle and Ginger left this morning, the bed. The only occasional times they'd get up were if they had to go to the bathroom, or a small brunch which Grammy would prepare. "What's wrong with her?" Pappy asked Uncle. "The usual, her parents," her uncle answered. "Lord, Lord, Lord, you have to help us. Ginger cannot function right without her parents," Grammy commented. "We oughta put her in the military," Pappy suggested. "No, Pappy, we just have to let her continue this. She will soon get better, trust me," Uncle suggested. "Good idea. I wish her parents could come back. We all do. We all miss them and love them very . . . much . . . ," Grammy paused, as tears were in her eyes . . . , "but sadly there is nothing we can do." Grammy removed her glasses and wiped off the tears with tissue. Pappy and Uncle comforted her. Ginger heard this all the way from upstairs and just sighed. Ginger took her locket from her chest. The heart-shaped locket just starred at her, and she stared back. She then went to her room to do her homework. On the side of her bed was a picture of her mom and dad and her in the middle. This picture was taken in Germany when the family went to see Grammy's old neighborhood and to celebrate her birthday. They were happier than ever on that picture because they were all a family, and Ginger was so cute when she was little. Ginger sighed, wishing she could take another picture like that, where they were all one big happy family. All she could do was cherish and dream about her parents, as if nothing happened (like the dream she had that Saturday before she went to see Lanely). Ginger finished her homework and then wrote in her diary. This diary truly was the connection between her and her inner truth. Without the diary, she'd be lost in the world, wondering where to go and what to eat. This time, Ginger did not write the sentence "Even though I am on my knees, I am working to climb on my two feet again (or however it goes)." It is one thing to write what's on your mind, but it is also another to speak the truth, and to speak the truth with zealousness. "Oh, Mom. Oh, Dad. Why did you have to go? I miss you so much! There's this big gap in my life without you, and I don't know how I can cover the gap! I love you so much!" Ginger was talking to herself physically, but mentally and even spiritually, she was talking to her parents. "We miss you too. We love you so much, Ginger!" she could hear both her mother and father say. Communication is powerful and a basic skill you need for life. Without it, you will just fall in a ditch without going close to the ditch. It is good that her parents did familiarize her with communication, but it is up to Ginger if she will benefit from it or manipulate her own path. Ginger put all of her books away in her backpack and got her uniform for volleyball ready. What was Ginger thinking? She can't be sad now; she has a quest to complete and a championship to win. Ginger added a few more words to her diary (she usually does), and then when she was just about done. Grammy had announced that it was dinnertime. Ginger went to the bathroom to wash her hands, and went to the kitchen table for dinner. Tonight they were having stir fry, cooked by Grammy of course. "So how was school?" Pappy asked her. "It was good. No complaints at all."

"Do you have a volleyball game tomorrow?" Grammy wondered. "Yes, Grammy," Ginger answered, taking a bite of stir fry. "We'll try to come," Pappy told Grammy. *Why not?* Pappy thought to himself. *I get to see my granddaughter on the court, plus I will have something to do.* Uncle and Ginger's grandparents decided not to bring up her parents, as it will make Ginger suffer greatly. When the family was finished eating, Ginger ran back upstairs. She went to where the family photos were, which were framed. There she saw that picture of her father pushing her on the swing. She also saw picture of her and her mother and father, and they were very happy together. Just looking at their smiles really impacted Ginger, because she can never take a picture with them again. Ginger has another flashback, this time she was at the hospital and so were Grammy, Uncle, Pappy, and Lanely. Her mother was in the bed, and this was her mother's last day. Ginger was crying so hard that everyone can hear her. "Mommy, don't go! Please! You promised to never leave me! Nooo!" Ginger cried that day. "Ginger . . . I will keep my promise. I . . . I . . . love you, and I know Pappy . . . and Grammy will take good care of you!" her mother said, very hurt not only from the disease, but also by her not seeing her daughter grow up. "Mommy, please! You said you will see me grow up! You said you'd watch me go to college!" Ginger shouted, crying even louder. She was only eight years old. "I know. Here Ginger . . . , take this locket . . . , I got it from Grammy when I was just a girl . . ." When Grammy heard that, she cried even louder than she already was. Ginger's mother took the locket off her neck, and with her strength, she put the locket necklace on Ginger's neck and kissed her on the cheek, and then Ginger's mother carefully laid back down. "Goodbye . . . Ginger . . . I love you so much . . . , and good-bye everyone. It has been so much fun . . ." Ginger just had tears coming down when she held the heart of the locket in her own two hands. But then . . . , Ginger's mother said . . . "I love you so much Ginger, and your father does too. Now, I can visit him in . . ." Beep! That was the sign of no pulse. "Where at? Noo! Mother, please come back!" Ginger was crying more, now. Her mother had just died, and now she was parentless at age eight. Lanely, Grammy, Pappy, and Uncle gave eight-year-old Ginger a big hug, grieving up on Ginger's mother as well. Ginger took a careful look at the pictures and saw her mother wearing the locket in all of the pictures. From the time Ginger received the locket to now, she has come a long way with just growing up and maintaining independence and self-respect. Maybe this is a message to her from her parents, and maybe this is just fate's revenge taking its toll. But whatever the case may be, Ginger is just glad to move on with her life and think of the happy times (even when there are none). Ginger gazed once more at the locket. The heart of the locket glowed for about ten seconds and stopped glowing. The locket sometimes does that, usually when something good is about to happen, or if Ginger has made a good accomplishment. The locket has only glowed a few times since she first received it, and she is trying to do good deeds to make it glow more. Usually, it glows when you least expect it, but it just depends on the day and time. Lanely's words and some words that Coach Hector was telling her earlier were soon to come true, and the locket was there to prove that. When Ginger looked at more pictures, she also saw some other family relatives, relatives you would only see at a family gathering, or a dinner party at one's house. The happiness of her family made Ginger smile again and maybe even throw a laugh in between; recognizing the family's silly moments. After seeing the glow of the locket, Ginger knew her life was about to change, and this time, it was going to change for the better.

CHAPTER 6

Teen Exclusive

Ginger hasn't had that dream, which is good, because it means she is not in much disbelief. At school the next day, everyone was starting to cheer for the volleyball team. The semi-playoffs game was just around the corner. Many kids were cheering for the girls today as they were in their volleyball uniforms. They were not only cheering to hopefully win the semiplayoffs, but also for the game after school. Just when they were entering the school, Ginger immediately spotted Todd's friends, with some other people. Remember, Todd is the most popular and cool kid in the school. In the group was Todd himself, Malcolm, Andy, Mack, Chad, the "Rockstar Kid," and The Wise. The Wise wears a mask in the school and never takes it off, and nobody knows why he does that. Perhaps it is to cover his identity or to make himself unknown to the world. Rockstar Kid has long brown hair, almost as long as Ginger's hair. He rocks at *Guitar Hero* and *Rock Band* and also at a real guitar. Chad is probably the second most popular kid in the school. He is pretty much known by everyone and has yellow hair and can get all of the girls. Andy and Mack have black hair. Mack is on the basketball team (so are Todd and Malcolm). They are both very cool. Before Ginger walks up to go up the stairs, she is stopped by them. "Hey, Ginger," Todd greeted her. Todd's friends behind him were just giving her a "flirting" smile. "Hi," Ginger responded. "Good luck with the volleyball game today," Todd told her. "Thanks," Ginger cried, giving him a smile, as Ginger walked up the stairs. Summer saw this and ran up to Ginger. "I think he likes you!" she teased. "He does not. It was just a simple hello," Ginger responded. "Okay . . . Anyways, good luck today. See you later!" Summer said, running up the stairs. "Bye!" Ginger called back. There was so much chattering when she was walking up the stairs because all kids were talking and were about to start class. Summer is a really nice girl and wouldn't hurt anybody (at least that was her reputation; which is fabulous). Just when Ginger reached the second floor, Luna caught up to her. Luna (as you know) is in charge of the book club and is very popular and cool in school and is Ginger's good friend. Luna goes to every party, every hangout (mostly at peoples' houses or on Main Street), and sleepovers. "Was Todd hitting on you? It was . . . , you'd better watch out!" Luna as well teased. "Shut up, Luna," Ginger said, but she was joking. "So was he?" "No. He just told me good luck. I'm going out with Bailey, anyway," Ginger reminded Luna. "All righty, then. See ya at today's game, Ginger!" Luna waved and was off to her class. Ginger waved back as well. When Ginger arrived to her locker, she spotted Bailey. "Good luck on today's game, cutie," he told her. "Thanks so much," she replied, as he kissed her on the cheek. Bailey was staring at her chest. "What are you looking at?" she asked him, being dumbfounded. "Nothin'. Good luck, Ginga'. See ya later, cutie," he replied, kissing her again and going to his class. Just when Ginger was going to class, she bumped into Stephanie and her best friend, Amy. "Oh, I'm sorry," Ginger apologized. "No need, Ginger, you're cool," Stephanie told her. "Good luck today," Amy added, as the girls waved and kept walking. Stephanie is the most popular girl in the school. She has straight blonde hair and shiny green eyes. Amy has brown hair, and she is always wearing tank tops. Her other close friends are Rachael, Joe, and Nick. Nick and Joe are friends with probably all of the girls in the eighth grade, and Rachael throws a lot of parties. At lunch time, Ginger sat with girls on the volleyball team (ten of them sit together, as they are all friends). Many students were coming to their table, wishing them good luck. The girls were all in their volleyball uniform. Ginger's closest friends, who were sitting next to her, were of course Meredith, Sally, and even Jenny. Summer sat with them as well, although she is not on the team. "Nick was so checking me out in science today, and he even picked up my pencil from the floor," Jenny said, eating some more of her lunch. Gossip. Typical. "Guys can be so cruel, but then they can be so sensitive!" Sally budded in. "Exactly. That's what makes them guys," Meredith cried, as the five girls laughed. "I'm glad I don't have a date at the school," Summer said. "But why?" Ginger wanted to know.

"Because sometimes he expects so much, and these guys in our school can be such perverts." "What a bad word, Summer," Sally told her. "It's true. Most guys are concerned with … you know …," Jenny said, not daring to say the rest. "Yea, especially the so called 'jocks,'" Meredith agreed. "True, but luckily us girls can stick together and keep our dignity!" Ginger announced the other four girls agreeing with her. Here comes Todd, Malcolm, and Andy. The other volleyball girls looked at him and breathed heavily. Ginger, Sally, Meredith, Summer, and Jenny pretended not to take any notice. "Hey, Ginger," Todd greeted her for the second time today. Ginger stood up, as the volleyball girls (all but her friends) watched him. "Hi," she greeted back. "So are you captain of the volleyball team?" Malcolm asked. "I think I am, yes," Ginger was shy. "Awesome," Andy added. "See you around," Todd told her, winking at her. Ginger slowly sat back down. The real gossiping was starting. "What was that for?" Meredith wondered. "I haven't a clue." Once again, Ginger was dumbfounded. She was being oblivious to the obvious. "Ginger, it's so obvious. Todd likes you," Jill, a volleyball girl, told her. Jill was not sitting far away from her. "How can you tell?" Ginger asked Jill. "Oh my gosh. He winked at you, and he said hi to you twice. He was flirting with you," she answered. "I wish Todd would flirt with me," a girl complained. "I'd love to totally go out with him. He's so hot!" another girl said. "Yea, his hair is so smooth," another girl agreed. "Well, I'm already going out with Bailey, and everyone knows that," Ginger cried. "Yes, but boys are attracted to you, Ginger," Jill answered. "Like who?" "Well him, and Eli," she answered as well. "I went out with him two years ago. We're just friends," Ginger commented. "True, but Todd was hitting on you," Jill cried. Ginger did not see it that way, nor was she accepting this. Next to Meredith sat Jason's other friends. They included him, Eric, Eli, Jim, Connor, David, Cody, and Jose. Eli and Jim were best friends. They had messy brown hair (the kind girls were attracted to), and those two were the best of friends. Eric and Cody are friends. Cody has black hair (which is short), and Eric has long brownish red hair. Jose was a Hispanic, therefore his skin was mixed. He has dark black silky hair and always wears sports shorts. Connor is short and has black hair. His mother passed away when he was little, but he doesn't show it. He is what is considered "normal" in the school, and he goes on Main Street a lot (in fact, all of these boys do). David is a little taller than Connor, and he has swirly yellow hair. He, too, can be described as "normal" (whatever "normal" may be considered as). Eli turned to Ginger and waved at her. Eli, Jason, Cody, and Jose smiled at her. Jason, Jose, and Cody turned to her and waved as well. Ginger could only smile and wave back. She still thought Eli was cute, but now they were just friends. From a glance, she could see Luna and about six of the girls reading. Luna has a book club at lunch and sometimes after school. They looked like they were very engaged to the book they were reading. Soon, lunch was over, and Ginger gave some of her friends hugs, and they all left for class. Band class. Ginger is not in this class, but band had to be the most dynamic class in the school. Sally plays the clarinet, Brianna plays the oboe, Hillary and Stacy play the flute, Connor and David play the trumpet, Eric and Cody play the alto saxophone, and Todd and Malcolm play the trombone. Jason and Andy play the baritone saxophone, and well Max, plays the tuba. Before class was starting, Hillary, Stacy, Brianna, and Sally were talking. In another group, Todd, Malcolm, Andy, and Jason were talking. "Dude, are you flirting with Ginger?" Malcolm asked Todd. "A little. I kinda like her," Todd admitted. "Well, you have to admit, she is hot," Jason agreed. "True, but why her? Aren't you gonna go back out with Stephanie?" Andy asked Todd. Todd was going out with Stephanie the previous year, and now they are not. "Naah, Stephanie is seeing someone else," Todd answered. "You gonna ask her out?" Jason asked. "Maybe. She shouldn't say no, she probably likes me," Todd answered. "I wanna go out with Ginger too. She has a fine ass," Malcolm admitted, as all four boys said yea and aaaahed. "I'd go out with her any day," Andy agreed, as they all shook their heads yes. Hillary and Stacy overheard this and approached them. "If you desperate guys are talking about my friend Ginger, you can forget it," Hillary told them. "Hillary, shut up, and go away," Jason told her. Hillary's bright orange hair fluttered through the wind from the door being pushed over. "Then why don't you stop talking about Ginger? She will say no," Stacy cried. "Don't be a stuck-up whore," Malcolm told the girls, as the four boys high-fived each other. "Do what you want, but Ginger will say no," Stacy told them. Joel crept up behind Hillary and tickled her on her side. This greatly startled Hillary. "Hey, Hillary. Gosh, you look fabulous," Joey said in his wannabe model voice. He always talks like that. Jason, Todd, Malcolm, and Andy just laughed. "Oh my freaking goodness you scared me," Hillary cried. "Wanna go out with me?" he asked her. He asks her this almost every day "No," she answered, rolling her eyes. "Aww, Hillary's getting mad . . . ," Andy teased, as Todd, Jason, Malcolm, and himself laughed and high-fived each other. Stacy pushed Andy to the ground. "Whoa," Todd said. "What's your problem?" Jason asked her. "You know damn well what the problem is. Now leave us and Ginger alone!" Hillary was angrier then mad now. "We never bothered you," Todd cried. "Well leave Ginger alone," Stacy blackmailed. "Okay, we will, just back off," Jason told the girls. "Yea, you girls need to take a chill pill," Joel laughed, as did the boys. Hillary smacked him, but Mrs. Alvarez saw anyway. "Hillary, no hitting in the hallway!" Mrs. Alvarez told her. Mrs. Alvarez has on diva clothes, with many bracelets. She talks like some sort of model. Mrs. Alvarez's personality and occupation just don't go together. By now, the second bell had rung, which means that the passing period was over. "Wow, Hillary. You're tougher than I thought," Malcolm said, as they entered the classroom. "I thought she was a wimp," Todd cried, as all five boys got their instruments. "Don't worry about them, Hillary," Brianna said, as the three girls were setting up their instruments Stacy and Hillary sat next to each other, and Brianna didn't sit too far away. "I know. They're just mean," Stacy told Hillary. It looks as though Hillary was about to burst into tears any minute. "I know. We just have to do everything we can to stay away from them," Hillary responded. Unfortunately, Joel sits next to Hillary, and he took his seat. Brianna went to her seat, and Mrs. Alvarez stepped on the podium.

The class was ready, and they had their music out. Joel was bothering Hillary when Mrs. Alvarez started talking. "Okay, class. Your concert is coming up soon, and we all need to be ready," she announced. Joel twigged through Hillary's hair. "Stop it!" she yelled out. "Hillary and Joel, stop it, or I will give you both a detention," Mrs. Alvarez said, as the boys were laughing, same with some of the girls. "But he . . . ," Stacy started. "Enough, now get out your music," Mrs. Alvarez finished for her. Andy, Malcolm, Todd, and Jason were still laughing. Eric and Cody were even laughing. "Shut up, it's not funny!" Sally told them. "All right, just chill," Andy told her. The boys were sitting in the back near the percussion, and the flutes sat right next to the podium of the left, the clarinets to the right, and the oboes in the center. The trumpets and alto saxophones sat next to the tuba, euphonium, trombone, baritone sax, and French horns. When band class was over, Hillary once again approached the four boys. This time she was with Sally. "Do not say anything to Ginger. It is none of your business," Hillary confronted. "Hillary, quit being a loser," Jason told her. "I'm not," she quickly responded. "Then quit actin' like one," Malcolm replied, as Hillary left, feeling angry. Sally stuck up her middle finger to the guys, and she, too, left the room. "Wow. Those girls are feisty," Andy cried, as the others were agreeing with him. The volleyball game was only just two class periods away, and what had seemed like a day of good luck to Ginger was merely a day of anxiety. She just wanted to make it to the semiplayoffs and win the championship. She herself was not excited as much as the school was about the championship, probably because she is the cause to win the game, and the effect of it is the school being excited. Unfortunately, she or any of the other girls could not see nor participate in the effect, because they were the cause. As Hillary, Sally, and Stacy were going to their next class, they were trying to figure out a way to "protect" Ginger for her own good. "What are we going to do? Those jerks are going to be mean to Ginger," Sally implied. "We're going to have to tell her," Hillary suggested. "But she'll treat what we say the wrong way," Stacy cried. "Well, we have to. This is for her own good. It's time to stand up against the jocks and say no!" Hillary cried, "Although they may be hot, especially Jason!" "Oh my goodness, yes! Andy too. His hair and eyes are dreamy!" Stacy exposed. "Have you forgot about the plan already?" Sally asked them. "Oh, right," Stacy said. "We should tell her tomorrow, today is too rushed," Hillary agreed. The second bell had rung, meaning it's time for the next class. "Okay, tomorrow! Bye!" Sally cried, as the three girls headed in different directions to their next class. Friendship is a very sensitive thing and involves no joke. What is a "true" friend? A "true" friend is when a person that you know well and long helps you with certain aspects of life, and to support you upon an obstacle. There is such a difference between "friend" and "true" friend, because a friend is just someone you talk to and hang out with a lot. A "true" friend is one that goes the extra mile to protect, or help their friend in need, which is really heartwarming and sincere. Hillary, Stacy, and Sally want to protect Ginger from those boys, because those "jerks" will just cause chaos and will not help Ginger at all (but this is only their opinion, and they only judge this by just seeing the boys at school). Ninth period came, and Ginger was headed for math class. In her class were Meredith, Summer, Todd, Jason, Amy, Chad, Mack, and Josh. Josh is Max's friend. In fact, Josh is Max's only friend in the school. Josh is a nerd and talks to no one. That is probably the reason why he is considered a nerd. Ginger entered the classroom, still talking to Summer and Meredith as the children took their seats. The math teacher Mrs. Divine stood in the front of the class. Mrs. Divine was a beautiful name because it describes herself, and many children in the school think so as well. "Okay, class, quiet down now. Thank you. For today, you can start your homework on the board. I don't mind if you work on small groups, as long as it's silent. You may get to work," Mrs. Divine announced, sitting at her desk. Ginger, Meredith, and Summer got in a group and worked together. Ginger is very smart; she has a 4.0 GPA. Her mother was really smart as well, and her father got a masters' degree in engineering anatogy. Ginger and Meredith were the only girls in the class wearing a volleyball uniform, and the rest of the class said good luck. The three girls were just talking and gossiping while doing their homework. Meredith and Summer were smart too. "I hope you guys win today," Summer cried. "We will. I'm concerned about next week, when the semiplayoffs will take place," Ginger cried, writing down equations from the textbook. "Well, it shouldn't be hard. If we win just one game in the semiplayoffs next week, we're in the playoffs automatically," Meredith replied. "True, plus we're still number one in our division," Ginger agreed. Todd, Jason, Chad, Mack, and Amy were sitting on the desk tables and counter, with math books open. The boys were just chatting with Amy and amongst themselves, and they were also texting on their cell phones. Summer turned to them and turned back. "Typical popular kids: always on the cell phone or sneaking," Summer cried, looking down at her textbook. "That's okay, as long as we are friends," Meredith responded, moving her red and curly hair out of the way so she could see the textbook. The boys were now staring at Ginger, Meredith, and Summer. Amy was just paying attention to her cell phone, and IMing her other friends. Ginger looked up and saw this. Ginger crossed her legs to get comfortable. The boys smiled and waved hi to Ginger. Ginger waved back and gave a small chuckle. Soon after, the boys were talking to each other, and so was Amy. Summer was puzzled. "What was that about?" she wondered. "They were probably just being nice," Ginger thought. "Hmmph, how nice," Meredith added, as the girls got back to work. Josh was working alone by himself. It was sad because all of the other kids were working in groups or partners. He was the only one working by himself. "Aww, Josh is working by himself. Poor guy!" Summer noticed. "Maybe we should ask him to work with us," Ginger suggested. The girls chuckled at this, because it would embarrass Josh if he was working in a group of all girls. It is bad enough he is insulted by the entire eighth grade, and the girls figured that asking him to work with him would just not help. School was over in twenty minutes, and at this time, Coach Hector got on the announcements, saying: "All eighth-grade volleyball girls please report to the gym with your things. All eighth-grade girls volleyball team report to the gym with your things." Ginger and Meredith stood up, and the whole class, except Josh, clapped for them. They cheered and said good luck. "Good luck, Ginger and Meredith!" Summer said, as both girls said thanks. Meredith and Ginger collected their books, and as they left, Todd said, "Good luck, Ginger." "Um, thanks?" she responded, as she and Meredith left the classroom. The classroom was still cheering from footsteps away. Ginger wondered, why did Todd only tell her good luck but not Meredith? Maybe it is because Ginger is the captain of the team, or he just didn't notice Meredith in the first place. Whatever the reason is, Ginger was utterly confused by it. Meredith waved Ginger good-bye, and both girls went their separate ways to their lockers. When Ginger went to her locker, Bailey was right there, and he had a flower in his hand. "Bailey! What are you doing here?" she asked him. "To give you this flower," he told her, putting the flower on the root of her ear. The purple flower (purple being Ginger's favorite color) was seen in her hair. "Thanks," Ginger told him. "Good luck, cutie," he told her, kissing her on the cheek, "I gotta go. See ya lata." Bailey quickly ran to his class, which he didn't even go to in the first place. That's just Bailey: he is just trying to be cool and a bully in the school. Ginger gathered her backpack and volleyball equipment and walked to the gym. Many other girls were already inside the gym, and some girls were walking as well to the gym. The girls were practicing around in the gym, and the janitors were setting up the benches to the side. "Hi, Ginger!" Sally happily greeted her. "Hi, Sally! Where's the other team?"

Ginger wondered. "They're not there, yet. I think we're playing Midway Middle School," Sally responded, as Ginger and Sally were bumping a volley ball to each other. They were already in their volleyball shorts and shirt, and so were the other girls. "Where did you get that flower?" Sally asked, noticing the texture of the flower. "Bailey gave it to me. Isn't it beautiful?" Ginger asked her. "Indeed it is." "He said it's for good luck," Ginger replied. Ginger already knew that her good luck was within the locket she was wearing, the locket that had her mother's soul and spirit upon. The locket is her only real connection spiritually, and her diary is a connection mentally. All in all however, she cannot connect with her parents ever again physically. In a couple of minutes, Ginger found herself bumping the volleyball with Jenny, Sally, Meredith, and even Jill. School was over in ten minutes, and at this time, Coach Hector blew the whistle, and the girls huddled upon one side of the gymnasium, the side without the bleachers. On the side they were on where the team players' side, right next to the scoreboard. On the other side of the scoreboard where the opposing team sits. "Okay, girls, you win this game and the game next week, you are in the semiplayoffs!" Coach Hector announced, as the girls cheered. "Remember, do your best, and victory will be ours for good!" he cheered, as the girls were getting more excited. "Now say the chant together on a count of three!" Coach Hector announced. "1 . . . 2 . . . 3 . . . USMS! Woo!" the girls and the coach said, as the volleyball girls took their seats next to the scoreboard. At that moment, the other school arrived. It was Midway Middle School, and they were second in the division, but so close to first. These girls were tough, fierce, and full of energy. The captain of their team is Mandy Liverstone. Her and Ginger have been rivals and enemies since the beginning of volleyball, when USMS beat MMS by a margin, and MMS was embarrassed. Here they are again! Competing. Ginger versus Mandy. School versus school. Sadly, one can only win, not two. Mandy approached Ginger near the water fountain and started messing with her. "Our team is gonna win. You can't stop us this time! Victory shall be ours!" Mandy told Ginger, "We've come a long way for this, and you won't ruin our championship." Ginger didn't know what her problem was and didn't care, so all Ginger said was: "Good luck." Ginger then took her seat. School was finally over, and kids were already paying to see the game. Janitors were cleaning up the floor and setting up the net. Mandy kept staring at Ginger and the other girls on Ginger's team. Mandy's expression was far from a happy smile: it was determination. Mandy has her game face on, and like Coach Hector, she wants to win the most. She will only be satisfied when the trophy is in her hands, and victory is hers. Only one can have victory and that shiny gold trophy, the other will just have a sign of defeat and sadness on their face. In just ten minutes, all of the kids were there to see. The school only needed to win this game, and the game next week to make the semiplayoffs, so everyone was excited and rambunctious. Ginger tucked her locket inside of her shirt, which was a sign that luck is on her side.

CHAPTER 7

Loving the Unloved

Ginger saw most, if not all, of her friends sitting down on the bleachers. She even saw Pappy, Grammy, and Uncle taking their seats, and taking off their jackets. They had arrived on time. Grammy waved to Ginger, and Ginger waved back to her. Some kids waved, intending on Ginger to wave to them. Ginger was focused. She has to lead their team to victory and let the school know that she is a champion. The girls now stood, and the timer was set. The teams were in huddles, as their coach was making an announcement before the game. "Okay, girls, this is it. Play hard, play strong, and most of all, do the very best you can, and be the very best you can be!" Coach Hector told the girls. "Be the very best you can be!" Is that even possible? Can you be perfect at whatever you wish to pursue? No. When Coach Hector said that, he really did mean what he said at practice yesterday. He really does want to win, and he wants no one to stop him. Coach

Hector has waited too long for this, and now his ambition of being a champion is about to come true. "He doesn't really think we are perfect, does he?" Ginger asked herself, as nine girls including herself took the position on the court. It's all about competition. Of course he thinks the girls are perfect; they haven't lost a single game, yet. Even so, they are not perfect. No one on this earth is. As long as the team won, that was all that concerned Coach Hector. He has worked so hard for this, and he feels that the girls are ready. Midway Middle School Girls took their place on the court, and now the people in the bleachers were silent waiting for the game to begin. An announcer was explaining the rules and procedures, and then the referee blew the whistle and gave Midway control of the ball. Mandy was tough throughout the entire game. Not only could others see this, she showed it during the game, because when the second quarter was over, Midway was up by six. There was no cheering going on at all from the bleachers, and Coach Hector had a gleaming look on his face. When the girls were getting water on a fifteen-minute break, Ginger was adjusting the purple flower on her ear and drinking more water when once again, Mandy Liverstone approached her. "Ginger, why don't ya just give up now? You lost. Do us all a favor and leave. In fact, go visit your parents. I bet they stink at volleyball too!" Mandy sneered, walking away. Some tears filled Ginger's eyes, but no one noticed. Many doesn't know a thing about Ginger's parents, and what she had said angered Ginger all over again. Ginger was not happy at all, and when the third quarter came, she expressed it. Ginger was spiking and spiking and spiking. When two minutes were left, it was a tie. The schools in the bleachers were cheering and were excited more than ever. "Okay, girls, less than two minutes left. All we have to do is avoid them from scoring and keep spiking. Have fun, though, fun is the key," Coach Hector cried. The coach from the other team had two simple words for the girls: "Stop Ginger!" The girls were back on the court, and the people were cheering again. Nobody scored, and in the last ten seconds, everyone was questioning each other. "Ginger!" Sally called. Sally passed the ball to Ginger. Ginger jumped up and hit the ball over the net really hard and with momentum. The other girls tried to stop it, but they couldn't. The ball hit the ground, and time was up. The whole school was cheering, and all Coach Hector could do is smile. Sally and the rest of the girls went over to Ginger, high-fiving her friends and other people. Ginger went to grab her materials when Mandy stood behind her and said: "It ain't ova, yet! We still have to play y'all in the semi-finals next week! Enjoy it now, but next week, we will win!" Mandy told her. "Whatever you say, Mandy," Ginger agreed, trying to ignore Mandy as much as she could. "Good job, Ginger! If you do this next week, we will sure win! You will lead us to victory, Miss McFraiddee! Thank you so much!" the coach told her. Ginger eerily smiled, and when children were leaving the gym, her grandparents and uncle were standing in the bleachers. Her Pappy started speaking German. Randomly, her grandparents and Uncle sometimes start speaking German or Italian. Ginger can speak those two and English. Grammy spoke German words to her as well, as they were walking to the car. They mostly speak one of these languages in public, to refresh on their skills, and so people cannot understand what they're saying, so they can be really personal depending on a situation. The family went to the car and got inside. Some other girls were waving good-bye to her, as they were happy to win. Ginger smoothly gave small smiles in the car going home. She was glad to win, and only one more game will lead her to the semifinals. At night, Ginger wrote in her diary. 'Another game won,' she thought, *and soon, victory will be ours.* Victory. A word that everyone wants and everyone sometimes feels. Unfortunately, if you are on a team of two or more, what must you do to feel victory, or even be victorious? Work. You must work to get the things you want. Work is not fun, but in the end, it most definitely pays off. If you have tried your best, but wasn't victorious, that is okay, because you gave it your all, and that is all a person can do. Things have gotten crazier at school the next day. The school mascot, a wolf, danced around the school, proudly taking pride in the win. Ginger walked in the school with Summer, Sally, and Meredith. Many kids came up to them saying: "Good job!" or "Great job, you guys!" Happiness has come upon Ginger? She felt like she accomplished a goal, not only for herself, but for the school as well. "Good job, Ginger," Todd said, approaching her. Meredith, Sally, and even Summer rolled their eyes. "Thanks," Ginger responded, a little puzzled. "No problem. Good luck in the playoffs." Ginger said thanks again, and she and her three friends were walking up the stairs, going to class. "Why did he just acknowledge you?" Summer asked Ginger. "I don't know.

Something's up," Ginger cried. "Yea, and it's Jill's message. He likes you, Ginger. Do not deny," Sally said. "He does not. He is just being considerate," Ginger tried to deny the situation. "The truth is the truth, Ginger. You just can't ignore it. He likes you, enough said," Meredith responded. Ginger did not believe it and did not want to believe it. Once again, she was being oblivious to the obvious. Anyone with eyes can see that he was flirting with her, and he was going to ask her out sooner or later. It was up to Ginger to accept or decline, but for right now, she was declining the idea. This isn't a bad thing, but soon the truth will be revealed. When Ginger went up the stairs, she saw Mrs. Robbin and Mrs. Duffy staring in a small window right outside their room. They are always doing this. What were they staring at? Why was it so interesting, or fun, to stare out of a window? These are the questions not only that ran through Ginger's mind, but the entire school questioned this. Ginger continued to walk up the stairs very slowly, as the two mysterious teachers stared blissfully into the small window. These two ladies must have a reason for staring out of that window, or an exact purpose of the matter. Every question must have a reason or a purpose to even get the answer in the first place. Nobody had an answer for this, only Mrs. Robbin and Mrs. Duffy did. For the reason being, it is still unknown to everyone. Really the whole thing was no one's concern, so Ginger moved on and ignored the two teachers. Before lunchtime, Ginger had gym class, and in her gym class were Meredith, Jose, Rachael, Jim, and Mack. Ginger only talked to Meredith in that class. She had more friends, but she considers them as acquaintances. They were in their gym uniform, and today was the PACER Test. This probably is the most annoying thing to do in gym, because the pacer test is for a grade, and it's frustrating to run back and forth on the gym court. The gym teacher was even worse. It wasn't Coach Hector; it was another gym teacher, Mr. Ukaletchii. He is Mongolian and Korean, and yet he is a gym teacher. He is strict and doesn't like to play games. "All right, listen up! The pacer test is important! It takes pride, dedication, and commitment. You will have a thirty-second break, now! Girls will go first," Mr. Ukaletchii announced. Ginger was talking to Meredith, and Jose, Jim, Mack, and Amy were just talking in a group, even though the boys were harassing her. Once again, that was just typical teens being themselves. Ginger, Meredith, Rachael, and the other girls were lining up, and getting ready to start the PACER Test. At the end of the PACER Test, Ginger had scored the most. She ran nearly sixty laps, and when she was running she was alone, the whole class was cheering her on. Rachael kept laughing, because she only scored a three on the pacer. When the pacer was finally over, Ginger was relieved. Ginger is also on the track team, and that is why she ran so fast, and was able to keep up with the pacer. When lunchtime arrived, Todd, Chad, Rockstar Kid, Malcolm, Jason, and Jose stood outside of the lunchroom, just hanging out as kids were filling up the seats in the lunchroom. At this point, Max approached them. "What do you want, kid?" Chad asked him. "To become your friend, please!" Max was always bothering them, and all Todd and his friends could do was laugh. "We're not your friends. Just go away. You're a nobody!" Todd said, as Max walked away. The guys were still laughing at that kid, as he was nothing more than dirt to them. "That kid has serious problems," Jose commented. "He sure does; and he stalks us," Rockstar Kid added. "He just needs a life and friends," Malcolm retorted, as the others were agreeing. Todd glanced, and he saw Ginger coming to the lunchroom with her friends (as many kids already were). She was with Brianna, Jenny, and Sally. The boys were too shallow to say nothing more than hi to Ginger, which is why Hillary's message to the boys about staying away from Ginger seemed to be working. "Hey look, there's Ginger," Jason pointed. All six boys just stared at her, mainly her boobs. "I gotta ask her out," Todd cried. Todd is the most popular guy in the school, and since he is popular, his friends are going to agree with him. "Ginger? What has she done to you?" Chad asked him. These guys mostly go out or have "dated" Stephanie's friends. They don't even know Ginger. The only thing they do know is that she is the captain of the volleyball team, which is enough for them to want to go out with her. Todd himself plays numerous sports, and so do his friends, and Ginger also plays sports, which is one thing they have in common. "She stole my heart," Todd answered Chad. "Ginger is hot," Jason added, still staring at her. "Aww yea. She seems cute too," Malcolm agreed. When Ginger and her three friends passed the boys, Todd just said: "Hey, Ginger!" Ginger and the three girls stop, as Brianna and Sally rolled their eyes. "Hi . . . ," Ginger responded. Ginger's blue eyes were ravishing and bright, and her golden hair was magnificent, which immediately made Ginger hot and attractive. "You play volleyball. Cool," Todd cried. "Thanks . . . ," Ginger then looked into the air, a little puzzled. All six boys solemnly smiled and were still staring at her boobs. "What are you staring at?" Ginger asked him. They didn't even budge. "Uhh . . . guys. Hello? Are you there? Guys . . . ," Jenny tried to get their attention, waving her hand in front of their faces. The guys finally blinked and smiled again. "So see ya later, then, and good luck with the volleyball semi playoff games next week," Todd told her. "Thanks," she said, still confused. "Guys can be so weird . . . ," Brianna commented, as the four girls walked into the lunch room. The boys finally walked into the lunchroom, and met up with Andy and The Wise at their table. Stephanie, Nick, Joe, Rachael, Amy, and more of her friends sat at the table right next to them. "Hey, you guys," Stephanie greeted. "Hey, Stephanie," the boys greeted back, sitting down about to eat lunch. Todd just cannot ask her out: he is too gutless at this point. "Hey, The Wise," Malcolm greeted. The Wise just waved in his mask. The Wise doesn't really talk, he is more of a sidekick. He gives advice to some kids, but he keeps his identity secure. Most kids don't know how he looks. He would be most great for a policeman or a secret agent. "Just ask her out. She's really nice and sexy," Andy told Todd. "I just can't. I don't know," Todd was officially going a little crazy. He sighed in relief. "She would say no anyway as she's going out with Bailey," Hillary budded in. Hillary is friends with Stephanie, and so is Shandi. "Bailey's an asshole. He thinks he's tough when he's not," Jose added. Todd's friends do not like Bailey, nor are they his friends. "Don't say that about Bailey. You wouldn't want to be insulted, either," Shandi responded. "We don't care," Chad told her. Shandi shrugged and turned back around. The tension between the jocks and the bullies were getting worse between each other, and after school proved that. Bailey and his two friends Billy and Jeff were in the school main hall, wanting to start a fight. These guys are huge, big, and tough. They will not leave without a fight. They will defend until they cannot defend anymore. Most of the time, Bailey and his friends get into trouble for silly and stupid reasons. It's all about the choices you make throughout life, and within them comes a consequence or a reward. But people are people. They can do whatever they want, whenever they want, and nobody can stop them. This is just a theory that people use to live their lives, and it goes to show you that this theory is invalid, as this theory has an effect on people being locked up, persecuted, or just dead altogether. This goes on every day in the world, and the questions is this: When will people learn to decline the theory and accept the truth? How can people see or know what rules to follow? People know these rules and their expectations, but they just will not apply. They would rather take the easy path and do whatever they want while ignoring the rules, which leads to chaos and pandemonium. You have to know your place and goals on the earth. You were called on the earth to do a good deed, but it is up to you if you are willing to accept the truth, and decline the invalid theory. Bailey and his friends choose to go with the theory, which results in conflicts, or making a mountain out of a molehill. Again, it is up to them to choose the path they wish to take. Just when all of the kids were leaving the school, it was just those three alone in the hallway. No teachers. No janitors. No students. No persons in sight. Todd, Chad, and Malcolm were about to leave the school while other kids roamed outside (Malcolm, Todd, and Chad were not expecting Bailey and his friends). Bailey and his friends are much bigger than Todd, Malcolm, and Chad. In fact, Bailey's body weight alone is the same size, if not bigger than Todd and Chad's body weight combined. Bailey wanted money from the boys (typical bully), and wanted to prove himself "King of the School," when the "King of the school" was obviously Todd himself. "I want my money, chump!" Bailey told them, pushing Todd to a locker. Luckily it was not that big of impact. "Back off. I don't owe you anything," Todd told him. Malcolm and Chad adjusted their backward caps, getting ready for a "fight." "He said he wants his freakin' money! Pay up or pay the price!" Billy told them. "Look, what's your problem? We don't we you crap, so just go away," Malcolm stood in, trying to avoid conflict. Jeff approached them nose to nose. "He wants his money, that's the problem," Jeff interfered. "And I also want'cha ta know," Bailey started, "that I am number one in the school, not you. So give me my money, and save yourself a trip from the hospital." Bailey was getting angrier and angrier, and he was also losing his patience. "After this, we'll see who's number one in the school!" Billy threatened, as the three bullies got their fists ready. Malcolm, Todd, and Chad just laughed. "Do you see yourself? You're just a retard. You think bothering other kids makes you cool when it makes you a loser," Chad told him. The three boys laughed even more, now. Bailey was furious. "Give me my money or pay the price NOW!" he demanded, being even louder. "Wow, just look at yourself. You really are a loser," Todd said, as Bailey threw a fist at him but hit the locker instead. "Are you okay, Bailey?" Billy asked him. Bailey's hand was hurt. "Yea I'm fine. I just want my freakin' money!" Bailey replied, trying to hold back the pain. "Give him his money!" Jeff threatened again. "Just shut up. You wanna start a fight, go ahead. We don't owe you anything. In fact, just go home!" Malcolm told them. This was enough to make Bailey try to grab them, but Jeff and Billy held him down, trying to make him calm down. Ginger was talking to some friends at her locker, and when she left to go home by herself, she saw the commotion. *Should I help them or go home?* Ginger thought to herself. When Ginger was in Second Grade and didn't know anybody she now knows, she would get teased. All of the kids would laugh at her. One time, another girl pushed her down to the ground, and everyone around her laughed and didn't bother to help her. They would just walk over her. Ginger would tell this situation to her mother, and all her mother told her to do was to be strong and never give up. Ginger thought about her tortured year in second grade and decided to be above the influence and went over to the group (after all, Bailey is her boyfriend). They suddenly stopped bickering when Ginger approached them. "What's the problem?" she asked them kindly. "Ginger, go home! Things are about to get ugly!" Bailey warned her. "I don't care. Whatever you are doing, please stop." One good thing about Ginger is that she can handle herself well, and that she is very strong. Being parentless has greatly taught her that. "He's right, Ginger. I'd leave if I were you," Billy agreed. Malcolm, Chad, and Todd didn't say too much of anything. They were just laughing at Bailey. Bailey saw this and took charge for the three boys. Ginger, however, pushed him back and slammed him into a locker. Bailey's back was in terrible pain. The boys were just amazed. How could a girl push Bailey, let alone slam him unto a locker? "Whoa," that's all Todd and the rest could say at that point. "What was that for?" Bailey asked her. "I'm sorry, but you were about to hurt him," she responded. "He should. These guys owe us money," Jeff explained. "No, we don't," Todd cried. "I'm not leavin' til I get my money!" Billy complained. "Me either!" Jeff agreed. Both boys were charging for Todd and Malcolm, but Ginger grabbed them by the shirt, and just like what she did to Bailey, she slammed both of them into a locker with her own two hands. Todd whispered, as he was really amazed. "Are you guys okay?" Ginger asked them. "No! Ginger, that hurt!" Bailey told her. "I'm sorry. Let's go home now," she replied, helping them get up off the ground. "Wow, Ginger, that was amazing! I never knew you could fight!" Todd complimented her. Ginger didn't see this as a compliment; she saw it as a stereotype. Ginger helped the three bullies out of the door. They were feeling a little light-headed. "It's gonna be okay," Ginger said, as they left the school. The bullies had forgotten what they were even fighting about. "Whoa, dude! Did you see that? She's a beast!" Chad commented. "I know! I never knew she could fight like that. She's always quiet," Todd cried. "Hey, man, she saved our asses. Those bullies would still be here wanting money!" Malcolm told them. Todd was even more attracted to

Ginger. "The way she stood up to us was hot," Todd admitted, as Malcolm and Chad agreed. "I have got to ask her out," Todd also said, as the three boys left the school, as if the whole thing had never happened. Malcolm, Chad, and Todd were just astonished. They couldn't believe what they had seen. A girl could fight or is tough? They had never really seen that! Nonetheless, they haven't seen a girl (one who is shy and sweet) who can stand up to three three-hundred-pound bullies! The three boys were relieved and mostly cautious. They just hope that the bullies will never talk to them again or try to bully them. Ginger said good-bye to Bailey, Jeff, and Billy and kissed him on the cheek and then she walked home. Ginger herself didn't know her own strength. This is probably what Lanely Tildon is trying to tell her. Lanely wants Ginger to see her strengths and benefits, because when she does, she can live life to the fullest. As the wind blew faster, and the birds were singing their afternoon songs, Ginger was starting to see her strengths and some of her weaknesses. The earth was most beautiful today, and the sun was shining the earth. Ginger didn't even know her own strength, but from not having parents, or someone to show her life skills at this point, it shows it has taught her the ways of the world. Ginger was starting to answer her parents' message left behind. She was seeing herself in a different way. If only she could answer Lanely Tildon's question, because that question is probably the same question that her mother would ask her. It does take time, though. Again, it could take Ginger time to figure it out, even in the "after life". Everyone should be able to answer these questions because they are a mere image of you and your character. Remember to ask questions about life, because the answer could fascinate you and the world.

CHAPTER 8

Broken Heart, Unbroken Certainty

Pappy and Grammy were watering some plants when Ginger arrived home. Grammy wore her cute and elegant gardening hat with flowers on the top, and Pappy wore his gloves. "Heya, Ginger!" Pappy greeted her. "Hi, Grammy. Hi, Pappy!"

"Ginga, you're late. Where've you been?" Grammy asked her in her creaked voice. "Oh you know, just saying good-bye to some friends," Ginger lied. She did not want to tell them that she was solving a "fight." Uncle wasn't home yet, he was probably at work. The next day was volleyball practice, only at 6:30 a.m. When practice was over and it was time for school, Ginger and some of the other girls were just tired and needed to rest. "I am so tired now," Meredith cried, as the girls were going to class. "I know," Jenny sighed. "At least Coach Hector is getting us ready for the big game next week," Ginger said. "Yea, we have to be extra ready to win!" Sally cried. "Okay, I gotta go to class. See ya later!" Ginger cried. The girls gave each other hugs, and went to class. When she arrived at her class, Hillary, Stacy, and Shandi approached her. "Ginger, watch out for the boys! They are up to no good!" Hillary frantically warned her. "What do you mean? Which boys?" Ginger was confused. She straightened out her long, silky blonde hair. "You know who we're talking about, Ginger. Todd and his friends!" Stacy told her. "Why are they up to no good?" "Because boys are stupid, that's why. We're your friends, and we just want to protect you," Shandi answered. "You've been warned. If those guys do anything to you, ignore them," Hillary advised. "Um, thanks for the advice," Ginger managed to say. She was out of words to say. Hillary and Stacy entered the classroom, saying nothing more, and Shandi went her separate way. Ginger saw Max enter the class, his head toward the ground. While the class was chattering here and there, Ginger went to the boy to try to have a bias conversation. "Hi, Max," she said to him. Max looked and ignored her by looking the other way. "My name is Ginger," Ginger thought he didn't know her. All of a sudden, she knew what to say to him. "I am not like the others. This wall separates us from greatness," she told Max, as he was still looking the other way. "This world may be treacherous, but you and I can handle it." "What did you say?" Max slowly turned around, seeming to understand what Ginger is saying. "You're not like the others?" he asked her. Ginger shook her head. "Oh." Max was confused by Ginger. He had never met an "outsider." He actually sees Ginger in a new perspective, one that the world cannot see. If Ginger said that to anyone else, they would just call her crazy, because those people are ignorant and too self-centered. They also fit in with this world. Ginger never thought she would meet someone else, other than Lanely Tildon, that can see herself in that new image, and can accept her inner feelings. This was like a bomb exploding in her mind. She couldn't believe that there is someone else in the world that can believe what she is going through, regardless of the person. Now she can see why Max gets teased a lot. She can now see the reason for him being a nobody at the school. He is travelling on a different path, a path that relatively no one can take. If Ginger didn't have friends or didn't play volleyball or was strong the way she is, she would be a nobody as well. Thankfully, that is not her case. She still feels a little bad about Max and his situation from the inference Ginger made. Max actually smiled, and Ginger went to her seat as class was about to start. Ginger has given him hope and courage. Just from her greeting him, they already have a connection that the world does not have, and the world will never have. When Ginger said "this wall," she meant the wall between reality and flesh. Flesh is powerful, but you don't need flesh to survive, you need a spirit. There are troubles throughout life (war, fights, depressions), but it only takes two people to look beyond and have faith to stand up to the world, and someday teach the world a lesson. It takes two people, however, and that is where Ginger comes in to help Max survive in life; let alone school, and prepare for leadership one day. That is what a "true friend" does and should do. Five seconds could change a person's life, and that is what happened to Max when she approached him. Now Max feels more confident than he ever did before, and it only took one person to do that. At least he is not the only one who considers himself as an "outsider." The only difference is that people not think or see Ginger as an outsider, but for Max, well, the world sees him as a nobody or a speck of dust. Ginger took her seat, and then Mrs. Smith began the lesson. She was lecturing about literary devices, and her face was turned to the chalkboard. Ginger received a text. It's a good thing her phone was on low vibrate. The text was from Hillary, and it read, "Watch out 4 them!" Ginger took a glance at Hillary who sat somewhere else, and she saw Hillary giving her hand signals, to beware of the boys. Ginger gave her a thumbs-up to confirm. While Mrs. Smith was still turned to the chalkboard, talking and writing notes at the same time, Todd wrote a note. He tapped a girl sitting next to her and whispered: "Pass this to Ginger." Passing notes in class is so second grade, but obviously Todd can only handle things this way. The girl took the note and passed it to other kids as the note finally landed on Ginger's desk. Mrs. Smith was still writing notes, as other kids were drawing, writing, sleeping, doing other homework, texting without being seen, or just not paying attention at all. Ginger saw the note and quietly unfolded the note so Mrs. Smith wouldn't take notice. The writing was in sloppy handwriting, but it was legible. The note said: 'Will you go out with me?' Ginger immediately looked at Todd, and he was the one who passed her the note. Ginger looked in Hillary and Stacy's direction, and they were shaking their heads no. Ginger tried to act snooty by rolling her eyes, and rolling the note in a paper ball, and throwing it away. Todd put his hands out, the sign that says on a person, "What the heck?" or "What was that for?" Jason and Malcolm were stumped as much as Todd was. "Why *would* she do that?" they thought. Todd automatically knew what the reasoning was, and he knew it was Hillary and Stacy's doing. Class was over, and Ginger walked out with Hillary, Stacy, and Luna. "I told you to look out. They were bound to do that," Hillary told her. Jason, Malcolm, and Todd approached the four girls outside of the classroom in the hall. "What was that for?" Todd asked her. "I told you to leave her alone. She's already going out with Bailey," Stacy answered for Ginger. "Oh yea, Ginger, thanks for covering for us, yesterday. You really are strong," Malcolm told her. Ginger took this as a compliment. Ginger just smiled, and the four girls walked away with pride on their faces. "Why did you say no to Todd? He's the most popular guy in the school! He totally wants to go out with you, Ginger," Luna told Ginger. "Because I'm already going out with Bailey, and Todd is a jerk," Ginger answered. "True, but still! You'd be the most popular girl in the school, not Stephanie!" Luna cried. "Luna, it's okay. There are many other girls in the school that like him. He can choose them," Ginger responded. "Okay, then. See ya later," Luna waved, as she was off to her next class. "Be ready, Ginger. He will continue to ask you out. Trust me, it won't stop here," Hillary warned her. "Oh yea. Has Joel been stalking you, still?" Stacy asked Hillary. "Yup. He called me twenty times yesterday at home," Hillary answered, rolling her eyes. "Sad. Oh well, bye!" Ginger said. "Bye! Remember, say no to Todd!" Hillary said, as Ginger hurried to her next class. It turns out that Hillary was right after all. In gym, Jose passed her a note asking to go out with Todd. Ginger of course threw the note in the trash, and Meredith told Ginger just to ignore Todd and his friends. Todd must really like Ginger, because in math class at the end of the day, Todd got caught passing the note, and he had to serve an after-school detention. Some teachers were strict about distractions in class. Ginger tried to not even look at Todd or his friends. What upset Ginger the most was that he kept passing notes to her, when he could just ask her in his own words. That shows some delicacy. Even so, Ginger would probably say no. Todd, Malcolm, Mack, Andy, and Chad were walking in a group going home. "I don't understand. She said no every time," Todd cried. "Maybe she just doesn't like you," Andy told him. "It's because of Hillary and Stacy. They don't want her to go out with you," Malcolm said. "And she is going out with Bailey. That kid's a joke," Mack added. "I know. I just have to ask her myself when Hillary and Stacy are nowhere to be seen," Todd suggested. "Good luck. She will still say no because she's going out with that douche," Chad responded. "Don't worry. I'll find a way. All right, later guys," Todd told them. "Cya." "Later, man." "Bye, dude." That's what they said to Todd as Chad, Malcolm, Mack, and Andy left the school. Todd left after talking with Stephanie and her friends. He just had to find a way to get Ginger to say yes, or in other words, try to manipulate her. Ginger hasn't seen Bailey all day. Usually he comes to her locker, or he spots her in the hallway. It is not like him to see his own girlfriend, and she knows Bailey is not absent, because she saw him at lunch, eating with his friends. Ginger caught up with Bailey after school. He was by himself, going home. "Bailey, wait up. Why did you just leave?" Ginger asked him. "Don't talk to me," he told her, not bothering to turn back to look at her. "What are you talking about?" Ginger was confused. "Why did you defend Todd and his stupid friends?" Bailey wanted to know. "I just wanted to stop the violence! It's not my fault!" she told him. "He wanted to ask me out, but . . . ," she couldn't finish. "You said yes, Ginger. I know ya did." "No, I . . ."

"Just leave me alone. You're good for nothing. Go away." Ginger was distraught but also a little confused. "What did I do?" she asked him. "Just don't talk to me, you good-for-nothing bitch!" Ginger took a huge gasp. She could not believe what she had just heard. "I can't believe you would say that about me," Ginger's face was turning red, and tears were in her eyes. Agony filled her spirit. "I just did. You know what, I'm glad your parents are gone! And they've never comin' back! So haha!" This broke Ginger's heart to the extreme. She was crying. "I can't believe you would insult my parents like that."

"They're never comin' back, so what does it matter? They wouldn't benefit you anyway."

"I wish you wouldn't have said that," Ginger cried, wiping off tears on her face. "Well, I did. Never talk to me again, you bitch."

"If you feel that way, I won't," Ginger yelled, leaving the school. What has gotten into Bailey? One moment they were just doing fine, and then the next moment Bailey hated her, and insulted her parents. Ginger was starting to think that the Enchantment Lanely Tildon had performed on Saturday to Ginger was nothing. Lanely said her days would be getting better, and so far nothing has changed. Ginger was starting to think that maybe she is becoming a nobody on this earth, or maybe it was fate. Can't you see? Bailey wanted to get rid of Ginger for good, but look who is right there to "take care" of Ginger. Hmm. Peculiar. Very, very peculiar. This was racing in Ginger's mind. But why did Bailey break up with her in the first place? Why did Bailey all of sudden did not like her? Ginger had a pretty good idea of what it was: he thought she was now going out with Todd, and what backed this thought up was the way Ginger stood up to Todd and his friends. Ginger kept crying all the way up 'til she got home. She just couldn't believe that Bailey would say that about her parents. They have done everything for her, and he is saying that they did not benefit her. What is also sad is that she had been called a bitch, and that Bailey didn't even believe her when she said she wasn't going out with Todd. Whatever the reason was for Bailey's crude behavior, she had to solve it really quickly, before things would end up getting worse. When Ginger entered the house, she was still crying, and her face was bright red. "Ginger, what happened?" Grammy asked her. "Love is what happened. In fact, love is not true at all." Ginger said no more after that, and trotted up the stairs to her room. Grammy, Pappy, and Uncle decided to leave her alone, because they don't know the real situation. They assumed she was once again grieving over not being able to hug her parents, like she could when they were alive, but that is not the case. Love is a word that changed to many people. How do you know if love is true? How can you actually tell? When a person loves a person greatly, gratitude comes on one another, and they both makes sure that nothing happens to each other. Clearly, love can be hatred. Any little thing that someone says can mess up a relationship, and soon start to hate. It is not cupid shooting arrows to find true love. In life, it is seeking beliefs and personalities. When this occurs, you must be careful from what you say. You also have to be careful of what you are telling to your spouse. People have no right to ridicule about a loved one who is dead, or just telling someone to go back to their country. It is mean, cruel, and simply shows hatred or jealousy. Nobody should ever say those two things to anyone, regardless if the person is mad, or has problems of his or her own. People interpret things the wrong way, and sometimes that happens with love, which could lead to a troubling relationship. That is why it's important to listen to what a person is saying, so you will not interpret or misunderstand the person. Ginger thought that Bailey truly loved her and would take care of her. In one day, it all turned into hatred. Maybe it had to take that to see Ginger's real destiny or where fate would take her exactly. The Enchantment seemed to have been working, but at the same time, it was doing absolutely nothing. Ginger was still utterly confused. She knew she had to resolve the situation. Ginger wrote in her diary for the rest of the night and was continuing to sob. She didn't care about Bailey breaking up with her (she cared, but wasn't crying about that). She was mostly crying at how he looked at her, how he totally alienated her, and the remark he made about her, and mostly about love and what made love real. Then again, there should be no love at Ginger's age, but Ginger felt the love within her. She couldn't even take her mind off Bailey. He treated her so well, and then he just left her. Ginger just couldn't believe it, or see him doing that. Once again, love can be hatred. All of this went into Ginger's diary, and she wrote nearly three pages. She also drew a picture of a heart, and three Xs on the heart, and a skeleton sign next to the heart. This was really what she had felt in her own heart, and it would take sometime for her to get it (if Bailey decides to apologize, rather talk to her for the matter). Ginger did not have dinner or dessert. She stayed in her room for the entire night. Grammy asked her if she wanted to play a good game of bingo, but she instead said no. So many things were on her mind, and what Bailey had done to her did not help her one bit. Bailey didn't care about anything. He wanted Ginger to suffer. He didn't care about love either. His spirit of hate affected the love, and as you can see, it caused sadness in Ginger's spirit. You can say that love is the Spirit Transporter, and it transports hate to people sooner or later. Believe it or not, this is true, and it happens every day and all the time. Love does not wait for anyone, and it easily turns into hatred, no warnings necessary. Ginger was even crying while she slept, and the next day, her face was pale red. Ginger didn't even want to see Bailey. She was more than mad at him; she was furious. "Hey, Ginger!" Summer greeted her. Summer quickly noticed that Ginger was crying for five minutes or had just stopped crying. "Aww, what's wrong?" Summer asked her as they entered the school building.

Talking would make Ginger feel worse, but she can trust Summer. "Bailey and I broke up yesterday after some argument. He called me mean words and insulted my parents!" You could hardly understand Ginger because of the crying. "Aww, I'm so sorry. You must be in terrible disbelief," Summer comforted her, as she gave her a hug. "I just thought Bailey was a different person. I guess I was wrong." "It's okay. You'll get through this, Ginger," Summer cheered her up. Other kids saw Ginger crying but didn't too much care. Soon enough, Ginger found herself surrounded by ten girls (also of which were her best and closest friends) as they hugged her and tried to cheer her up. "I'm never talking to Bailey again!" Ginger sobbed. "You don't have to either. After what he did to you, I wouldn't see the guy ever again," Sally added. "You gonna be okay, Ginger?" Meredith and a bunch of other girls asked her. "Yes, I will. Thanks so much," Ginger responded, wiping tears off her face. The girls were continuing to hug Ginger and cheer her up until the first period bell rang. It didn't take long for the news to spread. Ginger is no longer going out with Bailey, and now all of the girls are feeling her pain, and the boys; preferably jocks, want to ask her out. Nobody seemed to like or talk to Bailey and his chumps. He got what he deserved. Girls were still comforting Ginger. Ginger was covering tears in, and her face was more red than before. Ginger was sitting with Hillary, Stacy, Cindy, Meredith, Sally, Summer, Shandi, Jenny, Brianna, and some of the volleyball girls (these were mostly all of her closest friends). "I thought love was real. I thought the relationship we had was real. Now, I can't get over what he said. He insulted me and my parents," Ginger cried even more at the remark of her parents being brought up. "You thought that love was true?" Stacy asked her. "It seemed that way."

"Honey, please. Love is never true. People just want love to be true to live a perfect life. Love can easily turn into anger and bitterness, no matter how it may seem. One moment you love each other and want to have 'safe sex,' but then the next moment you are caught in the trap, and now you hate someone, and they hate you back," Hillary explained. "But he said my eyes were like shining diamonds with glittered grace," Ginger responded, crying more at that comment Bailey had told her. "Love is as strong as hate, Ginger. Sure you can say one thing, but that can mean nothing!" Shandi reminded her. "Don't worry, Ginger. We're all here for you. That asshole may have broken your heart, but look who is here to help fix the broken pieces," Stacy told her. Ginger lifted up her head. "Really?"

"Of course, Ginger," Brianna cried, and the rest of the girls said yea. "Thank you so much in my time of need." "Anytime, Ginger," Meredith replied. "And don't worry about love, it is very tough, as you can see," Jenny told her. Ginger's soul was now cleanseth. Ginger smiled now, her blue eyes were bright as ever would be. "Oh and you don't have to ever talk to that jerk Bailey ever again," Cindy told her. "I know, and I won't. After what he said to me, I'm never going to even look or work with him." At least Ginger could see how love works, and that the Spirit Transporter was no joke. Bailey broke up with Ginger, and now things will never be the same again. Will this benefit or torture Ginger? So far it surely hasn't benefitted her one bit. Ginger continued to hug the girls sitting next to and around her. Ginger felt good that she has support and people to care for her. Todd, Malcolm, and Chad came over to their table to see what was going on. Ginger kept her face hidden (which didn't matter because those guys already knew what happened and about the break up). "Looks like a love fest here!" Malcolm teased. "Shut up, you guys! It's not funny, now leave us alone!" a volleyball girl ordered. "Okay, okay, sheesh!" Chad told them, as the three guys laughed and left the table. "Those guys are such assholes!" Hillary said. "Yes, and they are annoying," Summer agreed. When girls and boys meet (especially at this age), there are many tensions in what is called the "relationship." That is only because the Spirit Transporter is causing the tensions by using personality and differences between the couple. It causes massive trouble, and someone has a crushed spirit (usually the girl). All because of the Spirit Transporter. The bell rang, and Ginger waved good-bye to her friends and gave more hugs, and then she was off to her next class. Todd still kept passing her notes in class to ask her out, and he hasn't yet once to ask her in person. Ginger thinks that Todd is being a womanizer. He just wants to go out with her because she is captain of the volleyball team, publicity, and she has the right "stuff." Why can't girls and guys get along and see others' personalities? Why must there be tensions? Why must the Spirit Transporter get in the way of peoples' lives for the worse? Boys don't even think about stuff like that. They only think about the girls, the looks, and what they must do to get the girl. Girls and guys have different minds, and when both their minds come together (in other words, the guy and girl get to know each other a little more), here comes the Spirit Transporter to turn it all into hatred and to cause a breakup or even a meltdown between the couple or spouses. Ginger tried to not even think about Bailey or the nice and sweet moments they had together. That was all gone now. Ginger thought, *Hey, it's time I moved on . . . I still have a life to live, and I can't let one guy stop me.* It was still too hard to not stop thinking about him and her hatred toward him. Hillary suggested that she get revenge, and she had some great tips on how to get back at a guy. Ginger didn't want revenge, because two wrongs don't make a right. Oh, how cute Bailey's eyes were! She had just adored his eyes and his lust of hair. She also adored him because of that one side of him he has opened up for her to see, and that no one in the school has seen. He had a very sweet side. A side that overcame him being a bully. It's too bad because none of that mattered. He had broken up with her, and Ginger could not turn back (no matter how much she wanted to). Bailey wouldn't look back, anyway, so it wouldn't make a difference at all. Ginger had felt much better when the day was over. After the comforting of her friends and the encouragement they had given her, Ginger started to shake things off her mind, which is a good thing. Volleyball practice today was yet brutal. Coach Hector was pushing the girls more then ever before. The championship was coming up, which meant the practices were only going to get more fierce. The competition was rising, which is the most fierce and challenging part. Everyone wants to win, and people would do anything to win. Coach Hector himself is competitive, and he wouldn't want that trophy to slip out of his hands (it already has for the past fifteen years). The girls were tired, but they had to push themselves, for they too want to see a good trophy in their hands. He has been pushing Ginger the most, as she is the star player of the team. Ginger can handle it, and it's only going to get tougher toward the championship. The girls were relieved after practice. "Good job, Ginger. See you later," Jill told her. "Bye, Jill," Ginger called, as she was drinking some water. "Great job, Ginger! Make sure you're ready for Tuesday, because that is the day our school will make history, and be in the finals!" Coach Hector cheered. "I'll definitely be ready!" Ginger responded. "Good. We're all counting on each other as a team! We will win the gold!" Coach Hector was determined. Ginger agreed with him, and then she packed up her bags and soon left the gymnasium to be headed for home.

CHAPTER 9

Revealing Messages

Pappy and Uncle decided not to go see Lanely Tildon that Saturday morning. They usually go sometimes, usually a Saturday or two per month. Pappy was still feeling a little weak and having some back pains. Uncle was starting to get stressed out from work, and even providing hospitality. It was half past ten when they arrived to the antique shop. This is their normal time of seeing Miss Tildon. When they opened the door, not much has changed. One difference was that there were about forty bottles of potions on a shelf and at least fifty lotion bottles on the shelves next to the potions, each lotion labeled a different flavor. In total, there were at least one hundred bottles of different potions and lotions on the shelf. This must've been brand-new, because the shelves with the lotions and potions weren't there last week. That is what Lanely was probably working on in that big cauldron from last week, and it sure took Lanely no time to create all of the lotions and potions. There were some customers looking and examining the new lotions and potions scattered around the shop or looking at unique antiques. Lanely owns the shop with her daughter Marie Tildon. Usually, Lanely is in some back room, and Marie is working at the register or guiding customers around the store. This had been true, because Marie was at the register and took a glance at Grammy and Ginger. "Can I help you, ladies?" Marie kindly asked. "We're here to see Lanely," Ginger answered. "She's in the back room where she keeps the cauldron," Marie answered. "Thanks," Grammy called back, as Grammy and Ginger walked in the backroom where the beads were. Grammy and Ginger walked through the beads, making some noise as they did. Lanely was sitting there with bottles in front of her, each with a different color. "Hello, Lanely," both Ginger and Grammy greeted, as they sat down in those same two chairs, as they had done last week. "Greetings." Lanely didn't bother to look up. She was mixing liquids into empty bottles, as if she was performing an experiment. Finally, she looked up, as her beads on her neck and wrist were shaking. "So how have things been?" Lanely asked. "So far so good, I must say," Ginger answered. "Has the Enchantment helped you or hurt you?" "Umm, I guess both." Ginger paused, and then sighed. "Actually, no. Bailey, (my boyfriend) broke up with me and said awful comments about me." "Oh, I see. Again, you must give the Enchantment time before you see real results. Good things come to those who wait." "I don't know what to believe anymore. Sometimes I just lose hope, and I get lost with certain things. I start to give up," Ginger cried. "Do you know why you are doing this?" Lanely asked. "Love. I thought love was true and that I wouldn't be fooled, but I was wrong. I guess I got carried away by 'true love.'" "Well, Ginger, the only true love is the love in your own soul and mind. If it is true to you, then it is true. If you think that certain things with love is false, it is false. You never can believe what a person says about true love. Only you can believe the truth and proclaim the truth," Lanely told her. "Did that boy make a comment about personal things to you?" Grammy asked in her German accent. "Yes, including you-know-who."

"Oh, now I see what happened," Grammy now sort of knew the full story. "Ginger, do you think that there is a difference between love and the soul?" Lanely asked her. Ginger had to think very carefully, because the answer was based on opinion and facts. "Um, the soul makes up love. You wouldn't have a soul if nobody on the earth loved you."

"That is exactly correct. Your mother thought that it was the love within the spirit which creates a real spirit. On that day she came in here and said, 'My daughter's gonna be someone someday. She may not have a father, but I know that my love has made up her soul to be what it is today. We may be struggling, but that is okay.'" Were Ginger's and her mother's synopsis similar? "And then I asked her, 'Do you believe her own spirit is true?'" Lanely continued. "'Yes, I do. I have done a lot or Ginger in her and my time of need. That is why when I die, I will give Ginger my necklace. That's how much I love my daughter!'" That made Ginger cry, because her mother had told that to Lanely the year before she died. "'Love cannot create a soul,' I told your mother." "The soul creates the love!" "What did she respond to?" Grammy wanted to know. "I told her! Love does not make up the human soul. It is vice versa!"

"Oh, I see whatcha mean now. Anyway, I promise to give my daughter the best life until I die!" "It just too bad she died so soon," Ginger said, wiping off tears on her face. Grammy started to cry as well. "Come, Ginger and Marybeth. Smell the cauldron. Smell the wonderful aroma!" Grammy and Ginger leaned in, and the fragrance was most delightful! Cherries and rose scents and the sweet smell of other fruits and flowers! Ginger had never smelled anything this good. "How do you feel now?" Lanely asked. "I feel much, much better. I had forgotten about what made me sad in the first place!" Ginger was almost in another world. "Sometimes simplicity of things is all a person will need. It is good for the soul," Lanely cried. Grammy had even felt a little light-headed. This was good, because Grammy needs true support and to calm down. "Do you understand more about love and its source? Do you realize that it can only be true if you BELIEVE?"

"Incredibly do, Miss Tildon. Thank you so much."

"Love can only come from the soul, and trust," Grammy added. "Watch this. This is how you know if love is really real or if it's fake," Lanely said. By now, Lanely Tildon stood up and put remedies of soap bars in the cauldron. She twisted her hands in some sort of wave emotion, and behold, a glowing pink light filled the area. This wasn't another Enchantment; it was the soul and love at work. It felt like waves were surrounding the room.

The force of the glow got brighter and brighter, and the scent smelled even better. "This is how you know love is true in your soul!" Lanely had to scream over the waves. Grammy quickly closed the door. "But this is the result of false love . . . ," Lanely's voice died down. The wind sped up, but nothing was blown out of place. All of a sudden, black smoke and clouds came bursting from the cauldron and filled the room. The result of this would be an emotional crisis, like the one Ginger was feeling. All of a sudden, one of Ginger's eye turned red, and she burst out a scream. This was what she was feeling from the break up. After Ginger stopped yelling and let all of her anger out, the pink glow shined over the dark and black smoke contents. "Ginger finally let her emotions out. It was not true, after all," Lanely cried. The glow and the wind had stopped, and now the room was back to normal. "Yikes! What was that? Ginger, your eyes were red! Are you okay?" Grammy was frantic, and she quickly grabbed her granddaughter to make sure she was okay. Grammy was breathing ferociously, but Ginger was just fine. "I'm fine, Grammy." "Miss Tildon, what was that?" Grammy demanded breathing heavily, wanting to know what happened. "It was my soul, wasn't it? When the black smoke came, it was my feeling of Bailey, and that the love that I thought we had was false. Is that it?" Ginger asked. "Absolutely, Ginger. That anger had to come out somehow," Lanely answered. Ginger stared at her necklace that was shaped into a heart. It hasn't glowed in a couple of days, now. "How can you see someone's soul?" Grammy wondered. "Emotions, Marybeth. Emotions. Actions speak louder than your words. To see it closely, you must perform it." Grammy was still a little brain damaged. What in the world was Lanely Tildon talking about? "I think I understand. That's exactly what I had been feeling. Now that I feel better, and I let the anger toward Bailey out, the light of my soul has returned," Ginger philosophized. Grammy relatively couldn't understand, nor feel the emotions, because it was Ginger feeling this, not her. "Yes, Ginger McFraiddee. You are coming along splendidly," Lanely complimented. "That was just amazing, Lanely. For the first time, I saw myself, even when I thought it would be impossible. Ginger couldn't even believe what she had saw herself. "You already did, Ginger. It was inside of you the whole time. It just sometimes takes even bad things to happen to us (like love) for us to recognize our own character. It may sound corny, but in the end, it certainly pays off," Lanely explained. "Certainly, Miss Tildon. Especially in the real world," Grammy added. "Yes, and to survive the world, you must know skills in life!" Lanely agreed. "But the real world is evil. People are hypocrites, and they think about no one but them damn selves," Ginger was irritable. "Unfortunately, that IS life, and that is how they *can* survive," Lanely told her. "Well, that stinks," Grammy moaned. "True, and as you saw, love will not help anyone whatsoever," Lanely cried, shaking her head. Ginger inferred that her parents had been wrong all along about love. But there is one kind of love. The love where you can go to your parents and hug them very sweetly. The kind of love where your parents can comfort their children and try to strive for the best in life. Ginger wishes she could do that, oh how she misses their hugs, and the advice they had given her when she was a young child. Such things of that nature make her see the world as it already is, and emotionally, she can tell that the world is from a "happy place."

"So, Lanely, do you think I'm ready to pick up my two feet, again?" Ginger asked her. "Your mother asked me that same question, and I will tell you the answer I once told your mother," Lanely paused for a second, "Only if you think you are ready. People cannot tell you if you are, and a sign of you being ready is you being a more better person than you already are, or learning from careless mistakes, which best describes you, Ginger."

"She is most right, Ginger. Everyone will mess up one day in their life, as long as they live and learn from the mistake, everything will be fine," Grammy emphasized. "Tuesday is the big day. The semiplayoff game. Everyone is counting on me. I'm so excited, and I don't know what to say, and other times I am just nervous," Ginger said, starting to breathe as heavily as Grammy did during the heavy wind and the pink and black glow (the seeing of soul). "Do you and your team really want to win?" Lanely asked. "Yes, we do. My coach is always pushing us to win. He has been waiting for this practically for over a decade, and so has the school." "Well, then, teamwork is the most important thing for victory. You have to have a passion for things, whatever it may be," Lanely responded. Ginger was striving to win, no matter what obstacle may get in her way. She knew she could do it, and now it will only take teamwork and the school support. Lanely poured more items into the cauldron, making the room smell more fresh than before. "Another scent product complete. Now I have to take it to my daughter for approval of the aroma," she said, as the contents in the cauldron began to stop bubbling. "Smells good, Lanely. What's the flavor?" Grammy wondered. "Magenta scent, a mix of raspberries and strawberries," she replied. "Interesting," Grammy was amazed. "There are many lotions and potions on the shelf. I came up with those since you were here last week. Doesn't take as long as you may think."

"Incredible!" Ginger complimented. "How could you perform that experiment with the soul while creating the scent thingy?" Grammy pondered. "The soul has nothing to do with the flesh or the outside of reality. What you saw was Ginger's soul and to see how she felt when she released her anger out on Bailey," Lanely answered. Ginger completely understood, and so did Lanely. Grammy, however, was still scratching her head. To be honest, nobody else in the world would understand, because they don't have the similarities between Lanely and Ginger. This makes Ginger think of herself as an outsider from the world, when the world accepts her as her own self. Lanely Tildon definitely doesn't see herself as an outsider, because Lanely knows all she needs to know about the world, and if anyone says something about her, she wouldn't care, because she knows her own self within. Lanely is sixty years old, yet even at a semisenior's age, she still gets humiliated by customers that come into the store, but she doesn't let them stop her. Lanely has important things to do, and nonsense is far from one of those things. It's almost been over an hour, and Grammy went to go look at some of the new potions, lotions, and scents. Grammy and Ginger would be leaving soon. "Do not worry about the Enchantment. It takes time and patience for things to happen. Light always shines through the darkness. Remember that." "Oh, I will, Lanely. I try to remember everything you tell me."

"Good. Do well on your semiplayoffs game on Tuesday. May the best be with you. In fact, I will see if I can make the game! I will try to take off work that day, but we shall see. Anyways, do well with that, and with anything you want to achieve in life," Lanely told her. "Thank you so much, Miss Tildon, and thank you for letting me release my anger out toward Bailey. I feel much better, now!"

"Anytime. See you later," Lanely told her.

"Bye-bye," Ginger waved, as she got up, and shook the beads when she left the room. Ginger caught up with Grammy when she was looking at the new scents, potions, and lotions. She held two bottles in one hand and a content of glass in another. "Hopefully, this will help the smell in the house, and Pappy needs a new back pain massager, or something soft for his old neck. This stuff should do the trick," Grammy said, as Ginger chuckled, and they both went to the cash register. Marie was still there, paying for the items. Sometimes it's good where you own a store where few people come to shop at. "Thank you and come again," Marie said, handing Ginger the bag with the items, and the receipt. Grammy and Ginger left the store, being very careful of the crooked wooden stairs. Rachael was having yet another party that Saturday night, and Ginger was not invited. It's mainly the same people at those parties anyway (Todd and his friends, Stephanie and her friends, some volleyball girls, Jason's group of friends, Luna and some blacks that go to the school, and other kids). Mainly the cool, popular, and jocks/preppies were invited. Ginger could care less, because those kids there were jerks to other kids (mostly geeks and nerds), but most of them would have a sleepover with some friends right after the party, which would upset Ginger, because some of her friends, not best friends, were invited to the party and were going to have a sleepover right after the party. But Ginger couldn't do a thing about it. Rachael really didn't even know Ginger, or she had just forgotten about her completely. Ginger decided to stay focused on what IS important, which is the semiplayoffs game and some schoolwork and projects. After dinner, the family watched a Western movie together in the living room. Family is always first, Grammy and Pappy decided to do this as one big family. They may be three generations of four people in the home, but one word separates the generation into one: family. Just watching Pappy smiling and laughing at the Western movie (classical and western movies were his favorites), and watching Uncle and Grammy enjoy themselves made Ginger enjoy herself as well. This is what a family should do, regardless of generation, size, divorce issues, or anything of that nature. Families are there to bring the people you know and love together and to rejoice and be happy. When Ginger would see family relatives, she would be so delighted. It would be as if they hadn't talked in years. Where does the time go? Grammy was volunteering at the Red Cross this week (which was only about five hours or so). While Grammy would be volunteering, Uncle would be at work, and of course Ginger would be at school, which means Pappy was in charge of the house since he was the only one there. Tuesday was the big day. Coach Hector called for volleyball practices before and after school on Monday, and another one this morning. It's a good thing the girls didn't have to run. He only wanted them to work on defense and basic skills. The girls came back and lined up for class in either a dress, usually worn on Sunday, or even a minisuit, as if the girl worked as an accountant. Ginger wore her volleyball shirt and short. Ginger's hair was in two braids, each braid has a purple colored flower to hold the braid (not the flower Bailey had given her). This attracted many guys, because she was the only volleyball girl wearing shorts that were really short. The other girl was just wearing a dress or skirt or suit of some sort. Meredith wore a red dress, Sally was wearing a long orange skirt, one which extended down to her knees, and Jenny wore a dress with stockings. "Whoa, Ginger . . . , you were supposed to wear a dress or something fancy," Jenny cried. "I know, but I kinda like this outfit better!" Ginger replied. "Oh well! As long as we win the semiplayoffs and the championship, we will be just fine!" Sally cheered, as the four girls cheered. "Can't wait to see the gold!" Meredith added, as the girls and other kids went inside of the building. Posters and signs and banners were hung up everywhere throughout USMS, all of which was to support the volleyball team. It was a big day for the team, the school, and especially a big day for Coach Hector. Ginger's outfit of short shorts that were jeans attracted tons of attention. The guys were just overwhelmed, not only of her being hot, but also she leading the team to victory. As Ginger was going up the stairs with Jill, Meredith, and some other volleyball girls, Todd was in with group of friends. "Whoa! Did you see Ginger?! Short shorts!" Andy commented. "I did. She's sexier than before." Todd added. "Dude, just ask her out. She may say yes if you, instead of writing notes," Jason told him. "Yea, dude, don't be afraid of her. She likes guys who are personal," Malcolm knew that for a fact. "Plus, she hates Bailey. He's a jerk, anyway. You have a chance!" Chad encouraged him. "I know. I just have to talk to her. You guys rock! Later!" Todd said, as all four guys said goodbye, and was off to class. Luna caught up with Ginger while she was walking up the stairs (this felt like déjà vu). "Good luck in today's game!" Luna encouraged her. "Thanks. Was Rachael's party fun?" "It was okay. Stephanie seemed to get drunk, and Hillary threw pie at Joel's face!" Luna laughed, as Ginger did as well. "Wait, Joel was invited?"

"Yeah. I don't know why, though," Luna said. "I wish I was invited," Ginger cried. "I'm sorry. Rachael doesn't know you that well. After today's game, you'll be known all over the school!" "Right, see ya later, Luna," Ginger waved. "Bye, Ginger." All of the boys were saying to Ginger, "Lookin' good!" or "Ginger, you're hot!" or giving her blown kisses. Some guys wooed or whistled. Ginger could barely get to her locker without them saying something every two seconds. Ginger just had to take it, because she chose to wear the outfit, and there will be an effect to it. Ginger was having another flashback when she got to her locker. This time, her mother was cleaning the floors one day, and

Ginger was sweeping. Ginger was just a little girl at the time, and her mother was wearing that locket. "Mommy!" Ginger called, sweeping more of the floor. Ginger's mother looked up with the mop in her hand. "Yes, honey?" she asked. "Mommy, when will daddy come back from the dead? Will I ever get to see him again?" Ginger asked her. "Umm, well, actually Ginger, no," her mother responded, straightening up her brown hair. "But Daddy has been gone for a year, now! I just want to see him again! Where could he have possibly gone?" Ginger wondered. "He's in heaven, honey. Oh, how we both miss him. I know it's tough, Ginger, but you'll see him again."

"When will that be, Mommy?"

"I don't know, sometimes I wish he could come back." "Can I visit him?" "Someday you will, Ginger. When you do, your father will be so proud of you! In fact, you will be the best volleyball player in the world!"

"Yea, volleyball! Woohoo!" Ginger had a passion for volleyball, even when she was a little girl. "Tell ya what, when we're done cleaning, let's go to the park to play volleyball!" Ginger's mom offered that day. "Okay, Mommy! I love you so much!"

"I love you too, Ginger. You will be the best volleyball player ever, and when you are, your father will be so proud!"

"Isn't Daddy already proud?"

"Of course, Ginger! He is happy for what you do all the time!" the widowed woman told her only daughter. "Yay!" Ginger cheered, as they continued to mop and sweep. Thinking about that day made Ginger happy and sad at the same time. Ginger's mother stayed positive all throughout her life, including when she was widower before she died. Ginger's mother always told her to never back down and to always follow her dreams. Ginger knew that after today, her father and her mother will be happier and more proud than they already are, and that she knew her parents would communicate with her with the locket she is wearing (regardless of where her parents are, whether heaven or hell or somewhere else). Ginger wishes that her mother and father would be sitting in the bleachers of her game and that they would be cheering her on throughout the game. Ginger left a picture of her, her father on one side, and her mother in another in her locker. When no kids were in the locker area, Ginger kissed where her mother's lip was, and where her father was. "I will not disappoint you today. I will make you more proud than before. I promise. I will not let you down," Ginger told her parents (as if they could hear her). Of course they said nothing. Her parents continued smiling in the picture, and Ginger too smiled in the picture, showing all of her teeth (she was very little at the time). In the background, the picture said "Welcome to Dublin." They were in Ireland for vacation to celebrate a family reunion. Most people Pappy knew, since he was from Ireland. Ginger took a long sigh, and then she got all of her materials to start the day. Will she ever see her parents again? Of course, the answer is not physically. How can she tell if her parents is actually there, sitting in the bleachers with the others? She can't. They are spirits, so no one knows. The only way she WILL know is that her locket starts to glow. Then again, that could be a sign of something else (something that Ginger wouldn't know). The purpose of the locket was to talk to her parents or at least try to figure out what they have left behind. Lanely Tildon won't tell Ginger the secrets her parents have left behind, especially her own mother, because Lanely decided to keep things personal, and that Ginger will need to find the answer on her own. But how can she find the answer that's not even within her? It's virtually impossible. That's what Lanely wanted her to find. Lanely knew she could, but unfortunately, Ginger can't do that by herself. She will need some help in her voyage against this world she calls of the "generation," which means it's her against the world. Why does Ginger think this? Nobody she knows thinks of her this way. She is pretty cool in the school, yet she considers herself from the world that is full of wonders. This world is magnificent, but if you were to ask Ginger, she'd say otherwise. This is all because of three dreaded words her parents died. But three more words will change her; it will make her see herself in a different way, and the three words are the volleyball finals.

Chapter 10

Popularity Cometh

The whole school was preparing for the big game. The bleachers were set up an hour before school was over with, and people, mostly parents and adults, came forty-five minutes early. Everyone was excited. At lunch, all of the girls were cheering and stood up to even dance (Ginger was a part of that), and the whole school was excited, yet nervous. Then the bell rang. Mostly all of the kids were rushing into the gym. Some teachers and staff had to accompany the students, so they wouldn't tear the school down nonetheless themselves or their peers. Ginger and the girls were sitting down in the chairs where they were the last game. All of the girls saw the students enter the gymnasium. Everyone in the eighth grade was going to be there. This was huge, especially for Coach Hector. Where was Coach Hector? He wasn't anywhere to be seen, and the game was about to start. The bleachers were as full as ten minutes from when the bell rang, and now, the net was being set up. The girls were chattering, and Ginger was just chatting with Meredith and Sally. "Where's the coach?" Jill wondered, searching around to see where he would be. "I don't know," Ginger heard a girl say. Nowhere to be seen. Nowhere to be found. By now, the other team had entered, and they took their seats, followed by their coach. The whole school booed as they sat down, and after five minutes of waiting, Coach Hector was found. Some people in the stands started clapping when he ran to the girls' team. Ginger scanned the area. Uncle wasn't there, he probably was still at work. Grammy and Pappy smiled and waved, and Pappy gave her a thumbs-up. Ginger scanned the gym and didn't see Lanely Tildon anywhere. This made Ginger a little distraught and even disappointed, but maybe things will change in the end. "She didn't show up," Ginger pouted. "Who?" Meredith wondered. "Lanely." Sally and Meredith are probably the only ones that know Lanely at the school. The other team took their positions on the court and same with the volleyball girls. The school started cheering again, as the game was about to begin. Still no sign of Lanely. This was one of Ginger's big moments, and Lanely wasn't even there. Ginger thought that maybe it's gonna be okay, and she would arrive soon. Ginger just couldn't get over her not showing up and even started to panic. This was just not the time nor the place for that; everyone was counting on the team, but mostly on Ginger. Nothing could be worse than losing when coming so far, and Ginger knew this. She and the school didn't want guilt on their faces, so Ginger knows she will have to shake it off before too late. This team looked more competitive than Mandy's team; in fact, these girls' faces were much fiercer than Mandy's team was. Probably because they too want to win the finals and have a chance to see Ginger's gold. Everybody wants to win, but sadly, there has to be a loser in the end. These girls were huge as well, which gave them an advantage of spiking, and most of all, power. Not one girl smiled or even dared to chuckle, and the opposing team's coach had that same look of determination like Coach Hector. They wanted to win. When the announcer had finished talking, the ball was given to the opposing team, and the game began. Silence. All you heard in the gym was the bumping of the ball and a cough from here and there. When the girls would score, the school would cheer a little. They are just too excited to say even a word. About a quarter of the first half is gone, and the other team is up by three. Lanely Tildon still hadn't shown up. This was making Ginger lose balance and coordination. She just couldn't concentrate and by the end of the first half, she had given up two points, and made one careless mistake from serving. They were down by five points, which was making the school a little shaky and more nervous than before. "Ginger, what is wrong with you?!" Coach Hector wanted to know. "I can't focus that well." "Well, you better! We still have two quarters to go! We are counting on you, Ginger!" he told her. Ginger got some water and got back on the court, as the second half began. Lanely had still not shown up. Ginger lost yet another four points, and the team only gained two points, meaning that they were losing by seven points when the second half was nearly over. The school went from cheers to boos in seconds. They were all booing Ginger. "Take her out of the game, coach!"

"Put in someone else!" That's what people were saying. When the girls got a five-minute break, Ginger was already exhausted. "Are you okay?" Sally asked her. "Not really."

"We can't lose, though. We just can't!" Meredith cried. "I know, I know. I will try again," Ginger replied, wiping sweat off of her face. "You know you lost, Ginger! Just give it up!" a girl from the other team teased, as all of the girls from the opposing team laughed at her. Sweat and more sweat crawled down Ginger's face from her forehead. Ginger was now overwhelmed. The school was still booing her and saying unwanted things. Some adults tried to stop that. Ginger glanced at Todd and his friends. Todd gave her a thumbs-up, not knowing if she spotted him or not. Ginger looked away, pretending that she didn't see him. The girls took their spots back on the court. When Ginger walked to her position, a few more boos came her way. At that moment, Lanely Tildon walked in the gym. Her African braided hair was in a ponytail, and she wore some casual sort of Kenyan or Ethiopian clothing. It fits her quite well. Lanely spotted Pappy and Grammy and quietly walked up the bleachers to sit next to them, carefully trying not to make any noise from the beads on the bracelets and necklaces she was wearing. Right when Lanely sat down, Ginger's locket glowed. The heart was bright red, and some people noticed. It made a small sound but then stopped after a while. Nobody knew what it was; only Lanely and Ginger did. Ginger finally spotted Lanely next to Pappy and

Grammy, and then she smiled. "Did I miss anything?" Lanely asked, whispering so no one would hear but them. "Not much, actually," Grammy responded. "Is Ginger's team winning?" Lanely wondered. "No, they are losing by seven points," Pappy answered. "Oh, dear," Lanely responded. Ginger felt different now. She was ready this time. When the other team served the ball, she jumped all the way in the air and spiked the ball, and it made a loud noise on the ground. From Ginger's face, she seemed angry, and everyone knew this because they were stunned. Nobody had said anything. They just stared. Coach Hector was the first to break the silence. He started clapping, and so did people of the school. They are still down by six, however. Ginger and the girls were on fire throughout the rest of the game. The only problem was that the other team could defend, and that they were on fire as well. By the third half, and with only less than a minute left, the USMS team was down by two points, and Coach Hector had called a timeout. "Okay, girls, we only need three points to win. No careless mistakes! Just do what we have been doing in practice! We can win!" The girls cheered and took their position on the court. The other team had their plot in mind: to take down Ginger. They know she is the best; everybody knows. If they can make her weak, then they can win. As the other team took their positions on the court, the crowd was getting more nervous. Three points didn't seem like much, but under a minute would be tough to do. Dead silence. For real, this time Ginger's team automatically scored a point from a bad play by the opposing team and from Jill spiking the ball down to the ground fifteen seconds left, and they were tied. The whole school was going crazy. They needed to win. It hasn't been fifteen years, and it can't be because they didn't make it into the playoffs. "Ginger, you spike in the last seconds. For now, we bump and pass until the last, last seconds we have come so far. Do not let them take away our championship!" the coach announced, as the girls agreed and cheered. The girls took their positions, and her team served the ball. When they got it back, they passed to each other. The people watching, and even the other team was confused. But the last three seconds, Sally had passed the ball to Ginger in the air. Ginger rose up in the air and slammed the ball to the ground, and the other team couldn't stop her. The ball bounced to the ground, and time was up. Ginger's team won. Everybody cheered now. Kids from the stands came down to where the girls were huddled. Ginger and the team chanted, "We're number one! We're going to the playoffs! Wooo!" No space whatsoever. Ginger just had to smile. What she had not expected is when two volleyball girls lifted her up in the air, and the girls were carrying her, as if she had been the MVP of the game. The girls and kids of the school were now cheering. "Go, Ginger!" "Without Ginger, we wouldn't be in the playoffs game!" Ginger just smiled and laughed. Kids were starting to leave when the girls huddled in and wooed. The other team had no choice but to leave the school and to accept shame. Summer ran to the girls, bumping into some kids. "Oh my gosh! Good job, Ginger!" Summer told her. "Thanks," she responded. Jenny, Ginger, Sally, and Summer were talking, when Stephanie and her friends approached her. "Nice job, Ginger!" Stephanie told her. "Thanks."

"Now we're going to the playoffs!" Amy bragged, as they cheered even more. Today only made Ginger more popular than she technically was. Kids were coming up to the team, especially her, cheering and saying good job. All of the kids left, and Ginger went to Grammy, Pappy, and Lanely. "Good job, Ginger. Your own strength was working for the good of you," Lanely congratulated her. "No, Lanely. Thank you for coming. I thought you weren't gonna come."

"But I did. Your necklace has glown as well," Lanely said. "I know. That's because I believed that I could, but I needed support," Ginger replied. "That's good, Ginger. I am glad you see that," Grammy smiled. "Well, sorry, Lanely! We're goin' out to eat and celebrate! See ya Saturday!" Pappy boasted, grabbing the coats. "Pappy, don't do that! No!" Grammy corrected him. "Oh, that is okay, Marybeth! I am sort of on a diet, anyway, but thank you for the offer," Lanely cried. "If you say so," Grammy responded. "Well, thank you for coming, Lanely. Full support is always the best!" Ginger cried. "Anytime. Bye-bye," Lanely waved, walking as Grammy, Pappy, and Ginger waved and left the gym behind her. Lanely was probably parked somewhere else when Ginger, Pappy, and Grammy arrived to the car. "So, Ginger, where'd ya wanna eat? How about some Irish potatoes?" Pappy suggested (He is from Ireland). "Or what about some good ole crocodile!" Grammy teased, as they laughed while Pappy drove out of the lot and got onto the road. "Surprise me!" Ginger offered. And so they did. They went to a steak house and took the food home. "It's too bad Uncle couldn't come. Where is he?" "Probably it was a late work day. It's not easy building in air!" Pappy answered. "So how has the Red Cross been?" Ginger asked. "It's been good, I must say. The only problem is that the people are crankier, and they just don't care anymore. I try and be the best I can to be a good volunteer," Grammy answered. "It's a good thing you're volunteering. It's for a good cause," Ginger responded. "And that she's getting a good pay from volunteering part time! Heh-hah!" Pappy bragged. "Money isn't everything, Pappy," Grammy reminded him. "To live it is!" Pappy insisted. Grammy and Ginger just had to laugh. It was dark when they arrived home. Luckily, Uncle was already home. "Didcha win the game?" Uncle asked. "Yes, we won! Now we're going to the playoffs!" Ginger answered, still very excited. "Very good! You ought to be proud!" "I am!" "I'm sorry I couldn't come. Sometimes life takes its toll." Uncle told her. "I know, but that's okay." Soon after, the family sat down and ate. Proud. It is a word to describe how you feel when you have done something great. It can be the feeling of achieving something that no one has even done before. You can smile and feel good about yourself for achieving this. It doesn't matter if the others are not proud of themselves, it only matters how you feel, and if you think you have made an accomplishment, and that you can smile about it. This is what Ginger felt. She hadn't felt this way in a while, and she was pleased to feel this way. Now she can smile and be proud of herself, and the school was proud of her too, which was the best part. Everybody was proud of her, including Coach Hector. This was probably the best feeling she had ever felt in a long time, and she does deserve it. Just the feeling of winning makes her jump for joy. The team hasn't won in over a decade, but now they have, and she was proud of it. Coach Hector was especially proud, because he finally saw champion not only in his team, but also to himself. Coach Hector was finally smiling and acting proud for once. Hard work *does* pay off in the end. People do not realize this, and they just give up hope, and sometime can be in a turmoil. When people take the time to work hard and do well (whether it's a career, occupation, school, home, family, etc.), they can smile and say, "My hard work has paid off." This is a feeling of one word. Proud. They are proud for what they have done, and that it has paid off. Anybody can feel proud, and it can happen anywhere, and definitely any time. Sometimes being proud doesn't need awards and recognition. It can just take a smile. Too bad most people want award and the goods, anyway. When the Spirit Transporter was glowing, proud was already in Ginger's eyes. She could see it. All she had to do was accept. Now, she will never forget this day. If only her mother and father were there to see her performance. If only THEY were there to have dinner, and to celebrate. But they are celebrating. In fact, Ginger already knew they were smiling at her, saying: "I have taught my daughter enough to live in the world." Now they too are smiling. They feel the same way she feels. As a matter of fact, they have been feeling this before Ginger was even born. This feeling can only be expressed in one word. Proud. They are always proud, and Ginger knows it. She cannot see it with her own two eyes, but that doesn't matter. She only needs to know that her parents are proud of her. When they are proud, she is also proud, and she has more hope of maybe even changing the world for the better. Inspiration can come from people around, but the source of it is you. Ginger could hardly sleep. She was so excited about the game, and the look on everyone's face. That made her feel really good on the inside, and it made everyone else feel the same, all because of one word: Proud. Things got crazy the next day. Everyone was still cheering, and even some kids from other grades helped cheer them on. Kids were bombarding Ginger, nonetheless the circle of girls on the team. Todd and his friends were in a group as usual. "Dude, just ask her out," Jason told him. "Gah, I can't. But I want to," Todd responded. "But you have to soon. That douche Bailey may go back out with her," Malcolm told him. "I will some day." "How about today?" The Wise offered. The others sorta laughed. "I will." "You should," Rockstar Kid told him. "Plus other kids like her, yea dude, you gotta hurry!" Mack warned. "Or else someone will be going out with her." Andy added. "I hear Nick wants to go out with her," Chad said. "That freak! He's going out with Melissa!" Todd cried. "But he may turn her down," Malcolm said. "Naah, he wouldn't break up with Melissa just to go out with Ginger," Jason inferred. "Yes, he would. He would do anything to go out with a better-looking girl," Rockstar Kid said. "Is Ginger better-looking?" Mack asked. "Duh!" the others went. "Melissa just has better friends," Andy said, the others agreeing. "But Ginger's a blonde." When Chad said that, all of the guys went "aaaah!" as if they were desperate for a girl. Melissa has burgundy hair. "All right, I gotta go to class. See ya," Todd told them, giving high fives to them. "All right see ya. Bye," they responded, as they headed to class. Ginger, Brianna, Shandi, Stacy, and Hillary, came in and were headed up the stairs. "Wow, Ginger, you're getting tons of recognition," Stacy told her. "I know, it's crazy. Everybody is just so excited!" "They should be. Because of Ginger, our team is unbeatable!" Brianna screamed out loud so everyone in the halls heard her. The girls and the others screamed and cheered all over again. "Okay, thanks," Ginger insisted. "Because of her, we're unstoppable!" Shandi yelled, the school agreeing, "Unbeatable!" Hillary yelled as well. "That's enough," Ginger offered. There was no stopping them. "Ginger and the team are number one!" All four girls yelled. Ginger had no choice but to cheer with the crowd. She also laughed, as she was feeling proud again. During the day, one of Bailey's other friends (not Jeff or Billy) offered to ask Ginger out. Of course she said no. Heck, she didn't even know the guy! She still does feel some affection for Bailey, and even though he didn't treat her the best, she still felt some sort of sympathy toward him and didn't want him to suffer that much. But then again, it was sometimes hard to consider the right thing to do. When Ginger went to get a drink of water, Elias was standing right behind her, his hair as "messy" as can be. Ginger was startled when she turned around. She jumped and nearly fell to the ground. It was just them two in the hallway. "Oh my God, you scared me," she told him. "I'm sorry. Are you okay?" he asked her. "Um, yes. Are you like stalking me?" Ginger wondered. "No,

I'm no stalker," he said. "Then what do you want?" Ginger asked, as she already knew what was next. "You wanna go out with me?" he asked. It took her awhile to answer. "Do you? I have to get back to class," Elias warned. "No thanks, Elias. You're sweet, but I can't go out with anybody," Ginger answered. "Oh. Is it because of Bailey?"

"You are a stalker!"

"What! No! The whole school knows!" Elias cried. "Oh. Well, I gotta get back to class. I would say yes if I wasn't feeling that way toward Bailey," Ginger told him. "I understand. Is it okay if we're friends?" Elias offered. "Sure. I'd like that," Ginger said. "Cool. Well, see ya later," he said. Ginger waved, and she went back to class, and so did Elias. She couldn't say yes to anyone, to be honest. She just wasn't ready for "love," or any signs of the matter. Elias seemed like a really nice guy, but Ginger couldn't handle it. She has to recover from Bailey before anything else. Happiness was on her mind, but Bailey had really broken her heart that day. That X, just goes to show you how cruel love can really be. But then again, Ginger knows that she must move on in her life, no matter what it takes. Lunch arrived, and Ginger sat with her usual friends. "Today has been just weird. Elias asked me out, and so did one of Bailey's friends," Ginger said. "You did say no to them, right?" Stacy asked. "Yup." "Good. Elias is a good-for-nothing jerk, and well, we know the incident with that crap," Hillary agreed, rolling her eyes. "Exactly, which is why I'm saying no to these guys," Ginger replied. "Good for you! Us girls will stick together from these guys who only like our looks!" Jenny agreed. The girls chanted "yea!" At that moment, a guy named Fred approached her. He was a friend of Todd (but never sat with them). "Hey, Ginger." Ginger rolled her eyes, and the other girls did as well, and looked away. "Did you come over here to ask her out, Fred?" Brianna asked. "Well, yea."

"Well, Fred, this is Ginger's response!" Hillary picked up a part of her lunch, stood up, walked to where Fred was, and smashed the lunch on his hair and clothes. Everybody saw and laughed. "What was that for?" Fred wanted to know. "You mess with my friend, you pay the price!" Hillary cried, as Fred walked away, embarrassed. Ginger and Hillary sat down. "What was that?" Ginger asked. "When a jerk like him wants to try to scam you and make you into a fool, you plot revenge," Stacy answered. "But how did you know if he was bad?" Ginger asked. "He's Fred, that's why," Jenny said. "And he's a huge jerk," Brianna added. "You should've squirted water at Elias's ass, then he would've known that you're the right type," Hillary told her. "Wasn't thinking," Ginger confessed. "That's okay, you have lots to learn," Stacy cried. At that moment, Shandi came to the table. "I'll take it from here. Thanks," Shandi said. "What do you mean?" Ginger asked. "Ginger, you can now sit with Stephanie's friends! Come on!" Hillary urged, as Shandi and Hillary literally carried her to Stephanie's table. Ginger waved goodbye to the others. "Oh, do I have to?" Ginger asked. "Yes! Ginger, you won our championship! There is a price of popularity!" Shandi reminded her. "And the price is a good price too!" Hillary added. Stephanie and her friends sat near Todd and his friends (the popular tables, so called). This was not good for Ginger, because Todd was trying to "flirt" with her, and now everybody knew. When Ginger arrived, everyone just stared, and there was already a seat with her name on it. "Hey, Ginger," Todd was the first to greet. "Save it, Todd. The answer is no!" Hillary snapped back. She already knew he wanted to ask Ginger out. The girls rolled their eyes as Ginger sat down, Hillary and Shandi sitting next to her. "Hillary's a whore," Andy whispered, sitting from across. The girls heard, but pretended to ignore him. Melissa, Stephanie, Nick, Joe, Amy, Rachael, and some other girls' Ginger didn't know were sitting there. "All of you. I'd like to introduce you to my friend, Ginger," Shandi greeted. "Hey, Ginger," they all said and waved. Ginger just waved back. "She's the girl who led our team to victory, and now, we're in the championship." Hillary added. "Oh yea, that's awesome!" Melissa told her. "Thanks," Ginger could only say that, because she felt a little intimidated. "So, Ginger, are you glad you won?" Amy asked. "Duh. Amy, you're so stupid. Who would be mad that they did win?" Stephanie questioned. "Well, I don't know. Some retard would," Amy tried to answer. "Well, Ginger is no retard. She's cool," Nick answered, as they agreed. "Aren't you captain of the team?" Joe asked her. "Yes, I am," Ginger answered. "Whoa, cool," Rachael cried. "Oh my God, you guys are like dumb. You just figured that out . . . ," Stephanie was being stuck up. Typical Stephanie. "You know what, Stephanie, you're stupid," Nick responded. "Pssh. Please. You didn't know that the earth was shaped in a circle," Hillary rolled her eyes. "So? School is lame. I don't care about learning,"

Nick responded. "Then that means you're lame," Joe replied. "You know what, Joe?"

"What?" Pause. "I got," Nick responded, as they all laughed. "Ginger, what's your phone number? I so have to add you," Stephanie told her. "All right." They exchanged numbers, and she did the same with Melissa, Amy, Rachael, and some other girls. She was now considered popular. For the rest of lunch period, the girls were just blabbering and gossiping about pretty much nothing (which they do every day anyway), but it all changed when Amy announced: "We're all going to Main Street Friday night. Hillary, do you want to come?"

"Duh. I'll be there."

"Ginger, what about you?"

"Sure, I'll go."

"Okay, great. Be at the theater at 6:30. I'll call ya." They were all in agreement. Only the cool kids go on Main Street. Only the popular kids go to Main Street and to parties, and now, Ginger was about to see this. The bell rang, and the kids were crowding into the halls. Ginger walked, but Hillary and Stacy caught up with her. "So, Ginger, did you like that table?" Hillary just had to know. "It was okay," Ginger answered. "It must be. You are so lucky. Stephanie wanted you to sit there, to be honest. She just had to add you to her phone. She only adds the cool kids!" Stacy told her. "Wow, I didn't know that much. I only sat there because she wanted me to!" "She only lets some kids sit there. Only the most popular kids can!" Hillary cried. "Wow! The game yesterday was a big deal," Ginger concluded. "Sure was, see ya later, Ginger," Stacy told her. "See ya," Ginger cried, as the three girls went their separate ways. Ginger couldn't stop thinking about them, and if this was a good idea for her to sit with them. Ginger really didn't care, she was now glad to be popular (or at least considered popular). Ginger spotted Bailey with his friends, and she had a mad glare. It was her soul causing this. It was just like what Lanely had been showing her the other day, how a person can make your soul in disbelief, and evil. But like Lanely had shown her, a light will come, making her forget the entire thing, and that is what happened, because Summer, Sally, and Meredith came over, and all four of those girls went to their next class as they talked. Maybe Ginger wanted to start going out again. But then again, maybe she wasn't ready. Let's just look at the reality part, Bailey broke her heart, and now that other guys asked her out (like Elias and Fred), she can now see why Hillary defend her. Hillary doesn't want to see her friend like that, all because of some guy who never even liked her. Now Ginger sees why Hillary is the way she is when it comes to these guys, and how words can make your soul filled with hatred and wimsiness. It took long enough for Ginger to realize this, and when she finally did, she was starting to not even care about Bailey. She was going to confront and compromise with him, but what would be the good in that? Nothing. He doesn't even care. If he did, he wouldn't have said what he said in the first place, and he would be the one to confront and come to an agreement with her. It doesn't matter anymore, as long as Ginger has that one word she will be fine, and that one word is: Proud. Ginger really didn't want another guy actually, for she was fearful of the consequence, but her winning the championship would make her attractive to guys, and maybe one guy would be the one for her.

CHAPTER 11

At First Sight

The next day was a drag. The only good thing was that no guy had asked her out yet. She hoped that no one would ask her out today. She hates turning people away, but this is only for her own good. A repeat of what happened to her would just be devastating, and she'd be in a huge dump. That is why Hillary, Stacy, and some of Ginger's other friends were helping her say no to other guys. It all changed at lunch. Ginger was sitting with her usual friends, and then another guy came up to her. She didn't even know him, nonetheless his name. "Ginger! Will you go out with me? Please?" This guy must've been a nerd. "Neal Shustangerman, why the hell are you here?" Stacy asked him. He had on some sweater vest with flooding pants. He is a nerd. "Because, I wanna go out with Ginger! She's preeety!" Neal responded. Ginger didn't even know his name until now. "And what makes you think she'd say yes to a nerd like you?" Brianna asked, as the girls laughed. "Come on,

Ginger. Please?" he offered a smile. Ginger shook her head no. "Pathetic," Jenny cried. "Please, give me something in return," this was Neal's last offer. "Oh, that's my job!" Hillary stood up and grabbed a liter of soda she wasn't going to drink, anyway. Instead, she poured the soda all over him. Everyone once again saw another guy get rejected. Kids "oooed" or said "rejected!" and called Neal names like "nerd," "loser," "dork." Ginger and Hillary high-fived each other and sat back down. "That's what happens when a guy tries to mess with me," Ginger commented, as the girls agreed. Todd and his friends saw that, and they were shocked. "Dude, did you see that?" Jason was astonished. "Yea. She's rejected every guy who asked her out," Andy answered. "She already said no to Elias. What's her problem?" Malcolm wondered. "Bailey. Duh. And don't even bother to ask out my friend," Stephanie overheard them from the other table, and budded in. "Ginger's your friend?" Mack asked. "Ya . . . ," Stephanie was being a jerk. "Are you still going to ask her out?" Chad asked Todd. "I don't know. She may say no to me. She's hard to get," Todd answered. "Good luck, though," The Wise replied. "The Wise, dude, will I go out with her or not?" Todd asked him. The Wise was his so-called "sidekick" and knew what was going to happen. Everybody at the table was waiting for the answer. "I'm going to throw my stuff away," Ginger told the girls. "Okay," they responded. When Ginger stood up, Hillary did as well. "Do you need me to go with you? Just in case."

"That's okay, Hillary. I'm fine," Ginger answered. "Okay. I'm just looking after my best friend." "Thanks, Hillary," Ginger cried, as she headed for the trashcan. "I don't know. Why don't you throw your trash away?" The Wise finally answered him. "What?" they all were confused. "Never question me," The Wise told them, as if he was the king of the school. Todd took his trash, walked to the trash can, and threw it away. Ginger came and threw her trash away as well. "Hey," he told her. "Hi," she responded. "Nothing's happening," Mack said. "Just wait," The Wise told him. "So you won the game? Cool," Todd said. Ginger couldn't help but to laugh. "Yep, it was me." "You know, you're kind of hot."

"I know," Ginger just laughed some more. "Thanks." She was actually smiling. "You seem a lot different."

"Different? What do you mean?" Ginger could now talk to him.

"I don't know. You're like, awesome. You're good at sports and everything," Todd answered.

"Thanks. You too, Mr. Captain of the basketball team," Ginger teased.

"And the football team," Todd corrected her, as they both laughed.

"You know, you're kind of sweet," Ginger told him.

"Really?" "Yea, I mean, I can talk to you just right."

"So do you wanna go out with me?" Todd asked her. Hillary and Stacy were giving her signals to say no from where they were sitting, but Ginger ignored them.

"You finally asked me," Ginger looked into his eyes. "I thought you'd never ask! Yes!" Ginger answered. Ginger and Todd laughed at the same time.

"Cool," Todd replied.

At that moment, Hillary got paranoid, ran over to Ginger with another liter bottle of soda. "What happened? I got nervous. Todd, she doesn't like you, now sit down, or I'll make you sit," Hillary threatened. "Hillary, you're too late. I said yes."

"What? I oughta spill this shit on your head! But 'grats, anyway."

"Thanks," Ginger responded.

"So I'll call you, then talk to you later," Todd told her.

"See ya later, Todd," Ginger cried, as Hillary and Ginger sat back down, and Todd sat down. "I said yes! I'm going out with Todd, now!" Ginger was excited. The girls were screaming, as they did feel happy for her. "I thought you weren't going out with any guys," Meredith was puzzled. "But look at Todd. He's soo cute. I couldn't say no to him."

"And he's the most popular guy in the school. That'll make you the most popular girl in the school too," Jenny cried. "Which is why she chose him!" Shandi said. "Yep." The girls screamed again. "I am so proud of you," Hillary told her. Ginger was receiving hugs from all of her friends. Maybe she *had* made the right decision, after all.

All of Todd's friends were high-fiving each other. "Dude, that was amazing!" Rockstar Kid commented, "I know. She said yes! I thought she was gonna say no," Malcolm replied. "She was onto me. The Wise, dude, how did you know?"

"I am The Wise. That's how," he answered, as they laughed.

"Anyway, thanks, man," Todd told him.

"No problem," The Wise cried.

"I swear you are lucky. She said no to everyone who asked her out!" Mack said. Not to Todd. When Ginger went to class, there was yelling in the halls. A child was racing down the hallway in tears and lots of emotion. It was a child with some sort of disability. Many eighth graders were watching this happen. Then the kid with mental issues fell on the ground and could hardly breathe. Teachers and students surrounded the child. The two mysterious teachers came racing to the child in their white lab psychologist coats. Ginger and some of her friends ran to the crowd as well. "Is he okay?" Mrs. Duffy asked. "I don't know. Let's just wait a minute," Mrs. Robbin cried. After a minute, the child with the disability was conscious. "Oh, thank goodness. What happened?" Mrs. Robbin asked the child. "I almost fainted," the child with the disability answered. "We must see the nurse then. You scared the entire school!" Mrs. Duffy cried. At that moment, the assistant principal rushed into the crowd, and the child with the disability was getting up. "Thank you, I will take it from here!" the assistant principal (Mr. Daniels) said, grabbing the child with the disability. Students, clear the halls!" Mr. Daniels ordered, as the students went to class, away from the crowd. Mr. Daniels held the child by the arm firmly, and the two psychologists followed. "Where are we going?" the scared child asked. "The nurse. How could you ladies let this happen?" Mr. Daniels cried. "We didn't. He had an emotional breakdown, sir," Mrs. Robbin answered. "We'll find out soon enough," Mr. Daniels snarled, as they were at the elevator. "What's wrong with that kid?" Sally asked. "He has a mental disability!" Ginger answered. "What does that mean?" "It means he's retarded. Well, I gotta go to class," Brianna cried. See ya later, Ginger," Sally cried. "See ya." Brianna and Sally went their separate ways, and Ginger went her own way as well. Brianna used a mean word to describe that kid, even though it was the truth. She could've said something else, but sometimes the obvious is the only truth. Ginger felt bad for those two teachers. Why would the assistant principal call those teachers "mysterious?" Why does everyone think that Mrs. Duffy and Mrs. Robbin? Ginger doesn't have any classes with them, but she doesn't see why they are left in the dust at this school. That is because these teachers are always staring at a window. Both of them. They do this every day, all the time. Maybe they are just like Ginger, after all. Maybe their soul has been hurt and now needs harvesting and manifestation. Ginger doesn't know them, so she cannot think for someone or think ahead. She can neither think for the future, because it hasn't happened yet, nor does she know what's to come. How can people be so mean and cruel? Oh yea, it's the world. Duh! This world is nothing compared to her dream she had a couple of weeks ago. This world isn't nice or beautiful like the way she wants it to be, it's wicked and terrible now. The source of it is the people and their doings. The wars, treaties, peace hearings, and terrorist attacks with evil in it have made the world where it's at today. People will do anything to survive and defend their country and try to rule all nations (we saw that in World War I and II and in many wars for nations). Let's just face it, Ginger's dream of the world being at peace, and that dream she had will never come true. There are seven billion people on this earth. People need to see the severeness of our planet and how peace would be great. How wars wouldn't be necessary. How people should love one another, regardless of one's race, creed and religion. How the light will shine on one's soul and deliverance shall come upon and arise up to be the very best. Well, we all want things. We all want to have the best, not only for our good, but for the world and our own nation as well. But that's not gonna happen, and we all know this. It's the truth. You cannot get mad at the truth, even though you may think your theory is valid. It's not about religion. It doesn't matter where you came from. It won't matter at the end who you hate, or who you just want to kill, or who you just don't like. It's about uniting for the better of people, especially Africa. Culture is not a factor. But what does it matter? That's the question that is proposed to the entire world. Why should a nation help a nation? Why is America helping other nations when they have problems of their own? Why isn't no other countries helping? Why are people so selfish? The answer is simple, and if you go to any country and ask these questions, they will say: "We don't care." People just don't care. They need to live themselves. Why SHOULD another country help one that is in desperate need? They won't because it's not their problem. Nobody cares. The only thing that people care about is themselves and their needs. That's why it doesn't matter. That's why the world will not unite together in peace. They have problems of their own. Oh well. Oh well. That is what people say when they give up or when they lose hope. But you can rise above the facts and knowledge, and help people in need. Donate to sick children or people in poverty. Donate blood. Donate food and shelter. Donate part of your soul. You can make a difference for this tragic world. It only takes one person to unite this world. It's up to you if you're willing to do so. It is also up to the entire world to finally realize and say: "This world needs my help and my country's help. If we change, we are one step closer to finally uniting with the world, and one step closer to having world peace." There are two-hundred-plus countries that make up our world and seven continents. Size doesn't matter. Peace does. One person and one nation is all it takes. It is important to care about one another. Like it or not, see it or not, we are all united. All of the countries united to make our world unique. People don't like to hear it, but that's because they can't handle that one word: truth. People really need to take this to heart. Lives are at stake. One is gone every four seconds. There goes another. And another. But when someone dies, another two are born. One day, someone on this very earth will make this world see its place, and where it needs to go. Religion has nothing to do with this; it's about uniting peace and power with the souls of people. One person can do this for the better. Are you that person? Do you have what it takes? Of course. Maybe Ginger sees that within Mrs. Duffy and Mrs. Robbin. But can she see that within herself? Maybe. But then again, it would take some time. She has the power, and so do you. All seven-billion-plus people on the earth do. It is up to them to decide their path. Mrs. Robbin and Mrs. Duffy may be absolutely nothing at this school, but someday, they could change the world for the better and unite those who really need salvation and understanding. You are not alone. Trust. Just trust. Trust yourself and have patronage within yourself and yours and other countries. The truth will always win in the very end. Statistics can only go so far. You can do the same. Ginger questions if those teachers are "outsiders," or if they are going through what she and Lanely Tildon are going through. But maybe not. They are teachers. They can't possibly feel the same thing, can they? Again, Ginger can't judge a book by its cover, especially a book that is mysterious or Ginger can just ask them their experiences, but that would just interfere within someone's personality. Ginger wants to get knowledge from those teachers only to see their experience their lives. Friday came. Finally today, Ginger decided to sit with Stephanie's friends, as they were deciding on what to do this evening. "Okay, so we'll meet at the cafe to get coffee, then we can decide what else to do when we get there!" Stephanie said. "Sounds great!" Ginger agreed. "Yea. We're gonna have lots of fun!" Melissa added. "Okay, whoa. That sounded so wrong." Joe cried, as they laughed. "Joe, you are so annoying," Amy defended. "Annoying but cute," he boasted back. "Okay, that's so not true!" Rachael cried. "That's because I'm cuter," Nick budded in, as the girls went wow. "Ginger, I'll text ya where we're going after school," Amy told her. "Okay," Ginger responded. "So when's the championship?" Nick asked her. "A couple of weeks," she answered. "Good luck! Our team shall go to victory!" Joe screamed out. Nobody was even paying attention to him. Stephanie and some girls were just talking. A person tapped Ginger on the shoulder from behind, which startled her a little. It was Todd. "Did I scare ya?" he asked. "Only a little." Todd squeezed in to sit next to her. "Todd, go away!" Stephanie told him. "Come on, Steph. Be fair." The girls said okay and made more space for him. "What do you want?" Amy demanded. Todd use to sit with Stephanie and her friends. Now he sits with his own friends. "Yea, Todd's cool," Joe cried, as Nick and Joe high-fived Todd. "Wait, so you two are going out?" Stephanie asked. "Yea," Ginger told her. Ginger stared into Todd's eyes and then smiled. "So are you going to Main Street?" Ginger asked him. "Yea. Are you going?"

"Yeah. See ya there."

"All right. Later." Ginger waved, and laughed a little. The other girls laughed as well. When the girls got up, they crowded the hall, and Todd and some of his friends joined the crowd of Stephanie's friends as kids were headed up the stairs or to their next class. Ginger was happy to be part of the "popular crowd." She had never thought this would happen, but she is happy that it did happen. Sometimes change really IS for the better. Max and Josh approached the group as everyone starred at them, as if they were stupid. "What do you want?" Nick asked them. "To become your friends. Please," Max insisted. The crowd just laughed. "Go away, kid," Malcolm told him, as they kept laughing. "You can get to know us. We're really nice," Josh cried. "We don't want to. Now go away," Amy said. "Please. Let's be friends. We can follow you anywhere," Max said. "Wow, you're a stalker. No one likes you. Just go away," Todd told them pushing Max to the ground. It took nothing for Todd to do that. The crowd laughed even more. Those two kids were in tears, and then they ran away. "Who were they?" Ginger asked. "Losers who are desperate for friends," Todd answered. Ginger felt bad for those two. They had no friends, no one to talk to, and nobody cared for them. They only had each other. Maybe they were outsiders too. Maybe they were just like Mrs. Robbin and Mrs. Duffy. Once again, Max and Josh could have a talent that no one knew about, and maybe one day, they could change the world. Ginger heard one kid in the crowd call them a "nobody." The answer is right there! The two psychology teachers and Max and Josh are considered "nobodies!" All this time Ginger was trying to figure out what a nobody actually was, and she had finally found her answer. But she can understand their feeling and how they don't fit in. could that prove Ginger is a nobody as well? Probably not. Sincerity and wisdom always make things seem true on the flesh, which is a total lie. Ginger added more people to her cell phone, and when evening came, she went to Main Street. Main Street was like the main street of the downtown suburban city. At the end of the day, the kids will play. All you saw on Main Street were teens hanging out, some shoppers and tourists, and normal people enjoying what Main Street has to offer. Main Street has a theater (which is where the teens hang out at). Pizzerias, ice cream places, bookstores, internet cafes, coffee shops, outlet stores, banquet and dining hall facilities, fancy restaurants, takeout foods, a game store, and more. It was the place to be and a place for everyone. One of the blocks on Main Street is made up of brick entirely. Main Street is just beautiful at night. Ginger hasn't been to Main Street that often. She went only a few times with Summer, Meredith, Jenny, and Sally. Most of the time, she and her friends have sleepovers during the weekend. Sometimes they even go to the mall to buy a few things. Usually Stacy, Hillary, and Brianna go to the mall. A lot of teens were hanging out on Main Street today. Ginger saw tons of kids outside of the theater and the pizza place that was across the street from the theater. Stephanie and some other friends were waiting outside of Starbucks. "Hey, Ginger. You're just in time," Stephanie cried. Ginger said hi to everybody. The same people that sat at the table on Friday were now in this group. Shandi was also there, and Ginger and Shandi talked. "So what are we doing first?" Joe asked. "Sometimes guys can be really dumb," Amy cried, rolling her eyes. "Let's go to Frank's Pizza Place across the street!" Melissa agreed. "All right," Rachael agreed. When the group arrived to the pizza place, Luna joined with them. "Hey, you guys!" Luna greeted. "Hey, Luna," they all greeted back, as Luna sat in the booth with them as well. "So how's your book club coming along?" Melissa tried to strike up a conversation. "Pretty good. If only more girls would join." "I'd join," Nick said. "You're not a girl . . . ," Stephanie said. "I know. But if I was, I would. Well, not like that, but . . . never mind."

"That's okay, Nick," Luna told him. "Anybody trying out for cheerleading?" Shandi asked. "Duh. I'm like the best cheerleader in the entire school." Stephanie bragged, although it was the truth, "I was head cheerleader last year, and the year before." "Well I was co-head cheerleader, so ha!" Amy tried to brag. "Wow! That's terrible!" Joe told her. "At least she CAN cheerlead," Rachael cried, as the girls laughed. "Shut up. We can play sports unlike you, guys," Nick tried to have a comeback. "Pshh. I can play tons of sports!" Luna said. "Luna, no you can't. I've seen you try to play basketball. You suck!" Joe told her, as they all laughed. "I've seen you try to hopscotch so you shut up," Melissa cried as they all laughed even more. "I was little," Joe responded. "Sure you were," Stephanie said. The talking continued, and then the waiter approached them. "We want to order cheese pizza with a pitcher of Sprite," Stephanie told him. Each person pitched in to pay. The waiter had left with their order. "So, Steph, who are you going to ask out or go out with?" Nick asked her. "I don't know. It's been a year since I went out with Todd. I'm thinking about Jason or Mack." "Jason is soooo hot!" Amy said. "I know. I'd faint if he took his shirt off!" Luna cried, as all the girls at the table screamed. "Ohhh, and his hair is sooo soft!" Rachael said. "Don't forget about his eyes," Shandi added. "I don't know. Mack is kind of hot too," Stephanie admitted. "Then ask him out!" Joe told her. "This is total girl stuff. You can't just ask someone out in a second," Melissa cried. "Yea, it does take time," Ginger added. "But how much time?" Joe asked. "I don't know. Weeks!" Luna answered. "Well, that's just stupid!" Nick cried. The girls just sighed and sort of rolled their eyes in a different direction. "You know what, Nick? You're stupid!" Shandi cried. "What the hell was that for?" he asked her. "She's telling the truth!" Rachael winked. Nick rolled his eyes. "Anyways, when is the next party?" Luna asked. "I don't know.

Dark Viper said he was having one soon," Stephanie cried. At that the moment, the pizza and pop came, and each of them took one slice, and some Sprite. Joe and Nick were eating like pigs. "It's called civilization, which you obviously don't have," Melissa commented. "It's also called food, Miss Anorexic," Joe replied. "Okay, that was not nice," Amy said. "Who said I was nice?" "Be quiet, Joe, or I'll spill all of the pop on your head," Stephanie threatened. Joe and Nick just laughed out loud. "She will," Amy commented. "Ya, don't get on her bad side," Luna added. After they ate pizza and drank the pop, they were back outside, near the theater's centre. They talked on and on, and even with some other kids. Suddenly, Todd, Chad, and Malcolm approached them. "Wassup," Chad greeted. "Hey," the girls, Nick, and Joe greeted. "What are you guys doing here?" Shandi asked. "We can't hang out here?" Malcolm asked. "Well, now that you're here, I guess so. What didcha guys want?" Stephanie asked. "To talk really. Like we always do," Todd said. Everyone knew the reason of them being there. It was to talk with Ginger. Todd solemnly hugged Ginger. Ginger smiled back and sort of laughed. They were "flirting." Typical teenage love (so-called love). Todd stood right next to Ginger. "We're going to the cafe. You guys wanna come?" Todd offered. (He was mostly asking Ginger). "Sure, I'll come," Ginger was the first to offer. "If that's okay with you, guys." "Of course it is," Amy told her. "I'm coming with," Luna offered. "Okay . . . oh see you guys later," Todd cried. "All right, cya," Joe said. Luna, Ginger, Todd, Malcolm, and Chad went one way, and Stephanie and her pals went the other way. When they've sat around a table, Ginger received a text from Stephanie, "If those guys do anything wrong, lemme know." Ginger responded, "Okay."

"So what did you guys want?" Luna asked. Luna only came to watch out for Ginger. All of them already knew that Todd wanted to talk to Ginger, his new girlfriend. Todd looked right into Ginger's eyes. "Wow. Your eyes are so beautiful," Todd complimented. "Thanks." Ginger smiled. "We should totally have another party. Like an eighth-grade party, I guess," Luna tried to suggest. "Luna, don't worry. Rachael and Amy always have parties. They had one last week," Chad reminded her. "Yea, but seriously. Another one wouldn't hurt."

"It's okay, Luna," Ginger told her. "So Ginger, you're pretty hot. Which one of us do you think is hot?" Todd asked her. "Todd, what kind of question is that?" Luna asked him. "I just wanna know."

"Chad by far! I'm sorry, Todd," Ginger answered. "Yes! I told you!" Chad bragged. "Whatever," Malcolm ignored him. "Typical guys. The lamer the stuff to talk about, the better," Luna whispered in Ginger's ear. "But that's all right, Ginger. Cuz we goin' out now," Todd hold her, holding her hand. Ginger pushed the hair behind her face. "Yep. But Chad's still hotter," Ginger laughed. "Oh, come on. You don't believe that," Todd was trying to sound gangster. Ginger just laughed at his humor. "You are so funny. Maybe I'll vote for you in the funniest list on the yearbook," Ginger chuckled. "I'd vote for you under hottest girl in the eighth grade," Malcolm told her. "No, you wouldn't. You'd vote for Shandi or Jill," Luna replied. "Just look at Shandi. She's hot. What guy wouldn't go out with her?"

"Don't forget about Hillary. She is like smoking. I would ask her out, but I'm going out with Claire," Chad cried. "Oh yea. Claire's a cutie. I'd grab her any day," Malcolm responded. "Okay eww . . . ," Luna and Ginger said at the same time. The guys just chuckled a little. Ginger received another text. It was from Amy, "OMG where r u? Come 2 movie theater."

"Oh, Amy wants us back at the theater. See you guys later," Luna read the text. "Okay, later. This was cool. See ya, Ginger," Malcolm said. "What? No hug?" Todd offered. "Of course." Ginger hugged him. "What about me?" Chad wondered. "Yea, and me?" Malcolm was the last to offer. Ginger smiled and hugged them as well. "Cya later guys," Ginger waved. "Later," the guys called back. Luna and Ginger left the cafe and headed back to the theater. "Wow, Ginger is pretty cool," Chad said. "And sexy," Malcolm added. "I know. She's even cooler than Stephanie. All Stephanie would talk about is gossip and shopping. That was fine, but she knew nothing about sports." Todd said. "Do you think Ginger does, though?" Chad asked "Dude, of course she does. Have you seen her play volleyball? She's a beast!" Malcolm commented. "Yea, and Jose told me she's the fastest runner in her gym class. I'm totally attracted to that," Todd responded. "I'm attracted to more preppy girls. Like Shandi," Malcolm said. "Dude, you've been talking about Shandi all week. Just ask her out!" Todd told him. "I can't. Shadi is hard to get. She doesn't even go out with guys that much anymore," Malcolm responded.

"That's because she acts like a go-getter. She just wants attention," Chad reminded them. This was true about Shandi. "Don't worry. It'll work out," Malcolm cried. "Yea. Just like it worked out for Ginger and I."

"If it wasn't for The Wise, you'd still be trying to ask her out." Chad said, as he and Malcolm laughed. "Shut up. At least I'm not going out with some freak obsessed with just hair and makeup." "She's not a freak. She only wants to look hot," Chad stated. "Most of the girls in our school *is* hot!" Malcolm cried. "Yea, like Stephanie's friends, Hillary's friends, and that one chick on the cheerleading team, Vanessa," Todd agreed. "Oh, the girls on the cheerleading team are superhot," Chad added. "I know. I got most of their numbers last year," Malcolm said. "Awesome," Todd commented. "Oh crap! I have a football game tomorrow," Todd realized. "Me too. I have one in the morning and one in the afternoon," Malcolm said. The boys sighed in relief. When you play so many sports, it will seem like you have no time on your hands. "Our team is undefeatable. Matthew Hopkins is a beast!" Chad bragged. "Oh, you mean that kid that goes to that Catholic School?" Todd asked. "Yea. He scored four touchdowns last week." "Our team is okay. I hate our coach, though," Malcolm cried. "Yea. It's like anything we do wrong, we have to run laps," Todd complained. Todd and Malcolm are on the same football team. "That sucks. Our coach is pretty cool," Chad cried. "Lucky. I'd give anything for a new coach," Malcolm said. "I wouldn't, actually. Our team is 7 and 1. A couple of more wins, and we'll be going to the championship," Todd opposed. "I'm just glad Rizza Corman is off our team. He couldn't even catch the freakin' ball!" Chad said. "Why is he off the team?" Malcolm asked. "He sucks, that's why. The coach got so mad at him, he nearly socked him in the face!" Chad answered. "Whoa. Harsh," Todd cried. "He deserved it, though," Chad said, as they all laughed. Malcolm received a text. "What was it?" Todd wanted to know. "My stupid sister. I have to go home, now see ya guys later," Malcolm said, as they stood up. "All right, cya," Chad cried. "See ya at the game tomorrow," Todd also said. The three of them high-fived, and Malcolm left the cafe. Todd and Chad also left the cafe and went to another place on Main Street (probably to see if their other friends were here, which they usually are). It was quite late by now. Ginger's grandparents do not agree about Ginger being up or outside at a certain time. Curfew has its limits. Uncle would be picking up Ginger (it would be too dangerous for her to walk home by herself that late). Although Pappy had a fit and a million reasons of why Ginger couldn't stay at Main Street too long, she would be surrounded by a group of people, which would be safer than her being alone. Luna and Ginger had just gotten back with the group. They were at some restaurant. A few other teens were here as well. "So how did it go? Good? Okay?" Shandi asked. "It was fine, I guess. Todd does seem compassionate," Ginger answered. "Todd? Compassionate? Please! He can be a total jerk!" Amy confessed. "And he can be mean to other kids," Rachael cried. "He was sweet when I talked to him," Ginger explained. "Ginger, lemme tell you about dating. I've gone out with Todd last year. Always remember these tips: Look hot (Todd loves girls who look their best). Talk about sports. (Todd is a jock, so he knows nothing about style and fashion. He only cares about the looks. If you talk about sports statistics, he will be more attracted to you, and he'll compete in sports.). And always remember, if he treats you wrong in any way, let us know. (We're Todd's friends. When I went out with him, he'd get mad at me for not knowing sports, or that I would get personal. He hates personal stuff. If he is mean to you, let us know. Then we can plot revenge)," Stephanie advised. "I know he won't be mean to me. I shoved Bailey and his friends on a locker."

"I find that hard to believe," Nick commented. "Anyway," Stephanie continued, ignoring that remark, "one last thing: You are in charge. (Make sure you assert yourself to Todd and always ask him for things. He thinks you're hot. You just have to use that to your advantage. Soon, he'll start to do what you tell him to do)."

"Thanks. I will definitely follow your advice."

"You should. Last year, I went out with Mack, her advice helped a lot," Rachael cried. "Too bad it only lasted a week," Melissa cried, as they laughed. "And he saw another girl," Luna added. "He still did what I told him to do," Rachael defended. "I'm sure he did," Joe replied. "Oh crap! I got that science paper due on Monday," Shandi whimpered. "Yea, and I have homework of my own too," Amy sighed. "Yea, I gotta get home before my mom freaks," Nick said. "Me too," Joe agreed. "All right, bye guys. I'm going home," Stephanie said. They left the restaurant, and just hung out. Nick, Joe, Stephanie, Shandi, and Amy had left already. Ginger, Luna, and Melissa talked, while Rachael went her separate way to text or do whatever with her phone. Luna and Melissa waved good-bye when Ginger's uncle arrived. Ginger waved and got inside of the car. Ginger was glad to have friends. She was not only glad to have the friends she already has, she was glad that she made new friends (especially popular friends), and she has a boyfriend. She just hopes that he's the right one. Todd is nice, he's the captain of the football, basketball, and the boy's track teams, and he did seem like a person to care and love. Ginger had forgotten about Bailey and the pain he caused Ginger that day. She moved on now. She has better friends and a better guy. The guy that's the most athletic and popular in the eighth grade. Friendship is a worthy thing. Some people couldn't live without friends, or they'd just be bored. Life is about finding people to talk with and becoming street and social smart in the world. Ginger forgot to ask Stephanie how her relationship with Todd went. People don't stay together forever, especially at a young age. But Ginger is different. She does have some things in common with Todd. They both play sports and are good at the sports they play. Having Ginger realize this can be a good sign of a great relationship. Friendship comes first and can lead to love (if the Spirit Transporter allows that). But one word makes Ginger feel the real feeling of friendship, and that one word is Shelby.

CHAPTER 12

The Destiny Virus

"Did you have fun today?" Uncle asked. "Yep. They are all really nice," Ginger answered. "That's good. I'm glad you're making more friends. Friends are really important to have."

"Uncle, I think you mean friendship," Ginger corrected him. "Yea." Friendship makes two people friends. You can't have a friend without friendship. True friendship matters a lot. One word that makes Ginger feels the hardships of friendship is Shelby, her dog. Shelby was a labrador who had embraced Ginger's life so much when she was a little girl. The family got him when he was just a puppy. Shelby had been with the family a year before her father died in that terrible accident. Shortly after Ginger turned eleven, Shelby ran away, and he never came back. Shelby and Ginger had been with each other for about six years. Both of them saw her mother and father die at that hospital. Both of them had a great bond with each other and established a good relationship and friendship. But then Shelby ran away, tearing Ginger's heart even more than it already did. She just can't get over it. She will never get over her parent's death or her dog that ran away from her, just when she was getting use to not having parents. But again, Ginger must learn to move on throughout the troubles in the world. It is sad that her family left her before she even became a teen, especially when she was two feet away from their death or her own friend running away from her. She still questions: Why would Shelby run away from her? Didn't he love her? Wasn't he her best friend? Ginger had known him for over six years. Why now? What made Shelby do such a mischievous thing? Ginger will never answer those questions. Ginger doesn't know where Shelby is now, or if he's dead. The minute Shelby ran away, Ginger and her grandparents went all over the city, and the Animal Protecting Agency to try to find Shelby. Many posters and signs were put up, and it didn't matter at all. Shelby was never found. Shelby was Ginger's guardian angel. All she had after her parents *was* Shelby. Shelby believed in her when she couldn't even believe in herself. He showed her creativity and performance by expressing values at such a young age. That is what you call true friendship. It doesn't even have to be a person. A dog can be anyone's friend, that's why it's referred to as Man's Best Friend. Pappy, Grammy, and Uncle don't remember Shelby, and Ginger usually never brings him up to them. Uncle doesn't like pets anyway, and Ginger still being upset about what happened to the pet she had, she and her folks were convinced at not getting another pet or animal for the house. Just looking at Shelby made Ginger smile. The true bonding they had just brightened up Ginger every time. But then fate came and took it all away. Ginger realized that Shelby is dead at this point (it's been almost three years since he ran away). In those three years, no one has ever shown her what friendship was. Lanely Tildon does show her certain things but not to the extent that Shelby would show. Ginger would always rub him, and he, she, and her mother would always walk a certain distance, so Shelby could get the proper amount of exercise. Ginger enjoyed doing things with Shelby, especially lying in the grass and just looking at the clouds. Ginger loved doing that when she was a little girl, and having her dog with her made it even more special. Even talking to Shelby helped Ginger on the inside and stronger on the outside. Ginger was just a little girl. She had no one to talk to. Her friends wouldn't have understood her as much as Shelby would. Ginger remembered skipping in a meadow with Shelby and enjoying nature with her own friend. All the good times and memories they shared. Too bad those times and memories are now down in the trash can, along with her childhood days. Oh well. What can you do? When you lost your loved ones and your special friend(s), all you CAN do is cherish the moments of the actual truth. No more can be told when death or tragic comes. It will happen to everyone. We may not like it, but again, the truth hurts. Most people think that humans are on this earth for a purpose. When a person fulfills that purpose, it could be time. That is opinion, however. The fact of the matter is to live life to the fullest. Never back down from anything. You may not know your future, and you're not supposed to know. You're supposed to make your future come true. Maybe Shelby was to only come to help. Ginger through her time of need, he saw both her parents pass on and he also saw Ginger grow into a near preteen. Could it have been his purpose? Or was it evil fate that wanted to see Ginger suffer more than she has? Whatever it may be, Ginger still misses Shelby and the laughs they shared. In just a blink of an eye, Ginger's family has left her. Though she hardly remembers her father, he was the provider for the family, and in that year he saw Shelby as a puppy, the family was at its best. Then came the terrible car crash. Life would never be the same again. Ginger's mother's life was in pieces. She too couldn't get over her husband's death. Now she had to raise her only daughter and take care of a dog that wouldn't stop growing. Only then the pieces of her life vanished when fatal breast cancer took her away. Ginger was still growing, and needed a parent figure. She was getting use to having one loving parent (the parent who taught her to be tough and to play volleyball) when she decided to visit her husband in heaven. Then her dog runs away from her. The dog that has shown her friendship and loyalty. The dog that taught her to become a hero. But all of that was in the past. Ginger knows that she can't keep holding on to these tragedies (even though it's hard to let go the loss of a family). She regrets to ever disrespecting her parents when she was a baby, but she knew no better. Again, Ginger can be thankful to have people who can help her through her life that seems to have been gone with the wind. Lanely Tildon may not be in the family's blood, but she knew her mother when she was just a teenager. She has seen Ginger since birth. Lanely knows the challenges Ginger faces ever since Shelby ran away. It's devastating to have even one parent or somebody special in your life at a young age. Lanely knows that. Lanely sees the connection of Ginger and Mrs. Fraiddee. Ginger's strength, intellect, and above all ego show this within Ginger. That is why Ginger can easily talk to Lanely about personal things (things that she would talk to, to her parents of Shelby). If you are a person going through this, you can understand the devastation feeling of a perished loved one. Ginger also had her and her uncle and grandparents to talk to, and they definitely understand the feeling of their close relationships gone (even though Pappy may seem skeptical about the whole thing). Ginger's friends really can't help her when it comes to the situation, mainly because they didn't even known Ginger's parents well enough. But then again, any support from someone does help a lot. Friends are important. But the *ship* in *friend* makes friendship extremely important. Shelby has shown Ginger friendship, and although he may not be with her today, she will always remember the times they shared; from the time she and her parents picked Shelby when he was a puppy to the time he ran away that cold, sad night. Times do go on, but never forget the past that you loved (this can even be "history" in the making, or what has been made). It was pretty dark when Uncle and Ginger made it back to the house. "How was it, Ginger?" Grammy asked her, straightening her crooked glasses. "It was fun, and I made new friends," Ginger answered. "That's good! The more friends you got, the more ya out of the house!" Pappy commented, as the family could only laugh. Silly Pappy. "Whatever you say, Pappy," Ginger laughed, running upstairs to her room. Ginger didn't have a lot of photos with Shelby. He was a part of the family, but when it came to photo time, he was somewhere sleep or something. Ginger went to the photo case where all the pictures were. She saw Shelby in a picture by himself and another photo with Ginger next to him. The one with Ginger in the picture with Shelby had to be taken when she was about ten years old. They looked so happy with each other. Shelby's large ears and hairy fur just warmed Ginger's heart all over again. Knowing that the love they had was something very special, Shelby smiled in both of the pictures. It made Ginger smile as well. For the first time in what has seemed like years, Ginger is smiling at her friend and at herself. That smile she has on her face shows and symbolizes that one word: Proud. Now Ginger believed again. It was as if Shelby was standing right next to Ginger. Sadly, those were the only two photos in the photo case where Shelby was in it. Ginger grabbed some old photo books the family kept (some of the photo books show Pappy leaving American heading to Vietnam to fight in the war. That's how old it was). The first photo book she picked up was titled "Ireland Summer Festival: 2000." The family took a trip to Ireland to celebrate a festival of the Irish. Dancing, singing, and parties were involved. And of course Ginger saw that picture of her and her parents and the "Welcome to Dublin" sign in the background. No photos of Shelby. Ginger looked through a lot of photo books and some film strips, though some were hard to see. Then Ginger saw a photo of Shelby, her when she was younger, and her mother. It appeared that they were at a beach. There was a date on the photo. It read, "7/13/2002." Now Ginger remembers! They took a family beach trip. Ginger's father had been passed away by that time. All three of them looked happy, and the water with rocks and the sand made the picture look even more beautiful. Ginger took that picture out of the book so she'll know where to find it. After searching more photos, she found one with her whole family (she, her parents, and of course Shelby). This was a much older picture, but it was still a special picture to have. Aww, Shelby was just a small puppy at the time. The new labrador was perfect to have in the family, and a smile every day from all four of them made life even better. Too bad that can't continue. Ginger saved this picture as well. She kept those two on her dresser, where she kept another picture of her and Shelby by themselves in some meadow (that picture was different than the four she had already seen). She decided to frame the two pictures she already had, so the moment with her old family (Shelby is a part of the family) could last forever. It was getting late, and Ginger had to go to bed. She decided that she looked through enough photos for one night, and she pretty much found what she was looking for. She was glad that her family took a lot of pictures, because the more pictures you take, the more memories and laughs you can have. Good thing Ginger had found these pictures. At first she thought that her grandparents got rid of some, or gave them to other family relatives to see. She was just relieved that the photos were still left unharmed, and that no photos were damaged. Ginger returned the photo books back where they belonged, and then got ready for bed. The weekend passed, and Monday was here all over again. Another week. A new day. Ginger was starting to think that perhaps the Enchantment Lanely Tildon had performed on her awhile back was starting to work after all. By now, it had been official. Everyone knew about Todd and Ginger. Hillary was still unhappy about it, but Ginger figured that she'd get over it soon. It now seemed hard for her to talk with her original buddies. But you can call that a fact of life. Now that she had new friends (popular ones at that), it would be hard. Little does Ginger know that her friends are happy for her, if not the whole school. Right when Ginger arrived at school, Stephanie just had to come see and talk to Ginger, along with Stephanie's friends. Ginger knew to take Stephanie's advice she had given her. Stephanie went out with Todd just last year, so if any girl in the school knows Todd that well, it would be Stephanie of course. After talking with Stephanie for a while, Ginger went with Summer, Meredith, Sally, and Cindy inside the building. "My mom and I went shopping yesterday, which was brutally boring," Cindy cried. "You went shopping with your mom?" Sally asked. "Well, it's something we do sometimes. It may sound weird, but it's now sort of a tradition and a little thing we do," Cindy explained. "Yea. I shopped with my sister last week. I definitely needed new jewelry," Summer said. "Cool," Meredith responded. "I only shop for clothes nowadays," Ginger said. "Me too. The other stuff I just don't need," Meredith admitted. "I think I may shop in high school more!" Sally said. "Yea, me too. The choices now are so limited," Cindy agreed. "I may shop. It depends on money issues as well!" Ginger admitted. "I'm getting new tank tops on Wednesday! Oh yea!" Summer bragged. "Woohoo!" the four girls cheered. "Okay, I'm going to class. See ya later!" Sally cried. "I'm going your way! Bye!" Cindy cried, as them two went their separate ways. Summer waved good-bye and went her way. Meredith and Ginger went the same way, and by now, they were walking up the stairs. "Is Stephanie actually nice?" Meredith asked her. "She actually is. We had a great time Friday night," Ginger smiled, as Meredith laughed. When she arrived on the fourth floor, she was startled by someone. A person had tickled her sides. It was enough for her to jump. Of course, that was Todd. "Are you all right?" he asked her. "Well, yea, I got startled. What do you want?" "Come on, Ginger. It was a joke. I'll walk ya to class," he offered. (They were in the same first-period class). Ginger had no choice but to smile and say, "Sure." Todd wrapped his arms around her, and they walked to class. There they saw Todd's friends in a group. "Hey, Ginger! Wassup, Todd!" Malcolm and Jason greeted. They both waved. "Did you see the game on Saturday? It was awesome!" Jason started a conversation. "Oh yea, I did! I wanted my team to win . . . ," Mack complained. "I know. They should've gone all the way. Oh well, there's always next year," Malcolm sighed. Ginger could barely understand a word they were talking about. She does play sports, but when it comes to tackle sports like football, she gets sidetracked. "So Ginger, do you play football?" Malcolm asked. "Of course not. Too much tackling," Ginger answered. "Are you serious? The way you pounded those guys on those lockers that day was amazing!" Todd complimented her. "Yea, and Bailey was almost crying," Malcolm said, as they all laughed. "Well, Bailey was bullying you so I had to make him stop."

"You sure did. Now that loser won't come near us anymore," Todd said, as they all agreed. The bell had rung, and kids were going to their appropriate class. "If you had the chance, would you go out with me?" Malcolm asked Ginger. "Of course she wouldn't!" Stacy answered for her. Hillary came showing up behind. "What the heck?" Jason wondered. "Ginger made a *bad* choice just saying yes to Todd, and now these freaks? Please! You'd be better off with a homeless guy in Downtown NYC," Hillary cried, rolling her eyes. "Hillary, come on. These guys are cute, aren't they?" Ginger asked her. "Well, of course we are. You're just jealous," Todd answered. "Jealous of what? The fact of insecurity and not caring for others? Stupidity and well . . . stupidity . . . !" Stacy wondered. "Hey I got a 3.7 GPA last trimester," Jason tried to defend. "Well, I got a 3.95," Hillary bragged. "Nerd," Todd commented, as those guys laughed. "I'd rather be smart than a dumbass," Stacy retorted. "I'd rather be that than a worthless whore," Malcolm cried. Todd wrapped his arms tightly to Ginger, as if they were to embrace. "Are you okay?" Todd asked. "Yea, I'm fine," Ginger smiled. "Cool," Todd responded as they went in the classroom. Stacy and Hillary pulled Ginger to the side to talk to her. "What the hell was that about?" Hillary asked. "Look, Todd is a really sweet guy. You guys may not like it, but we're sorta going out now."

"I know. We just want to protect you. And here's a small tip: Have your own personal space," Stacy cried. "Thanks for helping, though. For right now, Ima just take one simple step at a time," Ginger cried. "Wow! Ginger didn't even care that you tried to cuddle with her!" Malcolm said, as the three boys were talking in a little conversation. "I think she has a thing for you, dude!" Jason added. "I know. Soon I'll be able to feel her goodies!" Todd said, getting all excited. "Naah, she won't let you do that. She's too nice," Malcolm cried. "Maybe. All she has to do is lighten up a little, like the rest of the girls that are insanely hot!" Todd explained. "Naughty girls," Jason corrected him, as they gave a small laugh. "Just like when Amy took off her shirt at the Luna's party one time!" Malcolm said. "That girl had to be drunk. Or stupid," Todd cried. "Probably both," Jason admitted, as they agreed. Once first period was over, things moved pretty swiftly by lunchtime. Shandi was walking into the lunchroom with a book in her hands when she accidentally dropped the book. "I'll catch up to you guys in a second! Save me a seat," Shandi called, as her friends kept walking. "Okay!" the girls cried. Shandi grabbed for the book, but someone else had grabbed it instead. Malcolm did. "I think you dropped this," he said very nicely, handing the book to her. "I almost stepped on it. Sorry." Malcolm looked into her eyes, and all he saw was beauty. "Thanks," Shandi said, smiling a little. They were just looking at each other sincerely, as if the world was gone, and they were the only ones there. "You know you seem shy," Malcolm said, breaking the silence. "Hmmph. Oops." Shandi dropped her book again. It was clear, now. Malcolm picked up the book again, and handed it to Shandi. "I'll call you," Malcolm told her. Shandi smiled, wrote her number on a small piece of paper, and handed it to Malcolm. "Thanks, see ya later. And by the way, you're sexy," Malcolm told her, walking off. Shandi jumped in the air and ran to sit with her friends and to share the good news. You see, the Spirit Transporter works in many ways. The biggest way, however, is through connection, whether an object or human. Shelby helps connect with Ginger, and that's why they loved each other. The Spirit Transporter allows anything to connect, or anyone, no matter the race of background or thing or animal. What actually allowed the Spirit Transporter to allow Shandi and Malcolm to like each other? The book did. The book connected these two together, and it only took one simple object. Even objects can allow the Spirit Transporter to work within a plant, animal, or human. Objects can play a big role when it comes to things like that, and the flow of love will be even more magnificent. The Spirit Transporter works in all kinds of ways in the world, both big and small. It is everywhere, and the direct source is by far different and can sometimes even be mysterious or unknown. It just depends on fate (although that can turn in for the worse). For the first time, Ginger was sitting with Todd's friends. She felt a little terrified because she does not sit with them nor does she talk to them. But Ginger was going to be ready, and Todd and Stephanie's friends could "protect" her in any way. Ginger met up with Todd, and they walked to the tables where they usually sat. There were already some kids who were sitting there, eating their lunch. "Are you okay? My friends can sometimes be jerks," Todd told her, as they were coming closer to the table. "Yea I'm fine. They wouldn't bother me, anyway," Ginger told him. They finally approached the table, where some kids were, munching and munching away. They were immediately stunned when they saw a girl in a volleyball uniform approach the table. She usually never comes to their table. "Hey, you guys. This is Ginger, my girlfriend," Todd introduced her. "Hey, Ginger," they responded back. "Hey," Ginger cried, smiling. Her smile attracted all of those guys sitting at the table. They were probably staring at her tits. Todd put his arm around Ginger's chair. More guys started to arrive at the table, and they were all eating their lunches now. More talking and conversations were now in place. "Aren't these guys cool?" Todd asked Ginger. "Ya, especially football players!" Ginger answered. Some of those guys went "Yea!" or "All right!" These guys are jocks. Malcolm had a note of some kind in his hands and was showing the other guys. "So does that mean you're going out with Shandi?" Andy asked. "Yea. Ima call her tonight," Malcolm said. "Dude, that's awesome! She must like you!" Todd told him, as they high-fived. "Yea, she does. I can tell. She couldn't stop looking at me," Malcolm informed. "Nice! Hopefully Shandi didn't give you some crappy number," Mack said. "Naah. She wouldn't do that," Malcolm explained. Shandi glanced at him from the table she was sitting at and waved. Malcolm waved back, smiling a little. "Shandi's a pretty okay girl. She doesn't seem mean," Chad said. "Only when she's around her friends," Rockstar Kid replied. "Yea, but she seems nice," Malcolm said. "Are you sad?" Todd whispered to Ginger in her ear. "Why would I be sad?"

"I don't know. You're just so quiet," he answered. "I'm kind of tired. And I have volleyball practice all of next week," Ginger sighed. "Cool. I'm psyched about the playoffs," Todd said. "I just hope we win," Ginger cried "Of course we will. That Mandy Liverstone girl doesn't stand a damn chance!" Malcolm cried. "Yea, and we have an awesome volleyball player on the team!" Andy added. "Jill Wiselaw?" Ginger asked. "You, of course! You're a beast at volleyball!" Mack told her. "I guess I kinda am," Ginger sort of denied. "Are you serious? The way you spike is amazing!" Chad complimented, as the others agreed. "Plus you look so hot on the court!" Rockstar Kid told her, as the other guys shook heads in agreement. "Oh, shut up. That's so not true. The uniforms are gross," Ginger cried. "Oooh, naughty!" Malcolm announced, as they all "dog whispered." "You haven't seen the naughty side of me," Ginger winked (the guys probably did want to see the naughty side). Teenagers. My, oh my, oh my. "You should try out for cheerleading. The outfits are much, much hotter!" Andy suggested. "Just for an outfit? No way. Plus cheerleaders are too preppy," Ginger cried. "Yea, like that one chick from Midway Middle School. She's a terrible cheerleader, and she thinks she's the best!" Todd agreed. "Well all cheerleaders are like that (ones who don't go to our school)," Mack mentioned. "But you still should try out. You'd be great," Malcolm encouraged her. "Maybe I will," Ginger decided. Ginger had received a text. It was from Rachael, "If u need help, txt me. O, and watch out 4 u-know-who!'

Ginger turned to see Stephanie and laughed. Stephanie saw she got the message. "What does it say?" Todd wondered. "Nothing," Ginger was still laughing as she flipped the phone closed and slid it into her pocket. Todd noticed Ginger's locket. He thought it was cool, yet a little strange. "What's that on your neck? It's kind of cool," Todd noticed. "A locket from my great-great-great grandfather that was passed down in our family." Ginger's mother owned that locket the longest, which is why it was considered her before she gave it to Ginger. "Sweet!" Todd cried, holding up the locket so he could get a good glimpse of the locket. The texture and somewhat modern color caught his eye on the locket the most. "So what other sports do you play?" Chad asked her. "Track mostly. I also play soccer, tennis, and a little of hockey. I used to dance when I was a little girl," Ginger answered. "Wow, awesome," Rockstar Kid commented. "I know, that's cool. Do you play football or basketball?" Andy asked. "Not really. I get hurt in those sports," Ginger laughed a little. "Still cool, though. I can't even serve in volleyball," Malcolm admitted. "It's easy once you keep playing, especially a sport that doesn't require much running," Ginger explained. "True. Or a lazy sport like golf," Todd replied, as they all laughed. Soon enough, the bell rang, and lunch was over. The guys got up, and as Ginger started walking, Todd stopped her. "Oh, come on, Todd. I don't wanna be late for my next class." "Just one hug. Please," Todd offered. They both hugged each other, and then Ginger caught up with her friends and went to the next class. Maybe Hillary was wrong about how guys were. Guys can be passionate about things; they just don't want to show it. Hillary will see that her own advice could be wrong, and it only takes one person. Wednesday afternoon. Band class. The kids were lined up outside, talking as usual. Brianna and Sally caught up to where Hillary and Stacy were standing. "Oh my gosh. I am so happy for Ginger!" Brianna cried. "Me too. I think she feels great again," Sally agreed. "I just hope that Todd won't be a douche like Bailey was," Hillary snarled. "He won't. Trust me! Todd'll wish he was alive if he even thinks to bother Ginger," Stacy remarked, as the girls agreed. "I'm just glad to see Ginger happy again," Brianna commented. "Yea! She hasn't been open since her mother died," Sally cried. "Which is very sad. I'd be devastated knowing that I have no parents in my life," Stacy cried. "Me too. My mother has been the best influence in my life," Hillary agreed. Joel came approaching the girls in the middle of their conversation. "Look what the cat dragged in . . . ," Stacy rolled her eyes. "You're just jealous because I don't like you as I do with Hillary," Joel responded. "Ewwww!" the girls cried. "No girl likes you, Joel. That's why you're gonna grow up being a homo that you are," Hillary told him. "Just wait, Hillary! You will be mine! You WILL admit the truth, my Love!" Joel exaggerated, completely ignoring her comment. "Not in infinity years, moron!" Hillary cried, pushing him out of the way. "Just wait, Hillary! You just wait!" Joel yelled, as he ran to the back of the line. "When will he learn that you don't like him?" Sally asked her. "I don't know." "He'll learn soon enough when I embarrass him in front of the entire school," Hillary protested. "Good luck with that," Brianna cried. Mrs. Alvarez came to only see the students not cooperating with themselves. "Children, children, children! Is this how you line up in my class?! Is this how you line up in *any* class? It's time you start acting like prep high schoolers. You will be glad that you did," Mrs. Alvarez explained, trying to discipline (Mrs. Alvarez is not the "disciplining" type). "Eww, is that Abercrombie you're wearing? Eww! Hollister is much better!" Hillary got off topic. "No it is not, now get in line Hillary so we can begin class," Mrs. Alvarez demanded. "Geez. Someone is a liiitle cranky today," Stacy said. "Hey, I had no coffee this morning, only a glass of orange juice," it's easy for Mrs. Alvarez to get off topic, "now enough. We've wasted enough time. Get your instruments and sit down!" Kids went into the band room. "Without talking!" Mrs. Alvarez went on. Hillary and Stacy took their seats with their flute in their hand. At that moment, Andy and Malcolm approached the two girls. "Would you go out with Joel?" Andy asked them, particularly Hillary. "Eww, no." "Why would you guys come over here just to ask us that? You knew she'd say no in the first place!" Stacy responded. "Just to make you mad," Malcolm said, as they laughed. "Well you did, now go away!" Hillary stomped her foot on the ground. "Leave her alone and sit down. Hillary, please shush, or I'll have to move you down a chair," Mrs. Alvarez cried, as Malcolm and Andy went to their seats. Everybody was now ready to make music. Ready to see the magic of music and Mozart and Beethoven. Ready to see the Spirit Transporter work at its own risk (even when no one is paying attention to these things). Mrs. Alvarez held up her baton when Joel was pushing into Hillary as he finally found his seat.

"Are you finished?" Mrs. Alvarez rolled her eyes. She was annoyed. "Yes, Mrs. Alvarez," Joel answered. "Good. Now our performance is even closer than before. You know where to meet, where to go, and what to expect. I advise all of you to articulate and look the conductor while playing. Now let's begin." After playing new songs and Joel constantly annoying Stacy and Hillary, things were about to get a little bit crazy (as if it already wasn't). "Better. Much, much better," Mrs. Alvarez announced. "Not Hillary. She messed up the entire thing. That's why I'm first chair!" Joel bragged. Malcolm, Andy, Todd, and Jason started laughing. "Shut up, it's not funny!" Brianna cried. "I can laugh at what I want to laugh at," Jason yelled. "Not when it's at a rude comment!" Sally replied. "Oh yea, Joel, it's weird how you're first chair, because you're the only boy in the flute section," Hillary cried. "Oh wait, Hillary. That's right. Joel isn't a boy!" Stacy yelled out, as the class laughed. "Stop the nonsense right now! I'm really not in the mood today!" Mrs. Alvarez concluded. "I will when Hillary stops insulting our friend," Jason stood up for Joel. "What are you talking about? He and your friends keep annoying me every single day!" This made Hillary stand up. "Give it up, Hillary," Malcolm insisted. "Not until you stop annoying her!" Brianna budded in. "We weren't talking to you," Todd cried, as he too stood up. "Why don't you just go away, already?" Hillary asked. "Why don't you have a normal hair color?" Jason asked. "Why are you so annoying?" Hillary asked. "Why do you act like a jerk?" Jason asked. The argument went on and on, and Mrs. Alvarez wouldn't dare try to stop it at this point. It all changed when Jason asked Hillary,

"Why don't you go out with me?" The whole class sighed. "What the . . . ? I'm supposed to ask her that!" Joel interfered. "You already did, Joel. Many, many times," Mrs. Alvarez sighed. "Will you?" Jason asked. Jason knew she wanted to go out with him. It was just a matter of time. "Yes!" Hillary answered. "Cool!" Jason cried. "What?" not only was Joel surprised, but so was Stacy, Brianna, Sally, and some other girls. What happened to girls sticking together? Did it mean anything of no more boys trashing and dating girls? Sometimes the Spirit Transporter does change the mind of people.

CHAPTER 13

The Enchantment:
Part 2—Path of Grace

Mrs. Alvarez pretended like that scenario never happened when class was over. "What the heck, Hillary? What happened to the girl rule? First Shandi, now you! Oh my gosh!" Stacy cried. It's the Spirit Transporter. "I'm sorry, but Jason is a very nice guy. It won't hurt to give it a try!" Hillary said. "I just hope you won't get hurt. Guys can be such assholes!" Stacy warned. "Oh don't worry about that. He or any other guy knows not to mess with me or my friends. They can try, but it won't work in the end," Hillary told her. "Jason is nice and sweet. Maybe he will be the right one after all," Stacy said. "Trust me he will. Hopefully the other girls will understand. Now that we're boyfriend and girlfriend, everyone will know the truth," Hillary cried. "They will. Unless if they completely hate Todd and his obnoxious friends, same with Jose, Chad, Eric most of Jason's stupid friends," Stacy smirked.

Stacy was texting some of her friends, and Hillary was as well, telling them the good news. "They'll be nice. Or else . . . ," Stacy replied, still texting away. Jason was receiving high fives from his friends. "Dude, you're finally going out with Hillary," Todd congratulated him. "I know, plus Hillary's hot!" Jason added. "Duh. Her titties are huge too," Andy said. "How did she even say yes, though?" Connor asked. "Yea, she always says no to guys," David added. "Maybe he's just cool like that," Todd answered. "Do you think the 'relationship' will last?" Cody asked. "Are you kidding?! Of course it will!" Eric told him, as if he were stupid. "Too bad Hillary's friends are such bitches sometimes," Malcolm said. "That's okay. That means more girls for us," Andy insisted. "Plus girls are truly hot when they start acting naughty and really sassy. That's the best part about girls," Todd said. "And the looks," David added. "Duh," Connor responded. "I just hope Hillary isn't some psychotic freak who can't seem to live without me," Jason said. "Most girls are like that, especially Stephanie's friends," Cody explained. "But she won't be. She's very cautious when it comes to guys," Eric said. "She's paranoid of nothing," Todd said. "That's why no guy would ask her out. She'd usually say no," Malcolm cried. "Not to Jason, though," Connor cried, giving him another high five. "She can't resist guys. No girl can. Unless they're lesbian," Jason said. The bell rang. "See ya later," Connor, David, Eric, and Cody went to class as Andy, Jason, Malcolm, and Todd said bye. "Remember to practice your instruments every day!" Mrs. Alvarez announced, as kids were leaving the room. Hillary, Stacy, Sally, and Brianna approached those guys, seeming a little mad, but also a little concerned about something. "Oh no, here comes drama!" Andy teased. "First Ginger, then Shandi, now Hillary! What the hell is wrong with you, guys? We told you to stay away from us! Geez, so much for girls sticking together!" Stacy yelled at them. "What the hell is wrong with you! Maybe you're just mad that you can't get a date!" Todd explained. "It has nothing to do with that. Now stay away from us," Sally demanded. "Actually, we don't want you annoying us," Hillary corrected. "Which you've been doing," Brianna added. "Just don't annoy them, and don't use sexual harassments," Hillary told them. "Uhh . . . okay. So I'll call you tonight?" Jason offered. "Okay," Hillary smiled. Stacy, Brianna, and Sally rolled their eyes. The girls walked on atrociously, bumping into some of the kids. "Now I'll never get a date," Stacy's face looked saddened. "Oh yes, you will, Stacy. Even if we have to do a boy search," Hillary suggested. "That would be plain weird," Brianna acknowledged. "Oh well, I'm goin' to class. See ya later," Sally cried, trotting off to class as the other three girls did the same thing. Just like the relationships with Shandi and Ginger, it took no time for students to figure out that Hillary was going out with Jason. Once Luna found out, that was all she needed to know to spread the word (she is like the queen of gossip). Girls, mainly preps and popular girls, were congratulating Hillary and were giving advice and more pointless gossip. Jason's friends gave him fives and told him to give Hillary many, many gifts. Hillary is a shopaholic. Girls at USMS already knew to beware the eighth-grade boys, especially jocks and Todd's friends. Since a "relationship" is even more sensitive, the girls were being more cautious, so their hearts wouldn't be broken. Love may sound happy at the end, but it could even lead to hell if you're not careful. Of course this was the last thing on Hillary's mind, because she was still happy at this very moment. School was finally over, and kids roamed the halls. Ginger was going to her locker to get ready to go home, when Todd came and tickled her sides again. "Hey," he said. "Gees, Todd. You nearly frightened me," Ginger told him. "Sorry. You know, I thought you were tough." "I am, I just don't use my strength when I don't need it," Ginger answered, "You saw what I did to Bailey and his friends."

"Oh yea. That was awesome. He'll never bother me again," Todd complimented. Ginger gave a solemn sigh and started walking off. Todd used his body to stop her. He lifted out his arms and hugged Ginger. "Come on, Todd. I have go get to volleyball practice," Ginger told him. "All right, see ya later." Todd slapped on his cap, and Ginger gave him a kiss on the cheek. Luckily, this was not too much for him. Coach Hector was in a good mood yet disturbed. The team only needed to win this upcoming game in about three weeks from now. The only problem was that they would be facing MMS all over again for the championship. Two words made Coach Hector irritated from just thinking about it: Mandy Liverstone. She is the star player of MMS, but she does not get along with Ginger, the star player for USMS. Competition can lead to the loss of a winner. And that's exactly what its doing to Mandy Liverstone. Coach Hector knows Ginger and Mandy pretty much hate each other so much, ever since they saw each other. Even so, Coach Hector knows it won't interfere with their team winning. He has waited too long for this. After long and hard hours of stress and yelling and fierce coaching, this may be the victory he and the school will have. As the girls were stretching and getting themselves warmed up, Coach Hector couldn't stop thinking of the word he will always see in these girls whether they win or lose: proud. He knows within himself and as a person that he has worked hard and pushed the girls to victory and greatness. Hard work can pay off at the end. Whoops, mistakes in that sentence: Hard work DOES pay off at the end. They deserve the best; Coach Hector only sees greatness in all of these girls. But he sees a different kind of greatness in Ginger; greatness that separates her from the rest of the girls. There's something so unique that Coach Hector sees in her. That something will expand her path of destiny. Something that will bless her and make her name great and have her become a blessing. Something that no other person can have but herself. Not even Lanely Tildon can have this. Something that will have her see her true identity and recognize her own soul and spirit. That something is passion. A love for the game she plays. A passion to succeed in life. The love and passion for her and others. The Spirit Transporter Coach Hector does wonder, though: how can he only see this special kind of passion in just Ginger and not the other talented girls who are good and unique at things just like her? Is it because she's the star player? Could it be the flesh and blood mounting on a cold day in Coach Hector's heart? What could Coach Hector possibly have to see the effect of Ginger having a good life and destiny? What do they have in common? The answer is simple: the Spirit Transporter. Passion and Ginger's love of volleyball definitely symbolizes that. Coach Hector cannot see that in any of the girls on the team (anyone knows for that matter) except for Ginger McFraiddee. Come to think of it, those two mysterious teachers can relate to what Coach Hector sees in Ginger and what they have in common. Mrs. Robbin and Mrs. Duffy, the junior psychology teachers of the school. Or maybe Coach Hector was just drunk when he thought about the similarities. There are none. All of these things were racing in Coach Hector's mind, and when the girls were all warned up and ready to go, Coach Hector put on his game face, and he was ready for volleyball. "Huddle, girls!" Coach Hector blew his whistle. The girls made a circle around the coach. "As you know, the big game is in two and a half weeks. This game will let epiphany reign the school ground. It will determine triumph to the passionate. It will tell our school we can! We can win! We WILL win! We have made it this far, all we now have to do is grab the trophy, and claim success! Remember girls, do your best. MMS wants it as much as we do, but we have the pride, and that's something they don't have, and will never have. Determination is also something they will never ever have. So remember, do your very best, and in anything in life, because hard work *does* pay off. I am very proud of all of you, and I know that you ladies will be successful in whatever career you choose in your life. Thank you so much for a wonderful season this year, and all we have to do to finish the year is to WIN the finals which we will do! We are champions, and we will *win!*" Coach Hector announced, as he and the girls cheered. "A quick jog around the gym and let's get started!" Coach Hector blew his whistle, and the girls started running around the gym. "Wow, Coach Hector is really excited about the big game comin' up!" Meredith inferred. "Of course he is. We haven't won in a very long time!" Jenny agreed. "I just hope we *do* win. That Mandy Liverstone girl is one tough chick," Sally cried. "We will. I can take on Mandy by myself," Ginger replied, as the four girls laughed. The net was set up, and the girls played a regular game of volleyball. Coach Hector stuck to his word about determination, because all he was doing the entire practice was yelling and giving constructive criticism to each of the girls. He usually does this at every practice, but this was by far the worst. And it would only get worse until the finals. Everyone was just plain tired and weak when practice was over with. You could hear each girl breathing from twenty feet away. That's how terrible it was. It was like building a car by yourself with no help as fast as you could. Fortunately all of this hard work would be paid off when the team wins the finals. Hopefully. Maybe. Possibly. "My aching shoulders," Jill complained, drinking as much water as she could. "Trust me, we haven't seen anything yet," Ginger cried, as the girls took a huge sigh. "Well, he wants us to win" Meredith responded. "Obviously," Sally snarled. "I just hope we can handle it. I felt like passing out today. Geez, he couldn't stop yelling," Jenny complained, as the girls took another huge sigh. "And I nearly failed the serve. Maybe all of his coaching is hurting us and not helping," Jill cried, as the girls agreed. "We'll find out at the finals, when we win of course," Meredith said, as the girls drunk more water, and gained back energy. "Ugh, and I have a ton of homework to do when I get home," Sally moaned. "Me too. This is gonna be a looong week," Jenny mumbled, as the girls were gathering up their gear to go home. "Bye. Great practice today!" Ginger waved, as the girls waved back. Saturday came, which meant it was time to see Lanely Tildon. Since Uncle wanted more decorations for the house and some creative appliances, Uncle and Pappy decided to go to the antique shop to look for some decor for the house. Marie Tildon wasn't working at the register today, because Ginger nor her uncle or grandparents saw her in sight. Oh well. Grammy quickly spotted Lanely herself, placing colorful yet elegant candles on shelves in a section. "Oh, I'm glad you are here. I will be with you in the back room in just a minute," Lanely told her. "Thank you," Grammy cried, as Lanely kept placing candles on shelves. Grammy led Ginger to the back of the store while Pappy and Uncle were all over the store looking for appealing things. Grammy and Ginger sat down, and like last week and every week they come, a cauldron is sat on the table. A couple of seconds later, Lanely Tildon came inside and sat down in the seat. "How are we doing?" Lanely Tildon asked them. "Good, very, very good," both replied. "How is school coming along, dear?" Lanely asked. "Good. Coach Hector is really pushing us to do our best so we can win the championship game in two weeks," Ginger answered. "That's really great. I am happy to hear that. I will most definitely be on time for this game. Sorry about the last one," Lanely did feel sincere. "That is okay. I'm glad we won," Ginger said. "That's good. So everything is going well?"

Lanely asked. At that moment, the cauldron was starting to boil and bubble. "Well, I do have a new boyfriend. His name is Todd, and he is very sweet," Ginger answered. "I'm glad to hear. I guess you let Bailey go after all." "I had to. He was no good for me."

"You never know. People come into our lives for a specific reason, and that reason is to help us with obstacles in this wicked and wrecked generation," Lanely explained. "I know whatcha mean, Lanely. This economy is so terrible. One of my nieces is on foreclosure and is unemployed. The last thing I need to do is not get good advice," Grammy cried. "Depends on who you get the advice from," Ginger reminded them. "That is very true. We are the reasons of good health. We are the reasons of why the world is in the way it is today. We must be aware of our surroundings," Lanely cried. "Very, very true," Grammy agreed. "Ginger, let me ask you a very important question. Do you believe in Reincarnation?" Lanely asked. "No. I barely know what that is," Ginger answered. "It's when you believe in the afterlife, and when you believe that your loved ones can somehow come back," Lanely explained. "I wish that can happen with my parents," Ginger cried. "It can. Look what is on your neck. It tells the secrets of your beloved ones, and even the people within your life. You may not believe it, but the fact is people leave behind a secret, one that opens the door of Grace that has yet to open. I can tell you right now that your mother has left grace in that locket, Miss McFraiddee. It is up to you to find out what 'that' could be. It may take years, or even decades. But with the help of Reincarnation, it will tell a person's soul and mind to the people that can have a covenant with the Spirit Transporter. Also, it takes belief to shadow the wicked. It takes wisdom to cleanse the dirty universe. It takes Reincarnation to fully understand the Spirit Transporter. You may not get the art of Reincarnation, but when you get a little older, trust me you will understand completely. The one of a dead body's soul will come back to all of its family members and tell the life of the untold. Memories and secrets will be shared, and hatred will be transformed back into Love. Passion. Proudness. Reincarnation tells us about the past and our possible destiny. Reincarnation tells us about the unknown, and the untold. Reincarnation is the very key of the Spirit Transporter. Reality will someday meet with the soul, and both will create an eternal light on our world. Both will have people see God's good creation. Both will unlock a miraculous covenant in the entire world. Soon enough, we will ALL have a Spirit Transporter. One that will tell us all about our past and the presence. One that will have an Enchantment upon our lives. It may seem that you are an outsider, but just wait. One person is all you need. Like I always say, 'One person is all it takes to change the world.' Look at MLK or Barack Obama for instance. Even Langston Hughes or even a person as young as Shirley Temple. They all help us inspire our world, and bring truth to the lies. That Enchantment performed on you transformed your life, Ginger McFraiddee. It made you see the true power and potential within yourself. Sometimes dreams and fiction DO tell us about life as we may know it. They CAN come true. It's up to us to make that happen, especially in this wicked and terrible X Generation. It may sound impossible, but once grace comes, anything can happen. And you too Marybeth will have to see the power within your daughter and granddaughter, and see the love within your husband as well. Reincarnation will soon reveal a massive band of spirits and an equality amongst the flesh. Blood will turn another color. The stars will shine down on our torched earth. Death will have its last say, as it will be a shadow on the dawn. The sun will fade away, as she will create a brand new world, one that will have the devil angry. Leaves will rise to the occasion once more, creating an everlasting miracle on courage and the home of the brave. I can feel the Great Ambition of your parents, Ginger. They know what's best for you. All you have to do is unlock that locket of yours. The key to the locket however, is Reincarnation and believing within the impossible. Your diary is another key of the works of seeing and hearing your very own parents. It opens up the pages of your life, and how Shelby exposed and enhanced your life completely. He has shown you the beauty of nature, and how animals can communicate to us. Open the diary, and watch how Reincarnation will do its job and will show you your life with parents and a dog and how it greatly impacted your life for the better. This is no joke. Reincarnation will determine your life for GOOD. Spells and the arts of spirit will arise on our earth and will erase the souls of evil. The Spirit Transporter will save the world. You will be able to communicate with your parents. Oh Ginger, their message will just soothe your heart for the better. Believe me when I say that. YOU and I will be able to talk with the dead. We will reveal the secrets of your parents, and what their plan was for you." "Lanely, you actually believe in Reincarnation and talking with the dead?" Grammy asked. "I KNOW, Marybeth," Lanely answered. "But our loved ones are never coming back. How can you actually talk to them? Have you even done this before?" Grammy questioned. "No, I haven't. But I know it works. With the Spirit Transporter, anything is possible," Lanely replied. "Plus how can I actually reveal the secrets of my parents, or Shelby? How can I talk to them or even find out about their future plans for me?" Ginger wondered. "Your locket. And your diary. Those two things work together help reveal the secrets and to help us tell the stories of the past," Lanely answered. "But they have told me nothing so far. My diary won't help me, and this locket has just been there for irony. But that's all. When will I see the REAL thing?" Ginger asked. "When you believe. When you stop neglecting yourself to the righteous. Don't doubt the treasures, for they will set aside the truth from this generation. You just don't see how important those treasures are and that is normal at your age. When you see the benefits, the Spirit Transporter will do the rest, and then the Reincarnation will take place. It is almost like faith. That is the catch. It will not work out when you want it to, but it will believe me it will. You will see the powers and the works of faith, and how waiting will be the best thing you can ever do. In fact, the entire world will see the powers of Reincarnation, whether alive or dead," Lanely explained. "Wow, Lanely. I never knew you believed in this kind of stuff," Grammy was shocked. "The whole world will someday. Believe me, Reincarnation answers questions that no one thought of having the answers to. Marybeth, some time beliefs will shatter this world. Look at Israel. The only Jewish state in the world. Look at Hitler. He killed a lot of Jews during World War II," Lanely cried. "I know ALL about that, Miss Tildon. I had to escape from Germany during that crucial time," Grammy stopped her, "though I'm not Jewish." "Hard times are rough, Marybeth. You still made it through. I hope I do the same with my long lost mother," Lanely was actually feeling sad and lonely. "Whatever happened to her?" Ginger knew she shouldn't have asked this question, but curiosity got the best of her. "I don't know, really. Shortly after Shelby ran away, I took a visit to my mother at the nursing home. When I found out she wasn't there, one of her best friends told me she had went to London for a 'vacation.' She had been gone for nearly a year from whatever her friends were telling me. I tried calling her, but I never got a response. I'm planning on finally going to London to try to find her. Lord knows where she could be. I just hope she is some place safe, and the worse hasn't happened. I'm planning on going some time in January. But for now I must continue calling her or contacting her. When I do contact her, maybe some secrets can be revealed. She hasn't been to that nursing home since the year before I knew her or any of our family knew she disappeared. It saddens me to know that the worst has already happened to her within these four going on five years just about. With the Spirit Transporter, I know her heart is still beating, and that she is somewhere on this earth," Lanely said. "Don't worry, Lanely. We'll find your mother, I promise. When you get to England, she'll be the first person you see," Ginger cried. "I hope so," Lanely sighed.

"Wait why would she just disappear like that?" Grammy asked. "None of us knows. Only SHE knows. Ginger, do you have your diary?" Lanely asked, getting off topic. "I do! It's in the car. I'll go get it!" Ginger was all of a sudden excited. She grabbed the keys from Grammy, and raced to the car and back. Why did Lanely want to see the diary? To perform another Enchantment. To open up her mind to see the wonders and works of how she could possibly use the Spirit Transporter. "Ginger, you still seem mindless about the world we live in, and about your parent's blessing. Maybe this Enchantment will help you see things a little better than before. The diary of yours helps us communicate with your mind, and tells us how you feel (that's what a diary does). To see what you're thinking, we use the Spirit Transporter and the power of Reincarnation to help us. Our loved ones tells us about ourselves (they know more about as than we do mentally, because they have been there. This Enchantment will help you see your mind a bit clearly, and will maybe have you change your mind about the belief of Reincarnation. You may even hear your parents talk to you, or loved ones but that's if you really believe in Reincarnation). Marybeth, please turn off the lights," Lanely explained. Grammy did what she was told, and turned off the lights. "Ginger, place your locket and your diary on the table," Lanely kept explaining. Ginger was hesitant on doing that. After a while, she frantically placed the items on the table. "I don't know if I should do this. I don't want these items to get destroyed. They're the only things I have left of my parents," Ginger cried. "Don't doubt righteousness or the Spirit Transporter. You just have to believe," Lanely told her. Ginger just shook her head. At this moment, Grammy knew she had to step back to be out of the way for part II of the Enchantment. That is exactly what she did as well. "Stand up, Ginger. Come." Ginger stood up, and moved the chair. The cauldron started bubbling, this time louder than the first Enchantment. "See the power of the winds. And the transformation of your spirit!" Light was created from the cauldron. It was glowing bright yellow, and it was almost bright enough to blowout Ginger's eyes. "Now to add the finishing touches of the Reincarnation Enchantment," Lanely announced, a few seconds after the glow was officially created. Lanely withdrew two potions from her shelf, and the cauldron was shining and boiling evermore than before. "Love . . . ," Lanely announced. She poured a pink potion in the cauldron. It smelled really heavily, now. "Proudness . . . Ginger, you pour this one in." Ginger poured the bright gold potion into the cauldron, and the cauldron made a gold shine. Grammy was about to pass out. "Now we add . . . Passion," Lanely cried in her deep voice. Lanely created a light in her own two hands, a shiny purple light was seen in her hand. "Lanely, how are you doing that? It's impossible to hold light . . . ," Ginger was amazed. "Reincarnation. With it, anything is possible. Now do not question during the Reincarnation Enchantment," Lanely cried. After a few minutes, the cauldron was done gleaming, and it started to "ferment." Reincarnation was at its own works. "Now, Ginger, listen very carefully. If the Enchantment goes just right, you may even hear your parents talking to you, as if they were in this room. You may also see pictures, as if you were having a hallucination. These pictures will tell the stories of your loved ones. Pictures are worth a thousand words. Remain calm during the Reincarnation Enchantment. Are you ready?" these were Lanely's final words. Ginger took a deep breath, and held Lanely's hands. "Yes," she answered. Winds were getting much, much fiercer. Grammy could hear the bells from the front of the Antique Shop. Lanely and Ginger closed their eyes. More brightness came from the cauldron. "Love, proudness, and passion!" Lanely announced in a voice that definitely wasn't hers, "Reincarnation, reign on the almighty soul of Ginger McFraiddee and let her see the power and spirits of your creation!" A spiral of light and air formed within the cauldron, looking like a circle spiral. "Aaah, Spirit Transporter. Let your wisdom shine on Ginger McFraiddee. Let your establishment of hallucinations see her identity as a person. Let all evilness and hatred go away! Let the Lord redeem her parents and her labrador! Have them be reunited in a place called home! Let Ginger see the power of illusions of Reincarnation! I cast the Enchantment on Ginger McFraiddee now! I command the Spirit Transporter to work NOW!" The spiral was spiraling much faster than before. Arose from the spiral was the locket, and Ginger's diary. Lanely and Ginger opened their eyes, and saw the locket and her diary rise from the cauldron, as if it was magic. Disclaimer: it was NOT magic. The locket shone its heart, like it did at the volleyball game. Ginger's diary suddenly opened, and pages were flying across, as if someone was flipping the pages in the diary. From the pages, angel-looking creatures came out of the diary and were floating around in the air. They were the spirits of the dead. After the spirits stopped coming from her diary, the spirits came aiming toward Ginger's heart. She didn't feel anything: only a bit dizzy. Some light reflections from the cauldron shined on Ginger, herself. "Ginger, close your eyes and tell me if you see or hear anything. Your mind and soul has now been enhanced with Reincarnation and even hallucinating." Ginger once more closed her eyes, but saw nothing. "I see nothing," Ginger said. "Just wait a minute. The Enchantment has to take some time to kick in," Lanely reminded her. All of a sudden, Ginger saw loads of pictures. They were all coming to her, and a grey screen was the background. "Wait . . . I'm seeing something . . . something weird." A few seconds later. "I see me, Pappy, Grammy, me, and we are all at the house." "Mhmm, and what else?" Lanely wondered. More light from the cauldron shined on Ginger, as if more spirits were inheriting her mind. "Oh my gosh! It can't be! I see a picture of Shelby and I in the meadow! I was ACTUALLY rubbing his fur! Wow!" Ginger was excited. "Maybe this Reincarnation Enchantment thing is too strong," Grammy suggested. "Do not be a 'Saumuensh' (German for a "woman" being a fool) Marybeth. She's gonna be fine." Ginger saw a picture of her dancing and prancing around in a beautiful garden. Then she saw a picture of her having tea with Mr. Chippers and her parents. That was the most astonishing one. She already dreamed about that months ago it seems. Then she saw a picture of her and Shelby, lying down in grass. Like old times. She was wearing her locket, and it shined. That's when Shelby looked at Ginger with his bright eyes, and barked! "Wow! Shelby just barked at me! I heard it loud and clear! Wow this Enchantment did work!" Ginger cried. "I am glad you are seeing the works of Reincarnation. Now let's see if your parents, or Shelby, can communicate with you, or any other loved ones. Unfortunately, the longer the person has been dead, the more it is unlikely to communicate with them. If you believe, it will work. It already worked with Shelby, let's see if it can work with any other relatives!" Lanely added more of the liquid potion to the cauldron, and more of the bright purple light. It then immediately got on Ginger. Ginger saw more pictures, mostly ones of her and her family. After some pictures went away, her parents were seen enlarged, almost large enough to cover the grey background. "Ginger. Ginger, are you there? Can you hear me?" It was her mother talking to her from the picture in her mind. "Yes, Mother!" Ginger announced back (of course Grammy and Lanely heard her). "What is going on?" Grammy was lost. "Shh. She is speaking with her mother's soul," Lanely answered. "Ginger, our death was a message to you. To never give up. To never stop trying in life. You will be special, Ginger. I know you will. Remember, your father, Shelby, me, and the rest of your dead family members love you!" her mom said. Her father just kept smiling and blinking. Her mother was smiling as well. "I love you too," Ginger cried. Her mother and father blew her a kiss, and soon enough, the picture faded away, and the only thing to be seen was the grey background.

Chapter 14

Main Street Madness

Ginger opened up her eyes, and that's when she decided she had seen enough. The Reincarnation Enchantment had been completed successfully. "Miss Tildon, I would like to start hearing some thorough answers if you don't mind. What in the world is going on? And do NOT call me the 'S' word," Grammy demanded an answer. "Marybeth, it's like extracting lemonade from a lemon. Do you know what I'm talking about?" Lanely asked her. "No, I don't." "Ya see, your granddaughter has been given the strength to see Reincarnation, even though she already has the power to see this, she must be Enchanted to see what she already knows. When the time comes, you will see." "My time is almost up! This entire Reincarnation things seems like a bunch of . . . ," Grammy started. "Now Grammy . . . ," Ginger budded in. "Trust me, I know it worked. Now for your analysis: Did you hear anything at all? Did you see anything unusual? You can turn on the lights now,"

Lanely said. Grammy turned on the lights, and she and Ginger sat back down in the seats. "Well, I saw my mother and father in a picture, and they were smiling and blinking, as if they were actually here this very moment," Ginger said. "Did they say anything in particular?" Lanely wondered, as the cauldron was beginning to stop bubbling. "They told me to never give up, and that I will be special in life," Ginger answered. "Do you believe you will, now that you heard it from your own parents?" Lanely asked. "Yes, I fully believe now." "Good. Wow, the Enchantment did work to the fullest. Usually you cannot communicate with the dead on the first Enchantment. For some, it could take several years," Lanely explained. "Why is that, Lanely?" Grammy asked. "It's all up to your mind. And if you have enough faith and wisdom. Also, you MUST fully believe in the Spirit Transporter , or it won't work. This may seem crazy, but trust me when I say this: Every human being will see the works of the spirit and believe in it as well. Sometimes greater things come if we wait, and obey. This earth would just tremble if there was no soul to have." Grammy gave Lanely that puzzled look and just pushed her glasses up to her face. "Well, Lanely, that's definitely one good way to look at things in life. Let's just hope your theory is correct," Grammy instigated. "I already know it's correct, and I know because I have wisdom. That's what sets me and this treacherous world apart."

"I think what my grandmother meant was your way isn't the only way. Many people have 'correct theories,' but the only way to find out if you're right is . . . ," Ginger stopped. "Is death . . . ," Lanely finished for her. "Well that surely is a scary thing to hear,"

Grammy cried. "Unfortunately, it's the truth. The truth is always a scary thing to hear . . . ," Lanely replied, "Death and the truth is no joke, nor is it something to play with." "Lanely, do you think you will be able to communicate with your mother?" Grammy wondered. "It can ONLY work with the dead or in dreams. It is a mind communicator in a different language. But like I said, I can only hope for the best when I arrive in England when January comes," Lanely answered. "We all do, Lanely. It must've been the toughest of times going through what you're going through," Grammy cried. "At least your mother is still alive on this earth," Ginger commented. "All's well that ends well, dear," Lanely replied. Ginger just took a sigh. The light from the cauldron was gone and Lanely placed the two empty bottles used for the potion where they needed to be on the shelf. "Well, Miss Tildon, I'm glad you helped her in this . . . well . . . experience. Maybe it has taught her the values in herself," Grammy was looking at the bright side (as usual). "What if Reincarnation only works with Enchantment? What if there's no other way I can talk with my parents?" Ginger asked. "It depends on if your mind is open to the possibility. I can't make it work, your grandparents indeed can't make it work, and neither can anyone on the earth. Only YOU can make it work. Like I said before, you just have to believe," Lanely explained. "So it can work anywhere and anytime?" Grammy asked. "Yes. Just use words of wisdom," Lanely answered. "Lanely, I don't know of whom has tried that alone or by themselves. It has to be impossible known to mankind," Grammy kept trying to instigate. "Notice the two words you just said: Mankind. The whole purpose of this is to change that dreadful theory of 'mankind.' To let the world see what can be done through Reincarnation. To take back the good, which was stolen by the rotten," Lanely explained. "But how can one or two people do that?" Ginger asked. "What we just did. All in due time, young child. You cannot expect the best in two seconds. It would be worthless. Good things come to those who wait," Lanely responded. "We know. Trust me we know," Grammy was losing her patience and her self-conscience for the moment. "I am glad you understand. Sometimes understanding can take some time," Lanely smiled. Grammy rolled her eyes the other way. By now, there was absolutely no more bubbling or light in the cauldron. Lanely dumped the contents of the cauldron in a nearby sink and carefully washed it out (in case of toxins and poisons in the remains). "I just have one more question," Ginger cried. "And what would that be?" Lanely asked her. "What does my mother mean when she says, 'I will change the world?' How could I change this world?" "When spirits come together, this world will have no choice BUT to see the powers of Reincarnation and natural spirits of the just. Believe me, only a few people on this earth know and practice Reincarnation of the spirit. But only one will show this world the power of the almighty. The world has to see that it can be done. Your parents believe that *you* can change the world. Their ambition for you will lead to another dimension: one that will fulfill the world with the truth," Lanely explained. "But I don't know how I CAN do that. I barely know how Reincarnation works. Now we're talking about the world! There's no way!" Ginger was being doubtful. "And why can't you change the world, Lanely?" Grammy asked. "Anybody can change the world. It's up to them to make that decision. It's not up to anyone for them to decide. It's not even up to your parents (though they may want you to). It's only up to YOU. I keep emphasizing that because life gives you choices. No one else can let you choose them. Not even the dead. Why? Because they're not living in your soul. You don't have to do anything you don't want to do. It's up to you to make the decision and the right decision. You have the power to change the universe. That's what makes you unique. That's what makes you, YOU. I could change the world if that was my ambition. But Ginger McFraiddee can. That's her ambition. I am just here to be a guide to help her. Every story has a beginning, middle, and end. How can I know your ambition? Your parents have told you yourself. You don't have to if you don't want to. It is totally up to you!" Lanely explained. "Why me? Why just me?" Ginger wanted to know. "It's not just you. Everyone on this earth has the power to change the world. Sad that only a few *will* try to help change. Then again, maybe those people are oblivious to the obvious . . . ," Lanely sighed. "Let's not be cliché, Miss Tildon. It's the principle of the thing," Grammy warned her. "Or for the moment of the time," Ginger added. "Indeed," Lanely agreed. Grammy took a glimpse at her watch. "Well, we better be getting home. I hope my son found some decors for the house. Nice talkin' with ya, Lanely," Grammy told her, as she, Lanely, and Ginger stood to signal the door. "Anytime, Marybeth. You too, Ginger. I know the Enchantment has made great effect on your life, and it will in the future," Lanely cried, as the three ladies walked out of the back room, leading them to the actual store. "I know it will. The first Enchantment has helped my life a lot. This one will do no different than before," Ginger stated. "That's the spirit," Lanely said. "Now where did your Uncle and Pappy go? They were just here a minute ago," Grammy said, searching around the store with her eyes. "You know Pappy. Once he goes someplace, there's no certainty that he will come back," Ginger cried. Soon enough, Pappy and Uncle came strolling down an aisle with a shopping basket in their hands. They quickly spotted Lanely, Ginger, and Grammy, and then they trotted toward the ladies. "Did you get everything?" Grammy asked. "Just about. We're ready to rock and roll!" Pappy answered. "Yea, I think that's everything," Uncle agreed, double checking the basket to make sure everything was right and okay. "I just have one more question, Lanely. Reincarnation can bring the soul back to the flesh, or bring someone back to life. Do you know of anyone who has bought someone back to life? Can I do that with my parents?" Ginger asked. "I know nobody who has done that I can't even do that. But it can be possible," Lanely answered. "What's all this Reincarnation talk?" Pappy wondered. "Oh nothing," Grammy dropped the subject. Pappy and Uncle were a little skeptical about the situation. "Well, let's go," Uncle concluded. They all went to the front counter and paid for the items. Ginger helped sort out the items in bags. Lanely helped Ginger, Uncle, and Ginger's grandparents out of the door to the car. "Bye-bye. Have a great day. And always remember to enjoy life," Lanely waved good-bye from the entrance. "We will," they all responded, stepping on the creaked wooden steps. Lanely smiled and went back inside the shop. While in the car, Pappy and Uncle were still confused about the whole Reincarnation thing. "What did she mean by Reincarnation? Ginger, sometimes I wonder if Lanely is the right person you should be around," Pappy complained. "No, she meant that so I could possibly communicate with Mother and Father," Ginger replied. "That's the craziest thing I've ever heard!" Uncle commented. "I said the same thing," Grammy agreed. "Well, Pappy, you didn't see what actually happened. Neither did you, Uncle. You both should know by now to not judge Miss Tildon and all of her doings. It's great wonders of what she could do," Ginger said. "Well, it still sounds so absurd. I assure you no such thing can happen," Pappy argued. "Not if you believe," Ginger testified. "Very good, Ginger. Apply to what Miss Tildon taught you is very good," Grammy applauded. "There's no telling *what* Ginger learned from that woman," Pappy commented. "Now, Pappy. That's enough . . . ," Uncle told him. "Well, I'm just sayin'! Soon that lady's gonna be tellin' us that goats can fly on horses! Next the world will all of a sudden turn purple! I mean really . . . That lady is goin' bonkers! She's bustin' the crazy bubble!" Pappy insisted. "Now STOP it, Pappy," Grammy demanded him, "Lanely has known us and our daughter nearly half our lives. The least we should be doing is thanking her. You both need to be a little bit more sincere because it is just tiring. Maybe Miss Tildon needs to enchant you, Pappy." Pappy and Uncle just laughed even more. "I told you nobody understands me. I knew this would happen!" Ginger was about to sob. "It's not you, Ginger, it's Miss Tildon and her doings, that's all," Uncle explained. "But she is a part of me. Her doings can help me find the answers to what my parents left behind for me. And both of you just think it's a big joke. Well, it's NOT! Without her, I probably wouldn't know who to turn to," Ginger said. "Well here's a hint, Ginger. That locket you're wearing has a lot to do with your parents and what they left behind," Pappy told her. "I know that. Do you know the answer to what exactly they left behind?" Ginger asked. "Well . . . um . . . no . . . ," Pappy sighed. "Enough about these secrets. Just hearing about it makes me tick. Ginger, do you have any homework?" Grammy changed the subject relatively quick. "Um, none actually," she answered, giving a glare at her grandmother. Was Pappy telling the truth? Why did Grammy allow her not to hear the "secrets?" Only these three people in the car can possibly know something about her parents. Will Reincarnation give her the answer? Or will life once again get to the better of her and have the authority? Most likely life will win, it always does . . . Ginger gets tired of when unfairness strikes in her life (more of the bad kind), someone always says, "That's life, get over it" or "We're all gonna have to suffer reality" or "That's how the world works." She wishes that life didn't work that way, and that somehow she can change the wonders of this unfortunate and gruesome world. In her dreams . . . Ginger had no clue of what Pappy and Uncle bought. It looked like the house was arranged for a Barnum and Bailey preview. "Pappy, what in the world is all of this stuff?" Ginger asked, staring at new decorations. "Ask your uncle! He's the one that picked 'em!" Pappy answered, sitting down at the kitchen table. Uncle and Grammy came in with more bags in the hands. "What are ya talkin' about, Pappy? You picked it!" Uncle defended. "Sure I did . . ."

"There old, old antiques, hun. These are things your great-grandfather on your father's side would buy," Grammy informed her. "Oh," she replied, "how relaxing." "Her great-grandfather? More like her great-aunt Shusterton! That lady was a maniac over jewelry!" Pappy cried. "Who?" Ginger wondered. "She lived during the early 1800s. She would buy and sell jewelry in eastern parts of Europe. Some rumors say that she found $10,000,000 near Latvia, but of course that's false. She was a great and strong woman indeed. Lived to be ninety-three years old," Grammy explained. "She was also a freak who did nothin' but make jewelry!" Pappy complained. "She also made big money back then. Don't meddle," Grammy insisted. "Did you ever get to meet her?" Ginger asked. "Unfortunately, no. Your cousin Ronnie did. Oh wait, he died eighteen years ago," Grammy replied. "What? Cousin Ronnie wasn't even born during the Great Depression! There's no way in hell he met Aunt Shusterton!" Pappy mentioned. "I think you mean Aunt Brenda, Grammy," Uncle corrected her. "Oh yes. Yes, her. She died thirty-eight years ago, sorry got confused!" Grammy fixed herself. "Aunt Brenda didn't know where her own bed was, let alone her own name!" Pappy teased. "She had Alzheimer's. Don't fret. The doctor says you are at risk too, Pappy," Grammy demanded. "I don't giva . . . what the doctor says! Ya think Ima believe him!"

"Calm down, Pappy. Did you take your medicine?" Uncle asked him. "Only a dose," Pappy answered. Ginger, Uncle, and Grammy gasped. "Pappy, you know your daily dose of medicine! We don't want you to have a heart attack, do we?" Grammy asked. "Well, I'm sorry but that medicine tastes like . . . ! I'd rather . . . ," Pappy started protesting, with harsh words. "Pappy, that's enough! Now I'll get your medicine. You know what the doctor said," Uncle helped Pappy up to another room. Pappy mumbled more crucial words under his breath. "Sometimes I worry about Pappy and his health," Ginger cried. "Don't worry, Ginger. The government health care is taking care of him. Ever since he came back from the Vietnam War, he is terribly sick. But he will be fine as long as he takes the proper amount of medicine," Grammy cried. "That's good to hear," Ginger was relieved. Melissa had texted Ginger to meet her at Main Street once again at 7:00 p.m. Right before Ginger was about to leave, someone called her. It was her boyfriend Todd. "Hey, Ginger. What's up?" he asked her. "Nothing, really. About to go on Main Street with some friends. What about you?"

"Just chillin' at Malcolm's house. Some of my friends are here. We were playing football, but then Andy got hurt." Ginger could hear Malcolm, Andy, Jason, and Rockstar Kid in the background. Then she heard Todd say, "Shut up!"

"Wow, Todd. You are such a jerk!" Ginger told him. "I know I am. But I'm hot, so that's all that matters." "That you are." Ginger heard the other guys go woo. "Wait this better not be on speaker!" Ginger yelled. The other guys laughed. "Haha," he responded. "Oh my gosh, Todd, you asshole! I'd punch your face if I was there," Ginger was joking. "And a kiss," Todd offered. "On the cheek . . . ," Ginger returned. "All right. I gotta go. See ya later," Todd told her. "Bye-bye," Ginger said, sliding her cell phone down. Ginger put on her jacket and went outside. She walked all the way to Main Street, which wasn't far at all. At the center of the movie theater, she was greeted by some other friends Melissa, Hillary, Stephanie, Shandi, and Amy. "Hey Ginger!" they greeted her. "Hey! Where's Rachael?" Ginger wondered. "She couldn't come. She's grounded. No phone, no text, no friends, no nothing," Stephanie answered. "Well, that sucks. I'd probably die without my cell phone," Hillary admitted. "Me too. I never forgave my mom when she took unlimited texting away from me," Amy agreed. "Isn't it good to have phones," Shandi boasted. "Yea!" all of the girls responded. "Hillary, I like your hair color. Is it brunette?" Ginger asked. "Indeed it is. Got it done this morning. Thank you!" Hillary cried. "Good thing Nick and Joe aren't coming. They get really annoying," Melissa was relieved. "They were here with Tiffany and me yesterday. Of course they were being obnoxious to Midway Middle School girls," Stephanie cried. "They can't flirt with anyone but themselves, and besides, they're just in it for more popularity . . . ," Melissa already knew. "Duh . . . That's why they could be virgins when they grow up," Hillary computed. "They WILL . . . ," Ginger insisted. The rest of the girls just laughed. "It's fun being bogus to Nick and Joe," Shandi cried. "Please. They make fun of us too," Amy cried. "Only to Beth. She goes to MMS. And to Luna," Stephanie added.

"Why would anyone make fun of Luna?" Ginger asked. "Because Nick and Joe are weird. That's why . . . ," Hillary said. "Tell us something we don't know, Hillary. Like your boyfriend . . . !" Amy shouted out loud. The other girls oooed. "Amy, please. You don't even have a guy. So there . . . ," Hillary cried. "Sorry, Hillary. But Jason . . . I mean, really. That guy has no . . . class . . . ," Amy argued, as the other girls agreed. "But he's soooo hot!" Hillary said, sighing. "I know, I'd go out with him too," Shandi agreed. "I wouldn't. He's cocky, and we all know that," Ginger argued. "No, he isn't. Maybe you have bad taste," Melissa cried. "No way. Jason is cocky. Though he's hot, no thanks," Stephanie agreed. "But Ginger's going out with THE most popular guy in school!" Amy bellowed, as the girls screamed for her. "He's also a good kisser," Stephanie winked, "Trust me, Ginger. If he disses you, let us know." "It's okay, I can beat him up myself," Ginger raised up her fist, as the other girls clapped. "And then there's Shandi. Going with that wuss and "womanizer" Malcolm. He broke my heart severely when we were going out . . . ," Melissa was sad. "It's okay, Melissa. That guy was sorry when he did break up with you. He got his daily dose of black love," Shandi told her. "Oh yea. He started getting mad when Melissa said no when he had the nerve to re-ask her out," Hillary laughed, as the other girls did as well. "Malcolm does seem nice, though," Shandi cried. "Seems," Amy cried. "They're all like that. But of course, they're not . . . I can tell ya that guys are more of b—es than we are," Ginger admitted. "That's why girls can be more attracted to them. And guys can be more attracted to us. Get the picture . . . ," Stephanie winked again. "Aaaah, I know whatcha mean . . . ," Hillary agreed. "Guys are only attracted to our tits and things like that. Especially the ass. That's all they look at," Shandi cried. "Remember girl code, Shandi," Melissa reminded her. "Please . . . That stuff gets old," Hillary cried. "Never," Amy urged. "Let's go somewhere. It's getting cold out here," Stephanie suggested. "How about ice cream?" Amy thought. "I can't eat anything anymore. I'm anorexic again," Melissa said. "Yea, I'm on a diet. Went shopping with Stacy earlier. Was embarrassed to find out I weigh 91," Hillary cried, tipping her hat. "I weigh 95," Melissa said. "Well, I'm tempted for ice cream, let's go!" Stephanie agreed. The six girls walked and talked all the way to the ice cream parlor. Only Hillary and Amy were texting here and there. The girls took their seats. Right when Ginger sat down, she received a text. It was from Todd. "Where R U?" Ginger responded, "Main Street, ice cream parlor." One second later, "Cool."

"Who's texting you?" Hillary asked, sitting right next to her. "Todd."

"Ooo, secret romance! Priceless!" Hillary bragged. "He's just wondering where I'm at. It's nothing romantic," Ginger cried. "It's just top secret. Like Hillary and Jason," Shandi added. "Like you and Malcolm," Hillary defended. "Yea right . . . ," Amy bellowed. "Mhmm, just like me and him," Melissa cried. The girls just rolled their eyes. Stephanie received a phone call. "Hello?" Pause. "I'm at the ice cream parlor on Main Street." Pause. "It's all girls, stupid. A party? Next week?" Pause. "Luna's planning it? Oh cool! Can't wait! TTYL. See ya!" Hang up.

"What's going on?" Ginger asked. "Luna's planning another party with Rachael. We're all invited. It's next week. Luna'll text you on the details, or e-mail," Stephanie cried. "That sounds great!" Melissa cried. "I just loove parties. I can drink soda however much I'd like, and I don't have to worry about going a little too far," Amy said. "Like you did at the last party. Puh-leeze . . . ," Hillary told her. "Hey, that was not my fault. Everybody was crazy at that one," Amy protested. "You were the craziest," Shandi concluded. "Hopefully, it won't be a stripper's party or something. Luna goes a little bit too far at parties sometime," Stephanie cried. "We all know," Melissa cried. "Pssh. Nothing compared to Mandy at her party. Looked like she was New York's most wanted," Hillary bit her nail. "I hate Mandy so much. She makes me gag," Ginger said. "She does throw great parties," Amy cried. "We've been enemies since the beginning of time. I swear we will never be friends." "I agree 100 percent, Ginger McFraiddee. Of course, I'm better at everything I do, and I'll prove that at the volleyball game coming up," Mandy Liverstone chilled her shoulder and the rest of her body. "Go away, Mandy," Ginger ordered. "Why don't you make me?" Mandy pointed right at her chest. That was the target. Ginger grabbed a large cup of ice cream and threw it right on Liverstone's evil little head. The witch never wins in a princess happy ever after. "You've been served," Stephanie called out. Everyone laughed. All Ginger did was smile, evilly however. "Well, if you want to play it that way, fine. You'll be sorry you met me, Ginger McFraiddee. I ALWAYS get what I want, and if I don't . . . ," Mandy cried, grabbing ice cream from another table, "I will . . ." She threw the ice cream all over Ginger. Mandy got more ice cream and threw it at her, but Hillary got hit instead. The girls were just entertained and kept laughing. Hillary stood up. Oh dear. "Don't mess with the brunette hair, honey." Hillary smacked Mandy, and Mandy fell to the ground, splashing into ice cream and soda on the ground already. "Because it'll snap ya right back," Hillary sat back down. "Who did this? I want ze truth!" the store manager wanted to know. All of the six girls pointed at Mandy. Mandy stood up, wiping off her clothes. "Out with you! Never come back for the rest of your young life! Out withz you! I do not want to see you ever again!" the shop owner yelled. "It was her fault!" Mandy screamed. "Out! Now!" Mandy frantically ran out of the store, some other people, supposedly her friends, following her. "Way to go, Ginger! The biatch has been biatched!" Stephanie announced, as the girls cheered. "I told you, that's how much I hate that girl. She just drives me crazy!" Ginger cried. "Me too! She got ice cream in my hair. I would've beat her ass if I had to!" Hillary agreed. "Wow, Hillary. I've never seen you so tough," Shandi said. "Then you obviously haven't met me. I'm tired of people thinking I'm not tough," Hillary responded. Ginger was still mad at Mandy. She knew she could've fought her, but that would've been more chaotic. But she didn't care. She just wanted to prove herself to Mandy. Maybe that's not a good idea if you really think about it. "That'll teach her not to bother me ever again!" Ginger cried, as the other girls agreed. Amy took some ice cream from Ginger's shirt, and ate some. "Yum! Vanilla my favorite!" Amy licked some ice cream off her lips. The girls just rolled their eyes. "Hey, it's not that I don't like her, it's just I like ice cream!" Amy said. "Then buy some, Amy. The sooner you become lactose intolerant the better," Stephanie was annoyed. "Now that was really random, Amy," Hillary responded. "Honey, please. There's absolutely no need for jealousy." "Pssh, like anyone'd be jealous of YOU," Shandi budded in. "I second that opinion. A lot of girls are," Amy boasted. "Name one . . . ," Melissa cried. "Well . . . I can't think of one." At the next moment, the door opened, and Mandy threw more ice cream. It hit Amy by mistake. The girls laughed even more. "Yum! Vanilla, my favorite!" Ginger mimicked, scooping up some ice cream from her. "Oh now it's personal," Amy cried, getting up. Mandy swiftly ran out of the parlor as the manager stomped his way to the front door. "Don't come back here anymore you crazy girl!" he yelled out, "I will make sure that you are banned forever!" Amy sat down, and the manager stomped back to the back doors." Stupid rotten kids . . . Always ruining stuff. Now I gotta clean up that mess!" he muttered to himself. "At least I'm not the only one that hates her," Ginger said. "I've always hated her," Melissa admitted. "Me too. Ever since she came to this city," Shandi agreed. "Everybody does," Hillary added. "Can't wait for the party next week! It's gonna be great!" Melissa was excited. "Me either. Luna may even have louder music, and her parents may let us stay there and party all night! I texted all my friends about the party!" Stephanie cried. "Hopefully Nick and Joe can't come. They already ruined Eli's party that one time . . . ," Amy said. "Duh. They're gonna be there. They're at every party," Stephanie said. "Well, maybe they won't ruin this one," Melissa said. "They're Nick and Joe. Of course they're gonna ruin it . . ." Shandi said. "Hah, we poured punch all over them that last time and to Joel. It was so funny!" Hillary bellowed, as the girls were laughing all over again. "Joel is just gay," Ginger gossiped. "Tell us something we don't know," Hillary was the first to comment. "He needs to get a life, and get one fast," Melissa insisted. "And he needs to stop shitting over Hillary. She has a boyfriend now! For God's sake!" Shandi said. "He won't stop, now. He's so mad at Jason, he's threatening him with letters to back off," Hillary said. "What the hell? It's only been a few weeks or so . . . ," Amy said. "Not even that long . . ," Hillary mentioned. "Well, Joel has no life, and we all know that. The sooner he knows that, the better. As far as I'm concerned, we're *all* tired of his butt getting into people's business," Ginger replied. "Wow, Ginger. You must really dislike him," Stephanie inferred. "Well I'm tired of jerks who keep annoying us. It's getting old and really annoying." "Like your boyfriend," Melissa said. "Todd is really sweet. He just acts like a jerk when he's with his friends," Stephanie noted. "And he tries to show off nothing," Ginger added. "Typical guys, to be honest," Amy commented. "Especially the jocks!" Shandi added. "Eww, like Mack and Andy," Hillary complained. "The only thing that saves them is their cuteness," Stephanie said. "That's what makes us attractive. Guys can't resist girls who are cute, and I'll say it, who have big tits," Ginger said. "Duh, that's what makes girls, girls," Melissa admitted. "Guys wanna see girls and their undies and their bras and their tampons. It's a part of life," Amy explained. "That's why girls have to be careful of guys. They can be naughtier than us," Shandi said. "Yet they 'say' they protect us," Hillary groaned. "From other guys, duh!" Stephanie encountered. "It's good when girls fight over a guy, or when a guy fights over a girl!" Ginger added. "Depends on who, though. Some people ya just gotta watch out for," Melissa said. "Please, guys are more afraid of girls than we are afraid of them," Shandi made a good point. "How though?" Amy asked. "Because we're too much for them. It's simple, really," Stephanie answered. "Not really simple . . . ," Melissa stated. "Too bad guys can't just treat girls like normal people. I get tired of them doing stupid stuff to impress us," Hillary admitted. "But that's what you want to happen. The more guys are after you, the more they become in love with you," Ginger opposed. "Well, love can turn into hate easily, and we all know this from experience," Hillary sighed. "Hate is not what I want. I want happiness and peace," Melissa cried. "Me too. I wouldn't want to be turmoiled by love in any way," Shandi cried. "That's why you have to be careful. Guys are always on the case," Stephanie warned. "Well ya. We can't just let guys walk over us. Especially jerks," Amy subcluded. "And they never seem to mind their own business. They just *have* to know what we're doing, when we're doing it, and why. It gets annoying after so long, I just start to ignore it," Ginger explained. Stephanie opened up her cell phone and started texting away. "Me too. Like if Jason asks me what I'm doing, I just make up some excuse like shopping, so he'd ignore me, or to tell him. He asks me what I'm doing every day . . . it's like OMG . . . WTF . . . ," Hillary cried. "They're just curious and want to know what their

GF is doing," Amy said. "Well, curiosity killed the snail as far as I'm concerned," Hillary responded. "Um, Hillary. It's cat," Shandi told her. "Well, whatever. You know what I meant," Hillary snarled. "Haha, Hillary. I hear Mrs. Alvarez hates you so much, she may switch you out of her class, or fail you," Melissa imposed. "I don't care to be honest. She's just jealous of me because I have better fashion than her and way better makeup. Plus I have all Bs in my classes. One F won't do anything to tell you the truth." "All Bs. That's a surprise," Stephanie joked as the girls laughed. "My teachers are such easy graders."

"Yea, right. You probably bribe them," Ginger said. "That's good enough for me. An A or B is what I need," Hillary cried. Stephanie finally closed her phone and looked up, pushing her blonde curly hair behind her face. "We're still having the sleepover, right?" Amy asked. "Yea," Stephanie answered. "Well then what are we waiting for? Let's go!" Shandi called out. "Um, okay. Let's go then. I didn't want ice cream, anyway. Just needed somewhere to hang out," Stephanie said, as the other girls agreed. Good thing Pappy, Uncle, and Grammy were aware of the sleepover. She had told them before she left. The girls chittered and chattered as they walked out of the parlor and headed for Stephanie's house. *Maybe this will be fun after all*, Ginger thought.

CHAPTER 15

Pappy and the Vietnam War

Stephanie's house is a modest house. Of course, Ginger had never been, so it was all new to her. The girls ran up and down the main hall. It wasn't quite late yet. Stephanie's parents were really nice and sweet. Her mother had Irish red hair that was curled up like Stephanie's hair. She also wore clothes that appeared to be from a local department store and shoes that hadn't fit her size. Her father, however, looked much older, and most of his dark hair had grey spots. It looked like he hadn't taken a bath, nonetheless a shower, for at least a good while. Otherwise, they seemed like nice people. Ginger had never been on a sleepover with Stephanie and Melissa and Amy before, so she didn't know what to expect. The girls stayed in Stephanie's room from 9:30 p.m. all the way through the night. Luckily her room was big enough. Stephanie's room is pink everything. They watched some comedy shows, texted each others' friends, and of course, talked. A normal sleepover. It was as if Ginger had a sleepover with Jenny, Meredith, Sally, and Summer. No different. After what had seemed like hours of more pointless gossip, the girls were getting tired. Not time for bed just yet. Ginger received a call from Todd. "Hello?" Ginger answered. "Hey, Ginger," Todd called back. "What do you want?" Ginger asked him. The girls surrounded Ginger and her phone. "I just couldn't stay away from ya. Your MySpace pics are hot."

"Shut up."

"So, where are you?"

"I'm at Stephanie's house. We're having a sleepover. What about you?"

"Still chillin' at Malcolm's. We're watching random videos on YouTube and Adult Swim."

"Cool. Even though it sounds . . . stupid."

"Hah, I know." Long pause.

"So . . . ," Ginger started.

"Are you going to the party next week?" he asked. "Yea, are you?"

"Yea. Cool, we can go together."

"Sure." Pause.

"You know what I love about you the most?" Todd asked. "What?" "That you aren't afraid of anyone. You don't let anyone push you around. You can handle yourself. You know, I've actually never said that about a girl I really liked. You're just the beat in my heart."

"You know, I can hear every word you're saying . . . ," Stephanie budded in, as the girls laughed. Ginger ignored them. "I like that about you too, Todd. It's too bad we can't talk like this in person," Ginger cried. "I know. Then I could tell you how I really feel." "Me too."

"Oh, I gotta go. See ya, Ginger." "Later," Ginger chuckled. Hung up. The girls just laughed and screamed when she hung up. While they were doing that, Todd's friends however took it as some sort of joke. "What's so funny?" he asked them, slipping his phone into his pocket. They were in Malcolm's room. "Nothin'. Just the fact that you're starting to actually like Ginger more," Rockstar Kid answered. "What's wrong with that? Ginger is hot, and she's really sweet. A guy can't say that?" Todd asked. "You said that about Stephanie, dude. No offense or anything," Andy mentioned. "Ginger's different, though. Every time I see her, it's like, she is pretty," Todd answered. "Said that about Stephanie too," Jason added. "Dude, shut up. Ginger's way more sensitive than Stephanie, and you know it," Todd meant that in a good way. "Sorry, geez," Jason cried. "Don't sweat, man. We all feel that way toward a girl, especially a sweet and cute blonde," Malcolm told Todd. "I know. You can tell Ginger is sweet," Rockstar Kid was being dumb. "No duh, Rockstar Kid," Andy replied. "All girls at our school are sweet. Ginger has to be the winner though," Jason said. "Yea. Her and Amy," Malcolm agreed. "Naah. Amy acts all dumb, and a stuck-up control freak. That girl couldn't last with a guy for more than two minutes," Todd cried.

"Duh," Andy agreed, "besides, Amy is too dumbfounded."

"And she acts all Marilyn Monroe," Jason emphasized. "Don't forget perky," Rockstar Kid added. "Yea. Ginger is the sweetest girl there is. Except when she nearly beat Bailey. That fat ass couldn't handle it!" Todd cried. "Then he had the nerve to break up with her. How dumb," Andy said. "Bailey is no good for Ginger, anyway," Malcolm had a point. "He's just a piece of crap, and we all know that," Jason said. "Too bad he thinks he's king of the school," Rockstar Kid added. "He thought he was worthless when Ginger slammed him to that locker," Malcolm cried. "That's because he *is* worthless!" Todd replied. "He still doesn't know that, though. He still thinks he's king of the world," Andy said. "Doesn't matter. He has no friends," Jason reminded. "And he never will. Billy and Jeff just feel sorry for him," Rockstar Kid cried. "They'll get over him, soon," Malcolm said. "Just like Ginger did," Todd added. "Yea, that'll be sweet," Andy agreed with them. "I don't know why, but I'm starving!" Andy said. "Wow. That was so completely random as hell," Jason replied. "Yea, dude you're outta luck. My parents won't let you," Malcolm told him. "Unless we sneak it," Rockstar Kid suggested. "Yea. Good luck with that," Todd responded. "No, don't. My parents would go crazy as ever and probably would never let you in the house again," Malcolm warned. "Aww," Andy commented. Family Guy was on Adult Swim, but Malcolm and the guys were surrounding the computer, looking up videos, videos that really weren't appropriate. Todd kept texting away on his phone. As we already know, he was texting Ginger. "Wow, you're still texting her. She's probably sleeping or something," Jason cried. "She's at a sleepover with Stephanie and some other girls. It's crazy when it's Stephanie," Todd told them. "Hah. I bet they're having a 'wonderful' time,"

Andy mentioned. "Or a living nightmare. Remember her party? I'll probably never go back there again," Rockstar Kid added. "It was fun, though," Malcolm cried. "Except when she turned off all the lights," Jason replied. "That was funny. All of the girls were screaming!" Todd laughed, as the other guys laughed. That party WAS a living nightmare certainly. But that is beside the point. Are Todd's words true toward Ginger, or are they the devil's voice in a shadow plague? Hmm, hard to say. Remember, love can be hell's passion, or the Lord's wrath. It's all based on how you look at certain things or this world itself. Emphasizing the world brings up many great and harsh things. Spirits simply CANNOT depend on people nor vice versa. In that case, where is the source or clear evidence? There is none. To the human eye, at least. Maybe to the soul. Well, the soul provides Reincarnation and makes it true. Some might argue that statement. The only reason they argue is because the soul is unseen. Physical and mental things are two different things. The sooner scientists and professors see that, the better. Maybe that's why they haven't a clue of how the earth formed, or why earth can be the only place to live in the universe. What do they mean when they say. "Earth just formed out of nowhere." Obviously, those philosophers are not religious at all. It's only a matter of time until they see their philosophy is incorrect. How, you may ask? Through the one and only thing that can set this world. Apart from its natural substance. The Spirit Transporter. Maybe Todd is the right one for Ginger. Todd certainly knows she's the one for him. Mentioned before, it's only a matter of time. The night had grown longer when

Stephanie yelled, "Pillow fight!" Then she had the nerve to blast up the radio. The girls were all tired by midnight. Pillow feathers were everywhere! Stephanie's parents weren't so thrilled by it but whatever. The girls didn't care. Sleeping was a big issue when it came to bedtime. Although Stephanie's room was big enough, the five girls had to sleep on the floor, pillow feathers and cotton surrounding them. There wasn't any room to maneuver, but there was nothing they could do about that. Another problem was that Melissa snored from here and there, almost sending the girls haywire. Good thing she is not much of a light sleeper. Morning rose, and the girls had waffles for breakfast. After that, they were headed straight for home. Ginger just walked, like her grandparents and uncle had intended her to do. Sunday zoomed by quickly, and Monday was finally here again. Grammy decided to only volunteer to the Red Cross two days this week, which would be Wednesday and Thursday. Uncle dropped Ginger off as usual. Ginger was quickly greeted by her original friends. "Hey, you guys!" Ginger greeted. "Hey, Ginger!" they said in return. "It's good to see you guys again. It's hard to talk or text now. Todd texts me almost all the time," Ginger told them. "Oh, that's okay, Ginger. Todd can sometimes never shut up," Sally beckoned. "Especially when he's with his dumb friends," Jenny cried. "I'm so excited! Our volleyball game is next week!" Meredith was getting jumpy. "I know, I can't wait! Summer, you can come, right?" Ginger asked her. "Of course I can come! Wouldn't miss it for anything!" Summer smiled, showing her braces. "Cool," Ginger responded. "We'll easily defeat Mandy's team," Sally was confident. "Of course we will. We did it once, and we can do it again!" Jenny cried. "It's funny. Mandy is now banned from the ice cream parlor," Ginger stated. "The one on Main Street near the movie theater?" Meredith asked. "Yea that one," Ginger answered. "Why is she banned?" Summer asked. "She threw ice cream at me, and the manager saw and told her to leave and never come back. It was hilarious!" Ginger bellowed, as the girls were laughing at the incident. "She probably deserved it," Sally snickered. "That's what happens when evilness perpetuates triumph," Summer was using a metaphor. "Especially that slump Liverstone," Jenny also snickered. "At least you got back your revenge," Meredith was glad. "Let's just hope I did," Ginger sounded a little confused. The girls just had a good chuckle, and headed inside the building. New week. New day. New everything, it seems. Of course, there is one word a child hates, and that word is: homework. Another one word can send a child crazy, and that word is "project." But children all have to do it, whether easy or hard. Projects can spark a child's creativity, while homework can boost their brains for a test. The one project Ginger was about to receive would unlock some knowledge about the untouched past, and that simple project could be specified in the three syllables: Heritage. It all started in Lit Skills class with Mrs. Maalone. "Okay, class. As we know, heritage has taught values and culture to a country. That can include celebrations, holidays, national holidays, customs, traditions, and even through the wonders of art and literature. Heritage also teaches us ways to express these different types of views. Remember, culture and heritage can be two different views (depending on how you look at it). We will be doing something a little different with heritage however. What I'd like you to do is interview your parents," Mrs. Maalone announced, but she was interrupted. "Ehm . . . ," Ginger was annoyed. "Or guardian or relative of some sort," Mrs. Maalone corrected herself, "about what great thing they have accomplished. It could be a job of some sort, their hobby, or how they help influence themselves, and how they are a role model to you. It can be anything of their personal life or a real experience. When you have gotten enough information you need, write what your guardian did, how it has influenced you, and how you can learn from this. Also, think about ways you can relate, or how it relates to the family. When you have that, jot it down. It should be at least two pages long, and it is due to me Thursday typed. I will not accept this assignment later or unexcused. You will receive half credit if it's NOT at least two pages long, or if it's not in point twelve font. This assignment is due to me Thursday typed. Any questions?" No hands went up. "Okay, good. This will not be an in-class activity, so now, let's move on in our Lit circles. Your discussion questions need to be turned in by the end of this week. It would much be appreciated. Well, get into your lit circles and let's get to work." Kids were scooting desks over, and shuffling papers getting their lit circle book and papers. Mrs. Maalone was clicking and typing away at her desk while children were beginning to discuss. Ginger was already thinking of who to interview for the assignment. She could interview Lanely Tildon, but no one would probably connect with her in the class. How about Uncle? Although he was born from Italy and knows all about the Colosseum, that's the only thing interesting about him if you ask Ginger. She wouldn't feel that much excited for this interviewing him for this project. How about Grammy? Grammy's child story is a bit interesting to know. She has lived through World War II. In fact, she was born in Germany, right where the center of WWII had been. Her family was not Jewish, but since the führer Adolf Hitler, was attacking, and other countries were bombing Germany, Grammy's mother and father and some other family relatives decided to immigrate to Hungary (Grammy's family was mostly from Hungary and her mother decided it was best for Grammy to not be in war zones, and go to Hungary). But then again, Grammy gets all nonchalant when it comes to her unsatisfying childhood. She usually hates talking about her experience as being a child daring the Second World War or immigrating to Hungary. Grammy was out on the list. And then there was Pappy. He too was born during WWII (a few years earlier than Grammy), only he was born from Ireland, a country that was neutral in the war. His experience was nowhere near as bad as Grammy's. Ginger knew she wanted to interview Pappy. His story does inspire her in many ways. Pappy as you know served in the military for many years before he retired. Most of serving was during the Vietnam War. Being born into a World War and having to serve in another war is a very interesting thing. The best part about it is that Pappy is still alive, and Ginger can get the answers from how life was during tough and harsh times. The class would be very amazed to hear about a veteran's story, and how he helped change America. Veterans should get more recognition for doing what they're doing in America and other places. It shows loyalty, courage, strength, and most of all, patriotism. When you do something like that, you should be well known for that, because it isn't an easy task to complete. Ginger was getting goose bumps from just thinking about this assignment. She'd even forgotten about the lit circles discussion. "Um, Ginger? Helllo? Are you there? She must be daydreaming or something," Brianna concluded, as the other two girls and Brianna waved to see if Ginger was okay. "Do you need to see the nurse?" Sally asked. Ginger caught her sense. "No, no, no. I'm fine," she answered. "Thinking about Todd?" Jill thought. "No, about the assignment. I can't wait to interview my grandpa to see what interesting facts he tells me," Ginger answered. "Oh. Me too. Hopefully I can find someone who has been through cool events," Brianna agreed. "Same here. I get tired of pointless info from my family," Jill replied. "Especially if they're older folks or have been through a lot in the world," Sally commented. The girls nodded and closed their books when the bell rang. Ginger quickly ran home when school ended and darted right into the house, nearly knocking Uncle over. "Be careful, sweetheart. You could accidentally knock something over!" Uncle panicked in his near-perfect Italian accent. "I'm sorry. It's just I'm excited about an assignment at school," Ginger told him. "School assignment?" Grammy overheard, as she and Pappy strolled into the kitchen where Uncle and Ginger had been sitting. "You're excited about a school assignment? Sheesh! What have they been teaching you these days? Next you're gonna tell me flies have the power to destroy Neptune, or a giant wiener will topple the Empire Building! Or—," Pappy started. "Pappy, shh," Uncle told him. "Juss sayin . . . It can happen!" Pappy protested. "So what's the assignment about, hun?" Grammy asked in a very calm tone. "One of our teachers wants us to do a report on what our guardians or families have been through or a life event that has inspired me and or changed the world. I choose Pappy," Ginger explained. "Well, I'm honored. Really I am," Pappy gave a smile. "Well, that's good to hear," Grammy was happy for him. "So what exactly are you doing?" Uncle pondered. "A report on heritage in another view. Our class has to get facts from someone that has inspired me or that has done something magnificent in life; through childhood, adulthood, etc. Then we have to type it up as a report by Thursday. That's pretty much it," Ginger explained. "Interesting. Interesting, indeed," Uncle replied. "Well, Ginger, ya picked the perfect person to interview. Our family has so much heritage I don't even know where to begin! We can talk about the Irish festival a few years ago! Our Hungarian vacation! Or . . . uh . . . , whatever else! Where to start, where to start, where to start! Um, um, um . . ." Pappy was getting goose bumps himself from this assignment too! "You can start by taking your afternoon medicine. You know it's vital to your health. If you don't, we'll all be worried!" Grammy commanded, heading to the medicine cabinet . . . Pappy gasped for air and took the disgusting medicine. He gulped it down faster than a cheetah on steroids. "Now where was I? Oh yea! We could talk about . . . !"

"Pappy, calm down now! Let's go to your room and then we can talk," Uncle suggested. Grammy helped walk Pappy to their room, Ginger right behind them with a pad of notebook paper and a pen in her hands. Uncle went in the living room to watch television. He'd probably heard his father's life story many times now. Pappy sat down in the rocking chair they'd had. Grammy sat next to Pappy on the bed. "Marybeth, it's only an interview with me and mah granddaughter. I think ya's should leave!" Pappy told Grammy. "It's okay if she stays, Pappy," Ginger cried. "No, no, have your time. Even though I am concerned about you dear," Grammy insisted, making her way to the door. "Don't worry 'bout me, hun. I'll be fine," Pappy replied, as the door shut behind Grammy. "So, where should we begin?" Pappy started. "I'm thinking hmm. How about your childhood? I mainly wanna hear about that and your job experience being in the military, fighting in the Vietnam War, and what that was like. Later on you can tell me what inspired you then and what inspires you now as a veteran."

"That I can do, Ginger," Pappy responded. "Good. So tell me about your childhood life," Ginger said, already ready to scribble words on her notepad.

"Well, my childhood was not an easy one at all," Pappy began. Ginger was scribbling away. "Our grandfather side of the family is originally Irish, French, a little of Spanish, and Scandinavian from what I can remember. Of course your mother's side is mainly Polish, Italian, and some parts of eastern Europe, and maybe as far as some parts in Asia (we can ask Shanna Lou on that). I was born in Dublin, Ireland in 1940, right in the middle of the Second World War. Our family was poor from the potato famine, so my father and great-grandfather had to work their butts off just to survive. I'd work in the fields with the folks in Ireland during my young years. Right after I turned four, we had heard about the Americans going to France to invade and attack the Germans. This had scared my family very much, because they didn't know if the Americans would invade us next. Then the attack on 6/6/1944, also known as D-Day. Many people had been shocked, many killed, and many homeless. The war soon ended. Luckily our country was at peace. Then a crisis struck. My father had lost his job and was in total debt. Lucky for us, one of my father's sisters had a home in Italy we can stay in. That's when me, my mam and pap, and brothers packed and headed for her house in Rome. I was raised in Italy practically my entire life. When I was twenty-one, I met your Grammy, and we loved each other's so much! In a year, we got married near the Colosseum, and in another year, we had a child, who is of course your uncle. Since I was dependable, your Grammy and I decided to move to America to start a new life. In America, we had another child, this one a baby girl, or your late mother. We were happy. We had a home of our own, and two lovely children, and we lived in a beautiful place called America. It didn't last long, however. Before we moved to America, there had been a war going on in Vietnam. Technically, Vietnam was in a Civil War during the 1950s and 1960s. Since the French decided to take over Communist Vietnam, it was declared a war. This war was one of the longest wars ever in American history. Vietnam had been split into two parts, Northern and Southern Vietnam. They hated each other and were separated for a very long time. And here comes other countries to try and "take over" Vietnam or "settle" the dispute. Things just got much and much worse for Vietnam. Americans weren't concerned about Vietnam. They didn't care at all. The military did, however. Americans were already talking about invading Vietnam. Typical America, always gettin' in other country's businesses. If you were over seventeen and in good health, you were gonna have to get drafted to the military to help fight the war. About six months after your mother was born, I was drafted to corps, and I would have to have a military training camp for six months. It was required back in my day. I was devastated by it. My son was only two, and my daughter was only six months old when I had got drafted. I couldn't see them grow up or anything. I didn't have the chance to be a real father during the Vietnam War. All I was doing was fighting. Fighting for a country where I lived in. I didn't see your mother or uncle until they were in about third or fourth or fifth grade. They hardly recognized me. I was mad at myself for not being there for my children. They were fatherless all through their childhood. Grammy had to play both roles while I was gone. I wanted to see them at a young age, but I *couldn't.* There was no choice when it came to drafting in the war. It's either you do or you die. Either way, I knew I *had* to make that sacrifice. I *had* to choose which road to take. I *had* to choose to fight. And that's exactly what I did. No other choice. Surviving that six-month military course was tougher than actually fighting in the Vietnam War believe it or not. We had to learn AND know everything about fighting on ground and in air. They treated us like nothing at that camp. We only had one outfit to wear, and we had to wear it through the entire six months we were there. The beds were small, barely enough to fit a doll (let alone a baby). And all we were doing there was training. They did show us useful things like holding a gun in the proper position, managing military gear, hiking and walking in unpleasant situations, and firing missiles at the proper correct time. We never had a break, or a resting period. It was just training, training, training. The other bad things there were that we couldn't see our family or children until the camp was over with. After seeing the family for only seventy two hours, we were shipped to Vietnam. We also couldn't mail or write to anyone at the camp. It was like being in the middle of Iraq, you couldn't do a darn thang. You could only fight, or get killed and die. I felt devastated not seeing your uncle, Grammy, or mother. It put me to tears. It pains me just thinking about the whole thing. But I had to move on. I didn't have no other choice. After learning the basic techniques of military equipment and movement, we next learned about actual fighting and introduction to the air. We also learned about ambushes and hiding places and shelter ideas. Running and jumping with five-thousand-pound equipment was just tiring and unsanitary. We were only given two cups of water, each one served afternoon and before dinner, so we had to make it last. The meals there were atrocious. To be honest with you, it hadn't been a meal at all. Half of the time it had been raw, and if we were lucky, we'd get served a bread roll and some potatoes. I'd always fear about that training camp; it was in the middle of nowhere. The ending of the training camp had to be by far the worse. We were using guns, air missiles, cannons, and even ship equipment. The men decided to have a "practice war," which was like a war, only it was the men at the camp fighting against each other. We started a real fire, and about eighty men were badly wounded. Luckily there were no deaths. I'm just glad that I will never have to experience that training camp ever again in my life." "Can you tell me about the Vietnam War now? And how was your experience in that?" Ginger asked. She had at least a page and a half down on her notepad. "Sure! It was 1959 when this terrible tragedy started. It didn't end until April 30, 1975. About sixteen years. Can ya believe that? Sixteen years was the length of that war! You hadn't even lived that long yourself! The problem was that Vietnam had been split into two parts: North and South. North Vietnam was all communists, and the Southern half was strict government. The South of Vietnam was anti-communist, so they were fighting North Vietnam, while the U.S. was supplying their air superiority and power. The U.S. wanted to prevent communist take over from North Vietnam, which is why the U.S. entered the war. When John F. Kennedy became president, he wanted to keep the allies safe and protect the Soviet Union space. He knew he had to stop communist expansions from taking over the world. He and the US became forces with Southern Vietnam to stop Northern Vietnam, and their communism. Unfortunately for Southern Vietnam, their military was poor and broke. Just before Kennedy was assassinated, North Vietnam was starting to go crazy. The two Vietnam split countries, the US, and nearby countries had to declare neutrality on Laos so North Vietnam wouldn't go and attack them as well. Kennedy also created the U.S.-South Vietnam Air Force, which introduced air supply and more military. This is when the troops start heading for Vietnam. Lyndon B. Johnson became president after JFK's death. He was for this war greatly, and he let the war expand greatly all the way through. August 2, 1964 is where I remember an attack. The USS *Maddox* (an airship) bombed the North Vietnam cost, and it wrecked Northern Vietnam military equipment. In the following three years or so, the U.S. is just completely bombin' North Vietnam. South Vietnam economy was booming again toward the late '60s, early '70s. Because of that, they were able to send out more goods to other countries, in exchange for more troops. President Nixon is now president in '69, I recall. For the last year, peace talks were being made. He wanted Americans to support the war, and he wanted propaganda taking place through all of this. Unfortunately, there was secret bombing in Cambodia from North Vietnam, and no one knew about it. Not America at least. At last, peace accords were held in Paris, and in early 1973, America was not involved in the Vietnam War. By then in '74, South Vietnam forces were strong, but on 4/29/1975, the day before the war officially ended, there needed to be an evacuation from Saigon. There was so much conflict there. In the end, the communists did achieve what they wanted to achieve, take down Saigon. Over one million died in

North Vietnam, only about seventy thousand from the U.S. Military. Around two hundred thousand died in South Vietnam. Many more were wounded. And Vietnam would be a separate communist country and divided for decades. Now enough about that, now it's time for my role in the war. We finally left the camp. I saw my family for the first time in months. Too bad I only had seventy-two hours to be with them. Right after those three days, I would be spending my time in Northern Vietnam, supporting my own country. I had been in my twenties, so I could just about handle anything. Northern Vietnam leader was Ho Chi Minh. Ours was of course JFK, Lyndon B. Johnson, and the brave Dwight D. Eisenhower. Eisenhower pretty much led the attacks and battlefronts, while JFK and Johnson were commanding troops and seeking national help. I was in charge with air and flying for the first few years, and then I was with the military fighting on ground helping wounded soldiers all the way to the fall of the Saigon. While in air, I was battling Vietnam aircraft in North Vietnam, Laos, and neutral Cambodia. I remember in '71 we dropped bombs over parts of Northern Vietnam costs. Northern Vietnam was strong, however. They had came right back at us with shootings in the sky or bombings below. It did feel great to be in the air, hoverin' around in that thing, but smoke and fumes was a bad thing throughout the war. After being exposed to 'em a long time, I became very ill. Sadly it couldn't stop anything. The men and I did manage to take down some of the communist controlled areas, including some parts of the Soviet Union. I then was deported to a helicopter. Air Force attack by the end of 1976 and beginnin' of 1972. We were scouting for headquarters. Looking for places and communists to kill. Luckily more troops came from surroundin' southeastern Asia and Oceanic countries. They helped us out a bunch and saved us a ton of energy. After flying for about three years, scouting and fighting, me and some of my other fellow men were now fighting on ground for the first time in the war. We were looking for opposing troops in North Vietnam, and for a short while, looking in North Korea as well. Ten of the close men I knew had died during that time from surprise air attacks or dehydration. Sometimes it just takes sacrifice. After fighting about a year on ground, peace was being talked about. Even so, our men had to look for dead U.S. soldiers in Northern Vietnam and Laos and Cambodia. If we found a body, we would take it and bury it near the nearest woods or forest. We had to. It showed a sign of care. Most of whom we found were just wounded from an attack or a bombing. We were just glad to see them again. We hadn't seen some of them for years. Just seeing them smile made me and others there smile as well. They were well, confident, and strong. The American casualties were bad. Some four hundred men were gone. After finding and burying men on ground (and avoiding fights still going on and attacks) we got on a plane and headed back home on May 1, 1975, just a day after the war officially ended. I was so glad to be home with my family again. Your uncle was almost a teenager, and your mother was the cutest girl I'd ever seen. They didn't even know who I was at first, but we laughed, because they knew I was home for the first time in years.

They could finally play with Daddy. The war did change a lot between American manufacture with other with countries. The economy did build up from this war as well. Trading was good. It's still too bad that North Vietnam took over southern Vietnam, Laos, and Cambodia in the end. That's why Vietnam's flag is the way it is today, a flag with a yellow start in the middle. Back in the war, that flag was North Vietnam's flag. But now there's nothin' we can do 'bout that. I was just glad to see the folks again, people whom I never thought seeing again. I knew your Grammy went through enough raisin' your mama and uncle alone. I knew she was glad to see me again. The war had great affects on me, though. That's why I have this cringy voice, and it's hard for me to walk and move. After the war, I decided to stay in the military (one that was close to the family). I retired after forty years from being in the military. I done somethin' great for America, but I never get anything back in return. No gift basket, no blanket, no nothin'. Butcha know what, it didn't matter to me. I am glad to have a family who loved me, and moments to share with everyone. I had two adorable children who loved me. I had my life back. The Vietnam War has taught me lots of different things. The most important though is how to live life through tough times, like now with this economic recession in America. I know I can make it, I just have to believe. Like my theory says, 'It takes a man's life to learn life.' Some five million people died from the Vietnam War, but me being a survivor has taught me with words like 'I can,' or 'I can do it.' It didn't come to me soon, it took a while. So, Ginger, whatever is going on, look at it in a positive way, and know how to live life through the tough times, and always, always believe in yourself. Well, I think I'm just about done here. Anything else?"

"Thanks so much for your help, Pappy. I got down some great notes down. Now I can start my project!" Ginger said. "Anytime, Ginger. Glad to help!" Pappy responded. Grammy came through the door, holding a plate of tea saucers in her hands. "Everything all right in here?" Grammy asked, setting the tea gently on the bed. Pappy slowly took his cup, and swallowed it bitterly. Must've been his medicine. "It got quiet, so I was just wondering. Be careful, dear, the oolong may be too strong," Grammy advised. "We're doing fine. I'm just about finished." Grammy set down her teacup. "Everything's fine, Marybeth, now please," Pappy urged. "I better do my other homework. Thanks for the info and tea!" Ginger said, hopping off the bed and headed for the door. "Anytime, Ginga," her grandparents replied. Ginger went right up to her room, already excited about beginning to write the report. Pappy's life did influence her greatly. Mentioned in the beginning, it was he who decided she should stay with him in rough times. It was he who wanted to be the best grandfather figure there was. It was he who gave her courage and loyalty to others. Most importantly, it was he who saved her life from a terrible orphanage. Although Pappy is the way he is (grumpy and not amused at all), Ginger can look up to him not only from him being a veteran, and experiencing two historic wars, but also through his passion, his love, and his proudness. Maybe that's why the Spirit Transporter gives grief to Pappy. Maybe

Reincarnation and its soul have trudged through the valley of a believer. Pappy can never be a bad influence to Ginger. Sure he may say bad words in German, or frequently smoke beyond his medication, but the reality of the matter is that she is thankful to have such an accomplishing grandfather like him and to have married a wonderful woman like Grammy. Ginger had to celebrate from what she had learned from Pappy, because she wanted to just visualize these things and incorporate them to human life. All Ginger had to do now was try to put the pieces together to present the actual project. She was just glad to have been done interviewing. That would take the longest. The next two days Ginger devoted her time on working on the report for the interview. She had received so much information, she didn't know where to start! Like usual when she writes, words will just come to her like they always do. Every time she'd begin writing or thinking, it would always bring up Shelby. Pappy would always take care of the pup, and he would always sing him some Irish folk tunes before bed. That always put a smile on Ginger's face, knowing that Shelby was in a good and safe place. It depresses Ginger when he thinks about that dreaded day he ran away from the house. Now she'll never see him again. The good though is that Shelby is in a better place, looking at Ginger and only smiling at the moments to share. If only you could see the way Pappy smiled when he would see or catch a glimpse of Shelby. That bond was very strong. Now all is lost in a deep, deep trench. It pains everyone in the family to think about Shelby, and how much he influenced the family. All times end with a tragic blossom. As

Ginger was writing, she would have to stop and think about those good times with her dog and how he himself helps answer what her parents left behind. Could it be true love to answer these questions? What about identity to reveal the secret of Ginger's parents? How about the connections of faith and prosperity with Shelby and her grandparents, and even friends? You have to look at it in more than one way to find out the TRUE answer. On a biased view, the answer may be on the ground stomped upon many times. In other views, the answer could be right in your eyes, but again, there is more than one way to look at things (hint: The soul and spirit can be one way *if* you believe). Here we go again with that word "if." It shows up practically everywhere! So remember, do not look at an object or a thing in one way. There are many answers to a problem. Just depends on how ya look at it. Like the Holocaust, for example. Did it really happen? Were the Jews getting killed and other ethnic groups for no reason, or is it because people have their own knowledge? Unfortunately, we cannot answer for each other, we can only answer for ourselves. Even though there's thousands of articles proving the Holocaust happened, and that there are veterans who've SEEN this happen, people today are still denying the fact. People that haven't even been there or seen the terrible years of the Holocaust. This leads to other views and standpoint people don't care about. Was 9/11/01 caused by terrorists? What really caused the Great Depression in the 1930s? How could Germany be separated from its own continent for a long period of time? Why did slavery stop but lead to more segregation? What is really the answer? Most people don't want to discuss these things, but you know what, it's life. These things are real! The world can't keep tossing stuff in the trash, pretending it never happened before. We *need* to know the truth for the future. We *have* to find an answer to war, crisis, genocides, terrorists, etc. All these things, the world must know the truth. We can't keep hiding! It's time to grow. This is what MLK's dream is for us. This is why Rosa Parks didn't leave her seat. This is what FDR wants from us. To be leaders. To succeed to take back what was stolen. To uncover the answer from the very beginning.

CHAPTER 16

Party and the Date of Eternity

Ginger finally finished writing her report for the class. On Thursday, she was nervous to say it to the class. Natural. "Okay, Ginger McFraiddee, you may go next," Mrs. Maalone announced, as the class ended their applause for the last person that presented. Ginger scurried her way to the front of the class and took a deep breath. "My project is on my grandfather, and the reason I chose him is because he has seen and been in events like World War II. He's also been to at least six different countries, (Laos, Cambodia, Vietnam, Italy, Ireland, and U.S.)." "Very good. And what specific things did he encounter, or from what you can remember?" Mrs. Maalone wondered. "Well he didn't want to say specific things about WWII, he was a baby at the time, but I do know he's seen Auschwitz (I believe that's true), and he saw the Americans invaded in England for D-Day (he lived in Ireland at the time) and the actual attack."

"What's Auschwitz?" a student asked. "Auschwitz is a place where Jews and Gypsies and other people were taken in Poland, I believe, to work and do hard labor, and soon they'd get exterminated, gassed, or just killed. It was just living hell. Almost anyone who went inside would get killed or exterminated," Mrs. Maalone answered, "tell us about his life a little more, and why he inspires you, sweetheart." "He lived in Italy for most of his childhood after WWII. In his twenties, he met my grandma, they had a child (who is my uncle), and then moved to the US to have another baby (which was my mother). Shortly after my mom was born, the Vietnam War was going on, and my grandfather had to serve for the war, leaving my grandma to care for her two children all alone. Before he was shipped to Vietnam, he and other soldiers had to train and be equipped to fighting in a real war, so they were at a training camp for six months. He said that the training camp was worse than fighting in the real war. No food, scarce water, limited clothing, and a lot of moving and running around and carrying truckloads of military equipment." "So your grandfather is a veteran of the Vietnam War?" Mrs. Maalone asked, scribbling words on her paper. "Yes, ma'am," Ginger answered. "Wow. That IS something to be inspired by. Knowing that someone from a different country came to serve for America. Now I know the Vietnam War was tough for him," Mrs. Maalone stated. "Yes, indeed. He almost lost his voice and suffers from chronic heart problems," Ginger added. "I can imagine. The Vietnam War was one of the longest wars to occur in all times. The war was mainly communists trying to take over the world, which was a major issue in the Cold War (you'll learn more about that in social studies). Can anyone tell me what the war we're in now that's occurring in the Middle East fought about?" Mrs. Maalone asked. "Terrorism," the class answered. "Very good. 9/11 had a big cause to terrorism. Okay, Ginger, what makes your grandfather an inspiration to you? Last part and then you're done," Mrs. Maalone told her. "He does everything for me and makes sure I'm the best I can be. When my parents died, he'd decided to keep me and nurture me, instead of sending me off to an orphanage. When I need strength, courage, or even advice about life issues and motivates me to keep moving forward, especially for every tough time. My grandpa has experienced many hard things in his life, and I'm just beginning mine. He does know the worse feeling. I can look up to him not only as a veteran, or a role model, but as a loving, kind, and caring grandfather. That's why I chose him for this project. He inspires me to do my best," Ginger said. "Very good, Miss McFraiddee. We all need someone to inspire us in our lives. Good job. You may take your seat," Mrs. Maalone cried, as the class applauded. Ginger gave her report to Mrs. Maalone and sat back down. When Mrs. Maalone said, "We all need someone to inspire us in our lives," it can make or break a person. Some people in this world are more unfortunate than others. Some people just don't have a person to look up to or they have no inspiration from nowhere. Not to be biased or anything, it's just that little word that keeps appearing in the story almost all the time: truth. But inspiration comes from the inside. It can only start with one person: you. You can inspire yourself, or even inspire the world. Looking at someone else's success only makes us think we can't achieve in life. You should know this part, however. They're wrong. What they're doing in life has nothing to do with you. Do not listen to what people have to say when it comes to success, because they are wrong and are trying to make you into a hypocrite. Always remember where you're going in life and the path to travel. Success CAN be easy. If you believe and trust. Ginger was having a sleepover with Meredith, Summer, Sally, and Jenny on Friday night. The girls talked and laughed and ate lots of food. Saturday night was the big night. The party. Luna's house. It's a good thing Luna had a big home, because there would be a lot of kids attending the party. Usually the teenagers consisted of kids from MMS, USMS, and Saint Joseph Academy. Some kids were from a school called Grace Lauran Elementary located not too far from the city Ginger lives in. How does Luna know all these people? Tip: via MySpace, Facebook, AIM, Main Street, or just having a lot of friends. Most parties lasted until one in the morning. Crazy, right? Ginger just hoped that Mandy wasn't going to attend the party (if there was a party going on, Mandy would be the first to know). Maybe she'd get grounded or something. Ginger was psyched about the party. She hadn't gone to one in the eighth-grade year yet. Uncle dropped her off at Luna's house just when the sun was setting. Other kids were already piling into the house. "Call me when ya need to, sweetheart. I'll talk to ya later," Uncle told her, as Ginger hopped out of the car. "Okay. Bye, Uncle!" Ginger responded, closing the door shut, and sprinting to the house. Not a lot of kids were there, but the night was still young. Luna immediately approached Ginger, or spotted her for the matter. "Thanks for comin'! You're a little early, but that's okay!" Luna had on oversized uggs and stylish glitter on her face. "Stephanie told me around this time," Ginger confirmed. "They're comin'. I already texted her and everybody else," Luna replied. Ginger gazed at the others who were hanging out and munching on food. Nearby, she saw a familiar person's back, who was talking to some familiar faces she'd seen. "Mandy! You invited her? Why?" Ginger was furious. "Why not? She's the coolest at Midway, and she always invites me to her parties!" Luna said. "We hate each other! She thinks she's better than me when she's not!" Ginger answered. "Oh. Sorry then. Didn't know!" Luna cried. Some girls called Luna over. "Oh, hey!" Luna greeted, walking over to them, leaving Ginger by herself. Moments later, more kids started arriving. About fifty to seventy-five kids arrived, most from Midway and Upton Sinclair Middle Schools. Among them were Todd and his friends, Stephanie and her friends, some preps and jocks from Midway and USMS, and acquaintances of Ginger from USMS. The music was rising, and the teens were eating and talking and drinking and dancing. "Hey, Ginger!" Stephanie greeted her. "Hey!" she responded. Malcolm was standing right behind Shandi and Jason next to Hillary. "Isn't this awesome?" Amy asked, dancing to the music. "Sure is. That's why we came...," Melissa acknowledged. "Yea, Melissa. You're smart...," Malcolm cried. "Don't be mean, gosh!" Shandi responded. "Sorrie!" Malcolm apologized. "It's too bad that Mandy Liverstone is here!" Hillary cried. Jason tugged her hair. "Who cares about her? You're hot!" he told her, making her smile. "I'm probably never gonna forgive Luna for that," Ginger responded. "It was funny what you did to her last week," Stephanie admitted. "What did she do?" Jason asked putting his arms around Hillary. "She threw ice cream all over Mandy, and she got Mandy in so much trouble," Amy started. "Mandy is now banned from the ice cream parlor," Melissa responded, fixing her uggs. "Ha. High five, Ginger!" Rachael cried, high-fiving her. "She deserved it, though," Stephanie agreed, texting away, and drinking soda. "Now she'll never mess with Ginger, again. The slut," Shandi remarked. "What terrible language," Malcolm teased. "Shut up. She deserved it, and she IS a slut," Ginger replied. "Whoa. Ginger's violent!" Jason teased. "You know what? That's it! Guys don't deserve crap either if you ask me! They're just as horrible," Stephanie protested. "That explains you and Joe," Shandi rolled her eyes. "We're just friends . . . Honey, I'm sticking with girl power, you traitor," Stephanie responded. "Well, that's what happens when a guy gets in your life. It's what we do," Jason said. "Ya, well, it's annoying," Rachael cried. "It's not our fault," Malcolm said. "Girl convo! Please!" Melissa cried. "What's that suppose to mean?" Malcolm asked. "It means you and Jason leave. Girls only! Unless you're a girl," Melissa was running out of patience. "Fine. Don't appreciate us," Jason snarled, as those guys left, only to be greeted by other guys, including Ginger's boyfriend. And of course, he strolls his way to the group of girls. The girls just rolled their eyes when he approached them and groaned. "Can we please have some privacy?

Is that too much to ask?!" Rachael cried. "What? Can't I talk to my girlfriend?" Todd asked. The girls sighed. "Let's go. The more parties we go to, the less privacy. TTYL, Ginger," Stephanie announced, as she and the preppy girls trotted away. "I'm sorry. Those girls can be so uptight," Ginger told him. "It's cool. I've known them too long now," Todd chuckled. Ginger looked down, a little shy. "You seem intimidated," Todd cried. "No, I'm not. Haven't been to a party until today. I'm a little nervous," Ginger admitted. Todd opened up his arms and hugged her. They were hugging for a long time. "Parties are okay. Plus we have each other," Todd was being romantic. "Hah," Ginger commented. "You smell really good," Todd cried. "Shut up." More kids started showing up, and the music only got louder. The dancing got even more intense. Ginger and Todd grabbed some chips and ate. "Wow, Todd! Hang out with us instead of your girlfriend!" a huge jock-looking guy yelled, him and his six friends behind laughing. "Who are they?" Ginger asked. "They're guys from Midway. They were on the football team," Todd explained, "very funny, guys!" "Wow. You have cocky friends," Ginger told him. "I'm cocky, and you're going out with me," Todd told her jokingly. "That's because I like you so much," she replied. "And I'm like the sexiest guy here. Duh!" Todd bragged. Gingers smiled and laughed. "You know you're not like other girls I've gone out with. You're strong on the inside, shy and soft on the outside. That's what I love about you," Todd said. "I guess I can say the same about you too. I mean you're really sweet. I can't talk to most guys because they only stare at me. But with you, I can."

"Maybe it's because I see the inside of you completely. Most guys don't," Todd cried. "Same for you," Ginger smiled. "Hey, are you doing anything tomorrow?"

"No."

"Cool. Wanna go see a movie?"

"Sure."

"I'll call ya."

"That'd be great." Ginger laughed. "Yea. I'm looking forward to it. Just you and me." Ginger's first date! Ginger looked into his eyes, and smiled even more. "Me too." Everyone was dancing and partying and having a good time. After Ginger and Stephanie and some girls from Saint Joseph Academy were talking and enjoying the punch, Luna had an announcement to make. The music was turned down lower to hear her speak. "Okay, okay. Thanks everyone for coming to yet ANOTHER huge party of the year! Isn't this awesome!" Luna yelled. Everyone else yelled. "But we're not done partying yet! We still have a lot of dancing and fun to do! We rock!" Luna yelled, as all of the teens were cheering her on. The music was turned all the way up again, and the party was back on. Mandy was talking to a girl named Vanessa Timmington. Vanessa Timmington. She is a wannabe Stephanie and goes to USMS. Vanessa has always liked Todd and wanted to go out with him. You can say Vanessa is popular but Stephanie, her friends, and most of the girls hate Vanessa because she is too self-centered. The fact that Mandy Liverstone is her best friend only makes USMS girls hate her more. "Eww, look at Vanessa. Fake uggs, fake makeup, plastic lipstick, gross!" Hillary criticized. "You forgot ugly face!" Stacy added, as the girls laughed. "Stacy, where were you all this time?" Rachael wondered. "All over the place, really. Too many guys were talking to me about crap," Stacy answered. "And speaking of guys," Stephanie pointed to some of Todd's friends headed their way including Nick and Joe. "I thought you said Nick and Joe weren't coming!" Amy whispered to Stephanie. "I told them we were going to Main Street today! Luna must've texted them about the party!" Stephanie whispered back. "Way to lie to us, Stephanie," Nick cried. "Yea, good one," Joe said. "Like we keep telling you, we need privacy!" Melissa began. "You don't have to treat us like crap, though," Andy mentioned. "Hey, Tiffany! Oh, sure I'd love to talk!" Stephanie stalled; she and some of the other girls following her to a different group of girls. Stacy, Shandi, Hillary, and Ginger stayed. "Wow, you guys are beasts," Malcolm said. "We're girls, and we're definitely not beasts, so back up!" Shandi threatened. "Nice threat, Shandi," Hillary cried. Malcolm put his arms around Shandi. "It's okay. Stephanie and her friends are just mad they don't have dates," Malcolm said. "Um, we are her friends . . . ," Ginger stuttered. "Come on, Jason. Let's get some punch," Hillary told him. "Sure," he responded, going their own way. "Hillary! Wait up!" Stacy called. "Wow, Ginger was the only girl to stay," Rockstar Kid was impressed. "Ehem! I'm still here," Shandi reminded them. "They obviously don't appreciate us. Let's go!" Malcolm told her, and they went their way. "You can go with them, Todd. It's cool," Chad told him. "No, Chad! I'll get mad as hell," Todd cried. "So, Ginger. Out of all us guys, who's the most attractive?" Chad asked her, "Me, right?"

"I'd say Jason if he was here," Ginger answered. "Wow, I thought you thought I was," Todd cried. "I do. I do. I wouldn't go out with him, anyway. He's a jerk."

"What about me?" Mack imposed. "Maybe. But out of all of you, Todd is the most attractive," Ginger said, giving her boyfriend a hug. "It's only because he's captain of the sports team," Chad snarled.

"And a lot of other things. He's funny, sweet, and cute," Ginger said, kissing him on the cheek. "Good fight, you guys," Todd told them. "I'm cute too," Andy budded in. "Oh, I know you are." Ginger blew a kiss at those guys, which sent them spiraling in the air. Night was coming to the middle, and things were gonna get a little crazy. It all started when Vanessa and Mandy and their group of friends spotted Ginger talking to Todd and some other guys. This set Vanessa off. Those girls were headed over to give Ginger a little surprise. "This oughta be good. Ginger doesn't know who she's messing with!" Mandy cried, as the girls laughed. Ginger turned around, only to see Mandy, Vanessa, and those girls she had seen back at the parlor last week. Mandy made sure to speak loud to try and embarrass Ginger. "So, Ginger. You think you're all, that, huh? You won at the ice cream parlor, but you will *not* win the volleyball game Monday, and that's final!" Mandy yelled out, where everyone heard, and stared. Everyone gasped. "Yea. Ginger. It's time to see who the real loser is! Yourself!" Vanessa cried, as those girls and some other kids laughed. "What's your problem?" Ginger asked. "Her problem is that she's tired of losing to a girl with no friends!" Vanessa answered. "Vanessa, you can't talk. No one likes you. Mandy's like, your only 'friend.' Why did you even bother to come to our school or the party?" Todd asked. Vanessa was a new girl at USMS. "Shut up, Todd. This isn't about you! It's about your girlfriend!" Many cried. Before Ginger knew it, mostly all of the kids were standing around, yelling "fight, fight, fight!"

"So what are you gonna do? It's time I show you whose the winner at volleyball!" Mandy said. "And to prove who is REALLY in charge. Enough is enough!" Vanessa budded in. You won't believe what happened next. Ginger went to the table, grabbed the entire bowl of fruit punch, and aimed it at both girls. Everyone gasped. "Mandy, I knew you were always competitive," Ginger started, pouring punch on Mandy, enough to make her scream. Everyone else laughed. "But you'll never win. And Vanessa. Jealousy has made you the slut you are today!" Ginger dumped the rest of the fruit punch on Vanessa. Both Vanessa and the Mandy were yelling out swear words, mainly the B word at Ginger. Laughs were flying everywhere. "Ginger, you will pay! Mandy, let's go! Aaaagh!" Vanessa yelled, the two girls still jumping around. "Girls, let's go!" Mandy yelled, as the two fruit punch girls scurried out of the door, her "pack" following. The door slammed right behind them. Everyone was still laughing and making comments at those evil girls. Evilness can never win. But we will see how it ends on 'Dynamo Monday.'

"Woah. You really do hate Mandy, don't you?" Todd asked, taking both her hands. "Yea, and that Vanessa freak. I wish they would go away!" Ginger bellowed. "I know. I know. Lucky it's all over now," Todd cried. "I guess you're right. I can't even stand them!" "You're hot when you hate others!"

"Todd, nooo! Those girls drive me crazy."

"I love it when you go crazy."

"I love you too." Ginger kissed Todd on the cheek. "You're so sweet, Todd."

"I know I am."

"Don't brag, now. Just kiss me." Kiss on the face. Embracing. "Love is sweet, isn't it?" Stacy asked, watching Todd and Ginger embrace. "Pssh. It makes me wanna puke!" Amy said. "Amy, just because you never had a boyfriend . . . ," Rachael started. "Yes, I have!" Amy protested. "Amy, what are you talking about? No, you haven't!" a girl with braces said. It must've been a girl from another school. "Whatever you say . . . ," Amy was mad. "Name one, then . . . ," a curly blond haired girl told her. Silence. "Exactly, nothing," Stacy commented. "Pssh." "Ginger and Todd, foreeeeeever! Mr. and Mrs. Wyndelle! Haha!" Big, ginormous football players and b-ball players teased, as Todd and Ginger cuddled and hugged. "Shut up! God!" Todd told them. "Ignore them. They're immature as ever."

"Hey, those are my friends."

"I know, and they should care for you."

"Uh, yea. Too bad they're jerks." "Which is why I'm your girlfriend. I like jerks, to be honest. They express themselves on the inside."

"Oh well, come on, let's meet some of my friends!" Todd cried, as the two went over to his friends. Luna had another announcement to make. "Okay, I don't know about you but that was fun! Mandy and Vanessa deserved it!" Loudness of cheers. "Oh, and Ginger. You owe me $10.00 for the punch! Love ya!" Luna gave kisses to Ginger. She was joking. Ginger just cuddled with Todd, as laughs went around. "The night's still young, though! Paaaaarty!" Luna yelled as the lights went off. It went even crazier toward the night. A fat kid ripped off his shirt and ran around to be funny. Food was thrown all over the place. This was a REAL party! "Woah, Todd. Goin' out with a prep," a football player joked, ten other big guys laughing. "Hey! She'll own you at volleyball and track!" Todd cried. "Wait! You're captain of the volleyball AND track team?" another guy asked. "Yea, and she'll OWN you!" Todd answered for her. "Well, HELLO, Ginger! One thousand apologies!" the first guy apologized, the others doing the same. Ginger chuckled. "That's okay!"

"Yea, but that's awesome!" a third guy said. "Not as awesome being with the captain of a football and basketball team," Ginger said. "Not at awesome as DATING, the captain of the football and basketball team!" a fourth guy said. "No homo, dude," Todd commented. Ginger smiled. So the party continued on. Lots of dancing and the talking with different friends. Do girls wear any other shoe besides Uggs or Converse these days? Finally it was getting late, and the teens were headed their way home. Luna's house had been trashed by an unwanted zoo. Ginger got picked up and taken home. *What a great party*, she thought to herself. The next day would get even better. The Date. Ginger's first date at that. She'd never been out with a guy, so this was pretty big in terms of their relationship. Todd seemed open and intimate, but was Ginger the same? Could Todd actually open up Ginger's heart to see her true identity, or would Reincarnation give her that answer? Ginger waited anxiously outside of Main Street Theatre, where St. Epiphany Baptist Church once stood until the fire. Todd didn't know what to expect on this date. He's been on dates with several other hot girls. But not with Ginger McFraiddee. Ginger was different. She was affectionate and very close to herself. Todd knew he would have to be careful with her. But he did like sensitive girls (even though he has never gone out with them). But there is still that something Ginger won't tell him that's keeping her the way she is. *Maybe it's really personal,* Todd thought, visualizing all of the possibilities. Whatever the case was, he knew he had to be sincere. Ginger does get tired of cocky and rude guys. That's one conclusion Todd had made. "I'm ready. I'm ready. Let's do this." That's all Todd could say until he crossed the street to the Main Street Theatre, where the St. Epiphany Baptist Church to be until that fire. How droughtful. Todd spotted a blonde, straight-haired girl wearing Uggs and a pink Abercrombie jacket. Her head was turned away. Her hands were touching some sort of necklace. Ginger was fidgeting with her locket when Todd saw and finally recognized her. They both walked toward each other and held hands. "Hey," Todd said, the wind blowing his cinnamon brown hair. "Hey," Ginger responded. "Are you okay? You seem nervous. If it's too much for you, we can do it another day," Todd suggested. "No, Todd, I'm fine," Ginger laughed. "Cool. What are we waiting for? Let's go see the movie!" Todd cried, as they headed for the ticket inbox. When they went inside, Ginger went to go get the seats, and Todd got the refreshments. When Ginger sat down, Stephanie called her. The previews were showing. "Hello?" Ginger whispered, so others couldn't hear her. "So how's it going?" "Good. We just got the seats. Ima little scared."

"Don't be. It's normal to be a little nervous. I was when Todd offered to take me for ice cream."

"How did it go?"

"Good, actually. He really was sweet and kind. Just be yourself, you'll be fine. Even if you are with a guy."

"Thanks, Stephanie."

"Anytime. You'll be fine, I promise. I G2g. Ttyl!"

"See ya." Hung up. The previews were still showing when Todd arrived with the refreshments. "Thank you so much. You are the sweetest. I just love the theater butter," Ginger said, as Todd sat down with the drinks. "No problem. I got a medium in case you weren't hungry," Todd cried, smiling at her. "I may be a girl, but I eat like a truck driver," Ginger responded, grabbing a handful of popcorn and shoving it into her mouth. "Wow, we should have an eating contest. I'd so beat you," Todd suggested. "Haha, not true! I'd definitely win if the contest was a pie-eating one."

"No way. I can eat pie faster than a hungry lion or steroids," Todd said, making them both laugh. "You're funny," Ginger commented. "Thanks. And you're so hot!" Ginger was flattered by that. Ginger was shivering a little through the end of the previews. "Are you cold?" Todd asked her, putting his arm around her back. "A little. I wish I had a different jacket. Or a much cozier one." "Here, you can have mine," Todd offered, taking off his jacket. It was his USMS basketball team jacket. "Todd this is your basketball jacket. Are you sure you want me to take it?" Ginger asked him. "Sure, why not? I only let girls wear it from who I can trust, and who's really special," he told her, sounding deep. "Aww. Thanks, Todd!" Ginger said as Todd helped her put the jacket on. "You look awesome," her boyfriend told her. "Thanks." Ginger and Todd tried not to talk that loud during the start of the move. They just couldn't help it. During the dynamic and scary parts, they didn't dare to speak. In one scene, Ginger yelped and hid under Todd's arm to avoid seeing the movie. "It's okay. The scary part is over. Scary, huh?"

"Yea!" Ginger gasped for air, "luckily you can protect me." Ginger looked up at him. "Yea, I know. Movies can be so scary."

"Yea, Todd, I'm still cold," Ginger complained. "You can lean on me if you want," Todd offered. Ginger set her head peacefully on Todd's shoulder. "Much better." Ginger did feel comfortable during the movie. It's too bad the movie they saw was a really scary one. Ginger loves to watch scary movies though. A mystery can never be solved by the eyes of the flesh. Todd was starting to become vaguer with Ginger. Sometimes it only takes communication and collaboration. Todd was glad his girlfriend trusted him, and that they could talk about anything. At least there were no walls or barriers between the two. That always ruins a good relationship. The two talked all the way to in front of Main Street Theatre. Ginger was just laughing and listening to everything Todd had to say. She just enjoyed her new jacket. "Hey. If you don't mind, wanna get some ice cream? I'll pay," Todd offered. "Sure. I'd love to."

"Sweet." They both held hands and walked to the ice cream parlor. Ginger waited while Todd got the ice cream. They sat at a high table with just two chairs. Ginger told Todd all about Shelby and the experience she had as a little girl. She didn't mention her parents' death however. Todd was very passionate about hearing how Shelby ran away from home that night and how he never returned. He was so sincere about hearing the experiences Ginger had to go through as a little girl. Ginger scooped some ice cream in her mouth. "Wow. Ginger. I'm sorry to hear that about Shelby. I really am," Todd did have feelings for others. "It's okay. He was my best friend. Thanks for caring so much." Ginger dropped a tear. "You're gonna be all right. I'm here for you. Don't worry. It's okay to cry. It's okay." Todd grabbed Ginger's hands and rubbed them, comforting her. Ginger wiped off her face. "It's okay. Sorry I did that. Just a feeling."

"I understand. We all wanna cry sometimes. Especially at a loss. Oh, you got ice cream on your lip." Todd reached over, and the got the ice cream off her mouth. Ginger laughed, and so did Todd. "This has to be the best date ever," Ginger admitted. Todd stared into her eyes for a minute. "Yea. Me too. I can actually talk to you and share feelings. Most girls don't like to do that." "I do. I do. I never knew you cared so much."

"Of course I do. I care about you, Ginger." Ginger smiled, and they finished up their ice cream, talking at certain times. "So that's why you're always so quiet. I knew it had to be something. God, I'm so dumb!" Todd cried, making Ginger giggle a bit. "But there's nothing wrong with that. I kind of like quiet girls. Some girls like Hillary don't know when to shut up," Todd joked, as they both laughed. "Well, I guess it's natural. I'm just a quiet person." Todd stroked her face. "And that's what I love about you. And that you lead our volleyball team to victory." Ginger nearly laughed at everything Todd said. Romance has just begun. "Maybe we should hang out a little more. You know, talk, go out, party, I really like you." Ginger smiled. "I like you too." They started talking again, and the manager (the same guy from last week when he kicked Mandy out) took note of this. "Hey! Are you two gonna order or not? You come here to buy, not to socialize!" he yelled at them. "Um, we did, sir," Todd explained. "Look. I already kicked a girl out for stupid nonsense. Don't make me kick you out too!" he threatened. "It would suck for you," Todd replied. The manager took a good look at the girl. "Weren't you here last week when I kicked out that maniac?" he asked her. "Yea," Ginger responded. "Oh. Well, I'm watching you . . . ," he said, and then he strolled off. "Wow. That was weird," Ginger cried. "Yea. Really weird," Todd agreed. "Now I gotta ask you this. Are you cool with my friends? A lot of times they're jerks," he told her. "Yea, they seem fine to me. Even if they are jerks. Cute jerks."

"Cool. I'm just lookin out for ya," he said, taking her hand again. "Your hands are really warm. Or maybe it's just me," Ginger cried. "Probably you. My hands were cold as heck," he replied, as they laughed. "Now are you okay with my friends? Mine are a bit intimidating. Hillary wanted to throw soda all over you when she found out we were going out," Ginger laughed. "Yea, sorta. I mean, come on, they're not THAT bad."

"Yes, they are. They get mad at guys for no reason. Especially ones they haven't met."

"Don't worry. I'll get along with them."

"Good."

"So do you want me to walk you home?"

"I'd like that."

"Cool. Let's go!" Todd helped Ginger get up, and helped her put on the USMS Basketball jacket he had given her. Although it was dark, she trusted him by getting home safely. Good thing she didn't live far from Main Street. "Todd, I'm a little scared," Ginger admitted, as they were walking. The sounds of the night rustled in the airless and dark sky. "You're scared of the dark?" Ginger nodded. "Don't be. You don't have to be. I'm right here." Ginger looked up at him. "Thank you so much." That's all Ginger had the guts to say. They held hands. Ginger rubbed up closer to Todd. "I'm not gonna wash this jacket. It was given to me by someone special," Ginger told him. Deep. "Wow. You really mean that?" he asked. She said yes. And they hugged for at least two minutes. It was a start. *Ginger smells really good*, Todd thought. "You really are sensitive, aren't you?" she asked. "On the inside I am. Hard to believe since I never show it." They both laughed a little. "I'll never forget this night. Ever."

"Me either. You know, out of the girls I've been out with, I like you the most. No joke. I mean, there's this bond we have. I can't take my eyes off you," Todd told her. "I know, and it's so fantastic. I thought I'd never meet a guy like that. But I did today. Thank you so much, Todd." "Anytime, Ginger. Anytime." Soon they arrived to Ginger's walkway, leading to her home. Todd grabbed her closer to him. They reached the front step, hearing noises in the back. "My folks. They're crazy," Ginger said, as they chuckled. Next they held both their hands, and looked at each other in front of the front door. "I had a really good time tonight. This first date was the best date ever," Ginger cried. "I had a good time too." Both of them stood there blankly. Until Todd leaned in and puckered his lips. Ginger did the same, and they kissed each other on the lips. Ginger was speechless. She didn't know what to do or what to say. It was totally unexpected. Todd was puzzled by it too. This was all just love having its delightful moment. They both kind of stared at each other gracefully. "So I'll see you later then," Todd told her. "Okay. Yea. That'd be cool," she responded. "Yea. I'll call you . . . I'll call you . . ." After a couple of seconds, they both reached in, this time their eyes were closed. They kissed on the lips a little longer this time, but not much longer. The front door had just opened when Todd and Ginger were through kissing. Pappy answered the door, while Grammy and Uncle were standing behind him. All three of them gasped. Ginger and Todd felt very embarrassed. They both turned to look at the adults who were astonished. "I . . . I guess this was a bad time," Todd said. "No, it wasn't. It was just right," Ginger responded. "Who are you? And why are you with mah baby girl!" Pappy demanded, throwing out spit. "I'm Todd Wyndelle, sir. I'm sorry about going with her."

"Don't be. They just don't know you," Ginger did the best she could to try to interpret things to Todd. "Wait. Ginger I was going to pick you up. Is everything all right?" Uncle asked. Todd noticed that the man had an Italian accent. "Everything's fine. He just walked me home," Ginger answered. "Fine? That's not fine! Walking with another guy AT NIGHT? No way! Someone coulda snatched ya up!" Pappy complained. "It's a good thing that didn't happen," Grammy commented, "and that you're okay." Todd turned his attention back to Ginger. "Today was awesome. I'm glad we finally talked. See ya later, Ginger. I'll call you. Take care, everyone," Todd said. "Bye, Todd," Ginger said. They hugged, and then Todd left. Ginger went inside, and Pappy slammed the door shut. "Okay, before you get mad at me . . . ," Ginger started. Too late. "That's the guy? Who the hell do you think you are? First you're goin' ter a party and now this! Gosh dammit! You walk with him home, you kiss him, AND you were with him all this time! I oughta give ya a good damn spankin'! And a butt kick if yar lucky!" Pappy was furious. Ginger was in tears. "You said I could go with him."

"I would've said no until I saw him!" Pappy replied. "Why don't you like him? He's really nice." "He seems like a bad influence. I will not tolerate that in this house! Not in mah house!"

"Now, Pappy, you oughta give Ginger the benefit of the doubt. As long as she's safe, everything's all right," Uncle defended. "That ain't the point! She could've been killed! I'm only doin' what's best!" Pappy said. "Well, she wasn't thankfully. And if she's fine with the guy, I am too. As long as she's safe. It's her choice, Pappy," Grammy explained. Ginger wiped off her tears. "I'm sorry, Ginger. I guess it's gonna take me awhile to get it all right," Pappy said. "It's okay. Just give Todd a chance. He's really nice," Ginger said. "I'll try. It will still take meh some time!" Pappy responded. "All's well that ends well. Now let's play a good game of bingo!" Uncle suggested, as they all agreed.

CHAPTER 17

Mandy vs. Ginger

Ginger didn't want to tell anyone about that kiss. She wrote all about it in her diary, telling about how sweet he is, and how she is starting to actually "like like" him. Before, Ginger really wasn't into him. Sometimes you can knock out your own blessing. Todd had felt something as well. He just didn't know how to say how he felt or what to say. He had never kissed Ginger, and now that he has, he can feel that close bonding between him and Ginger. Todd could barely find the right word to say to her after the kiss. Just talking to a girl that clearly understood him, and a girl that looks for the inside in a guy was really amazing to him. He could understand Ginger in a sort of secret way. Todd knows how hard her life has been. He has learned from one's experience. Although Ginger didn't tell him that much info, it was enough he needed to sort of get a feel of Ginger, and how his girlfriend is like. Going out with a totally different girl who is quiet, within herself, and solemnly nonchalant can bring wonders to Todd. Maybe that's why he likes her so much. Being different from everybody else can be rewarding. Just looking at Ginger's bright blue eyes made Todd want to talk to her. Whatever she'd say would make Todd more curious. He really wanted to get to know her. Todd's friends had been looking for him that night. He told them he was sick and couldn't go anywhere. Good thing no one saw him. But of course that kind of news would spread somehow. Ginger and Todd had took a picture together at the parlor. Todd decided to post it on MySpace, because they looked so happy together. Ginger WAS the girl for Todd. That was his conclusion. Just that one date had decided it, he had thought. What separates herself from the other girls? BEING herself! You may not understand now, but later you will. Monday came again, and this day was the BIGGEST day ever! The volleyball finals. School vs. school. Purity vs. Evilness. Coach vs. Demon. Ginger vs. Mandy Liverstone. Everyone was preparing. From the school decors to the mascot to the principal doing the school dance to the spirit team performing their own jam, everyone was ready, especially Coach Hector. Many feelings and tensions were already being aroused. Nervousness, relaxation, competitiveness, and athlete's foot were all symptoms of today's game. At lunch, all of the volleyball girls sat together at a table, as the kids were cheering and dying for autographs. This meant Ginger couldn't talk to Todd like she wanted to. While Ginger and the other volleyball girls were celebrating, Todd was with his own friends. He had hoped none of them knew about the lie he told. "So,

Todd . . . How was your date with Ginger?" Stephanie asked him from the other table. The guys heard this and gasped. "Stephanie, you suck!" Todd replied. "It's called payback. Haha. Saw you guys in the movie. I didn't wanna tell you I was there, so I hid and texted her. Ginger looked so cute with Todd!" Stephanie continued, as the girls at Stephanie's table awwed. Todd blushed a little. "Dude, you went out with her? Nice!" Andy was the first to comment. "Yea, I did. I was never grounded," Todd cried, seeming a little upset. "Dude, there's nothing wrong with that," Jose told him. "Yea, Ginger's hot," Mack cried. "Why didn't you tell us?" Malcolm asked. "Because I thought you guys would laugh or something. I kind of got nervous."

"That's natural with every first date, dude," Jason replied. "Plus Ginger's cool. I would wanna go out with her myself. Nothing's wrong with that," Jose said. "I guess I tweaked. Sorry, guys," Todd apologized. "No sweat, man. It's all right," Malcolm told him. "Yea. First dates are always the hardest," Andy agreed. "So how was the date?" Mack just had to know. "It was pretty sweet, actually. We saw a movie, and then we went for ice cream. She likes to talk a lot. And she hates self-centered guys and bullies. I thought she didn't want to go, but she did, which was awesome."

"Did you kiss her?" The Wise asked. This was the first time he had said anything. All the guys started laughing, even Todd himself. "Yea, but for only two seconds."

"On the lips?" Jason asked. "Yea. But for only two seconds!" All the guys gave him a high five. "Dude, that's beast! And on the first date!" Jose complimented him. "Did she actually want to kiss you?" Malcolm asked. "Yea, she did. She totally wanted to when she first saw me."

"That's cool! Ginger doesn't even like to kiss that often. You're so lucky. Usually she'd turn you away," Mack said. "She did, though. All she was doing was looking into my eyes and stuff. I can tell she really wants me."

"So how is she? She a slut? Talks too much? Do you really like her too? Like what?" Mack just needed to know. "Yea, I do. You can talk to Ginger about basically anything. Most girls don't care. And she's no slut, dude. Just a little shy."

"Wow, that sounds pretty good, yo. Are you gonna go on a date with her?" Jose asked. "Hell yea. She's totally awesome."

"So who do you think is better? That one chick from Hadley School you went out with, Tiffany, or Ginger?" Jason asked. "Ginger, definitely. Those girls acted like total whores and losers, and they wanted everything. Ginger's not even like that!"

"So you 'like like' her?" Andy asked. "Yea, I do. Who would've thought one date would make me attracted to a girl who doesn't know me?" Todd was clarifying his mind. "I guess girls are attracted to you," Malcolm concluded. "Yea. It's too bad Ginger and I can't talk right now. She's very interesting (in a good way)."

"It's cool that you're into her. Most girls take advantage of other guys," Jason cried. "Like you and Hillary?" Malcolm teased, as they laughed. "Hey, Hillary's rich. She never asks me for anything," Jason commented. "Wait 'til we get to high school," Andy cried. "If it even lasts that long," Jason responded. "Wait, dude. She's wearing your basketball jacket! Whoa!" Malcolm glanced over and saw Ginger wearing her volleyball jersey and Todd's basketball jacket. "It's official. What can I say?" Todd questioned. "Haha! That's beast!" Jose complimented. "Go, girls! Go! Go! Go, USMS! Go, Wolves! Go! Go! Go, USMS, we can't lose! Go, Go, Go, Wolves! Woo!" the volleyball girls and some other kids cheered. The second mascot was dancing on the table, as kids were throwing confetti all over the place. "Go, Wolves! Woooo! Hip Hip . . ." Jill started. "Hooray!" everyone else went. "Hip hip!" Jill went. "Hoooray!" "Hip hip!" "Hoooray! Wooo! We are going to win!" Cheers cheers, and the more cheers. Soon lunch was over, but the yelling and cheering did not stop there. The volleyball girls literally had to walk in a big clump to avoid mosh pits. Ginger was walking with Meredith, Jenny, Sally, and Cindy. "So I was at the party, and like they were like, 'OMG Cindy long time no see!'" Cindy bragged. "Wow! Go, Cindy! Go, Cindy! Go, Go!" Meredith cried. "That's awesome, Cindy! You go, girl!" Jenny told her. "I know, thanks." "We're so gonna win the championship today!" Ginger bragged. "I know. I'm so excited! Hip hip, hooray!" Sally cried, as the girls cheered. "Hip hip, hooray!" they cheered. "OMG! Ginger, is that Todd's basketball jacket?" Cindy asked. All of the girls paused at the top floor, gazing at Ginger. "Um, yea it is. He gave it to me to wear." They all gasped. "Are you serious! When was this?" Sally asked. "Saturday at Main Street. We were on a date," she whispered. The girls were just amused by this. "A date with Todd Wyndelle! And your first one? Ginger, that's great!" Jenny complimented. "Thanks! I love this jacket. Especially knowing that it came from someone great," Ginger replied. The girls felt the jacket and its texture. "Do you 'like like' Todd, Ginger? It's obvious that he 'likes likes' you," Meredith wondered. "After the date, and seeing that he is sincere, and he does care about things and me, I am starting to 'like like' him," Ginger responded. "Ginger, that is so sweet. I could almost cry," Sally was being a drama queen. "Oh, stop it, Sally," Cindy bellowed as the girls laughed. For the rest of the day, the school was cheering. All was cheering and in a happy mood except for two people. They were staring in a window, as if nothing has happened. The two mysterious teachers. Mrs. Robbin and Mrs. Duffy. They didn't seem to care at all. They probably didn't even know there WAS a big volleyball game today! They were shunned from the world. In it, but not OF it. If that was the case, what were they of? Only they know. Only the window can tell their story. Things happen for a reason. Not to be biased, but when something happens, or when someone does something, it's for a reason, which leads to an effect. Think about that for a second. "Things happen for a reason." Is it bias, is it a theory, or is it a fact? It depends on how you look at it. School was finally over. The volleyball girls were already in the gym getting warmed up for the game. The stance was ready in advance. Parents were already in the stance watching (or guardians and family relatives) when kids and teachers came rushing to the gym. In less than five minutes, the entire school was packed inside the gymnasium. Students and faculty were scrunched into the seats. There was barely any room for anyone. Some were standing up in open areas around the stance and even near the court. There was a lot of yelling and talking and screaming and cheering in the stance. Grammy, Pappy, and Uncle made sure to get there early and to get good seats. Smart idea. Lanely Tildon was also with them. Ginger took a glimpse and immediately saw the four toward the front rows. She was exceptionally glad that Uncle showed up this time, and Lanely Tildon was on time for the game. The girls took their seats across from the stance. The mascot of the team was performing for the audience, and the people were still arriving in the gym. There was a long line of people and kids waiting at the register. Some figured they probably couldn't get in after all. Coach Hector was shaking recklessly. He'd come so far to winning. He even took some water a few times and splashed it all over his face. Ginger saw almost everyone from school there. She saw Todd's friends, Stephanie's friends, Summer talking on the phone, Mrs. Alvarez painting her nails and even Mr. Daniels standing up, talking to other staff members with a soda cup in his hands. Everyone who was anyone was there. Even Max and Josh, the two loser kids! All except for the mysterious teachers. No surprise. But no one cares about those teachers. It's all about the volleyball team winning today's game. By 3:35 p.m, everyone started to settle down a little. Still no Mandy Liverstone or her team in sight. Maybe they were late for dramatic tension. Extremely late at that. Ginger noticed that Vanessa was sitting with two other girls. It looked like they were talking to themselves and not even cheering or throwing small amounts of confetti like the others. Vanessa was probably routing for the other team and Mandy, anyway (Mandy was probably her only friend out of all the girls on both teams). 3:44 p.m. One last chance. This is it. This is what Ginger McFraiddee, Coach Hector, and the entire school has been waiting for. Then the gym door bursts open. Mandy Liverstone and her coach and team decided to show up. MMS Team. The girls took their seats. Dead silence. Ginger tucked her locket in her shirt. Mandy Liverstone couldn't take her eyes off Ginger. It was time for revenge, and A LOT of it. After the party and the incident on Main Street, she figured Ginger needed and deserved her wrath. Mandy Liverstone was not mad, oh no! She was furious! Only this game could decide the true winner and who actually deserves wrath. Once again, this game was practically a show down between two highly competitive girls. But said earlier; only ONE can win! Mandy was tired of being the outcast. She would do anything to win this game. She was hungry for victory. And nothing would or could stop her. Except for the girls who hunger and thirst for righteousness. The visiting team could not have a chance to warm up since they were unreasonably late, which gave USMS some sort of an advantage. 3:58 p.m. The girls took their positions on the court. The entire school was at a moderate tone when it came for cheering, and everyone was looking at the game and not elsewhere. Mandy had her game face on right when she walked through that door. No other girl on MMS thought this was a joke. Neither did the USMS team. The game started off slow, and gradually began to speed up. Timeout was called by MMS in two minutes of the game, and everyone else went back to socializing. "Ladies and gentleman! Welcome to the District GG Midwest Competition Conference,

Volleyball girls edition. Our final teams are teams from Midway Middle School." There was an announcer greeting. The table was set in the middle of the gym, next to where the girls sat. Nobody clapped for MMS. "And . . . Upton Sinclair Middle School!" Everyone cheered, much louder than before. "Today's game will decide who wins the final conference and takes home the looovely trophy!" Two ladies bought out a gold trophy, a huge volleyball on it with "First Place" written on a plague. Everyone gasped at it. The ladies set the trophy next to the announcer. Coach Hector was ready to take that trophy and run. But he kept his cool. "Both teams have come a long way, but only the humble can take home the trophy and have pride in their school! Especially you, USMS, you haven't won in years!" That wasn't needed to be mentioned. It made some people angry, especially Coach Hector. "Nonetheless, good luck. And have a great game. We've already started, but it's just gettin' started! Woo!" the crowd was loud. The referee blew his whistle for the girls to have a timeout. When the timeout was over, the girls were back on the court, ready as they would ever be. Coach Hector's teeth was clinging. Same with some of the students in the audience. Quietness. Except from the girls announcing that they were open. MMS scored the first point. An incomplete move was made by USMS. Mandy gave Ginger a glare (an evil one at that). Then she grinned hastily. What a lousy girl! Who does she think she is, anyway? The referee blew the whistle, and the serve was made. Bump. Bump. Pass. Bump. Then the ball was headed to HER. She rose up and slammed the ball down, hitting a girl on the chest. But it still counted. USMS earned a point. The crowd of course went wild and out of control. But MMS wasn't giving up just yet. Not now, anyway. The score was tied 1 to 1. Still the first round and then two more after that. Mandy wasn't going down without a fight. That's just how she was. Toward the end of the first round, it was mainly Ginger and Mandy spiking the ball back and forth. But then Mandy tricked Ginger, and passed it to another teammate. That teammate spiked the ball to the ground! 2 to 1. "Nice, Liverstone!" Ginger told her from across the net. "Thanks, McFarty! You're not taking my trophy away from me!" Mandy was being stubborn. "We'll see about that . . . ," Ginger replied, as their team rotated. Both girls were not happy AT ALL! It started to look like Mandy was on steroids. She was sweating and on some adrenaline rush. But it didn't stop Ginger or the rest of the team. Mandy simply CANNOT carry a team all by herself. It takes teamwork. Before you, knew it, the first round was over. Mandy's team was up 3 to 1. Still not over. Vanessa even had the nerve to go over to where the MMS team was sitting, and start talking to Mandy and some other girls! She was even cheering them on instead! That backstabbing traitor! Mandy and Vanessa were socializing as if nothing ever happened. But Ginger couldn't worry about that. During the end of the first round, the team had called for a time-out. "Okay, girls. Defense is key. We've been losing good points and back passes because of no D. Now remember, pass and THEN go for the shot! One thing we have that the other team doesn't have is teamwork! Now go out there, play your best! And win this game! The championship is ours!" Coach Hector commanded, as the girls cheered on, agreeing with his statement. The girls took a two-minute break, then it was back on the court. 4:21 p.m. "And the game resumes!" the announcer announced. Coach Hector was trying to look at the game, but he couldn't take his eyes off that trophy. It was just too good for his liking. He wanted it so badly! Badly, badly, badly! Ginger was getting worn out by all of the excitement. Everyone was counting on her for the best. She wouldn't want to ruin a game herself. Coach Hector would be devastated. Grammy, Pappy, Uncle, and even Lanely Tildon would pass out. Then again, life isn't perfect. You can't have what you want. The second round began, and that's when things got a little bit more crazy (as if it already wasn't). Every time Mandy passed, bumped, or spiked the ball, she'd have a mean comment about Ginger, or some girls on Ginger's team. Mandy was supposed to have been taken out for foul language, but the coach insisted. The score was 6-2 when Coach Hector spoke to the judge personally and when Mandy wouldn't stop. Mandy sat out for nearly five minutes, letting other girls in the game, which was a big mistake. Since there was no Big Mouth Mandy to complain every second, Ginger had no trouble concentrating. At the final minutes of the second round, the score was 6-5. Mandy apparently was a huge distraction to Ginger. At the end, the score was 7-5. The team started to have doubt. They figured they could not possibly get in the lead now. Coach Hector wasn't willing to just let go of the trophy that fast. It ain't over till the fat lady sings. And that's how everyone wanted it to be. Someone started chanting: "USMS! USMS!" Now the entire crowd was clapping and cheering that chant. They were just so excited. The end of the season was finally here. "Ladies and gentlemen! This is it! The last round! How will it end! I don't know! None of us knows!" the announcer was trying to act all surprised. "We know! Get to the game, ALREADY!" an angry woman in the stance yelled, as everyone agreed and started yelling. "Okay, okay!" the announcer screamed, "Round 3! Last round! Girls, please take your positions!" The girls entered the court, looking fierce as they ever have. Meredith, Sally, Jill, Ginger, Jenny, and the rest of the girls were ready. Coach Hector was ready. Of course, Mandy and her team were ready. Who was their biggest supporter? Vanessa was. "This is my court, Ginger. You'd be better off leaving!" Mandy commanded her. They were talking from across the net to each other. "And you better not show your ass to Main Street ever again!" one of Mandy's teammates cried, as the girls laughed. "I'll get you back for that punch, McFarty! Me and Vanessa will!" Mandy boasted, and then the ref blew the whistle. The ball was served. Nervousness and teeth gnawing. Even the school mascot participated in that. When there was only five minutes left, the score was 9 to 8, Mandy's team in the lead. Fierce. "Okay, girls. Huddle up! This is the moment of truth. I (well not I), we, have been waiting for this moment for over a decade! Don't let us down, girls! And remember, have fun! McFraiddee, are you gonna be okay for the last part of the game?" Coach Hector asked. "Yes, sir!" "Good! McFraiddee, Stewart, Jones, Miller, Walters, and the starting four! On the court now!" The girls and Coach Hector cheered, and then the nine named girls took their positions on the court. The cheering started once again from the stance at the last minutes. Mandy was on fire! She'd scored three points in a single minute! But Ginger rebounded two points toward three minutes left, and then two more points were scored by other teammates. 5:49 p.m. Thirty seconds left. Score: 12 to 12. The last time-out of the game was now. Todd went over to Ginger; as Ginger drank water and Gatorade. "I'm really, really nervous!" Ginger told him, panting like crazy. Todd gave her a shoulder rub. "Calm down. We only need one more point. You can do this. We're all counting on you," he told her. Then Ginger took a look at Todd. "Is this how you feel when you're in a basketball game?" she asked him. "All the time. You'll be fine, I promise." Todd took her hands and rubbed them together. Then the whistle blew. "All right. I'll see ya later. Go, Wolves!"

"Go, Wolves!" Ginger agreed. Then Todd gave her a kiss on the cheek, and ran off. Ginger smiled for a quick moment, but then wiped off the smile as she returned to the court. "The last thirty seconds left. Play ball!" the announcer yelled, as the ball was in play. It was just bumping and bumping as twenty seconds passed. Ten seconds left. The ball was passed to Mandy at that point. Mandy jumped up, and bumped the ball. Mandy bumped up the ball, and then she bumped it again to Ginger's team. A girl on the team was too slow, and missed the ball by that much. The buzzer sounded. "And MMS wins the conference!" the announcer yelled, as the coach of their team and the girls huddled and celebrated. Vanessa went over and joined the girls in the victory. Ginger was disappointed. Coach Hector was the most. Coach Hector was so disappointed, he walked off and was not seen anymore. Another year wasted. "Like I said, Ginger, the better girl wins!" Mandy bragged. "Haha!" Vanessa retorted. The team was just sad. Those girls all sat down in dismay. Right before the MMS coach could touch the trophy, Summer and some other girls from the stance walked over to the announcer and so-called judges! "Hey! Mandy cheated! That point doesn't count! She bumped the ball twice before it went over the net! It's an illegal move!" Summer pointed out. Nobody seemed to notice that. Little conversations and disputes started in the audience. Ginger looked up when she heard that. Mandy ran up to Summer and the other girls. "No, I didn't! I only bumped it once!" she explained. "No, you didn't! We all saw you, Mandy!" one of the girls said. At that point, the audience was yelling. "Redo! Redo!" The announcer and the two other people were debating frantically. Finally, they had come to a deliberation. "Mandy, you did bump the ball twice yourself, which is illegal. The final point does NOT count! We will have a 1 minute redo. First one to score or the highest after one minute wins! Girls, take your positions! We will begin after a five-minute break," the announcer said. The audience and the girls were relieved. MMS, however, was not. Their coach was arguing with the announcer and the other two "judges." Mandy, Vanessa, and some other girls from the opposing team scurried over to where Ginger, Jenny, Meredith, Sally, and Summer were talking at. "Nice try, McFraiddee! It's not over! You got lucky THIS time!" Vanessa laughed in an angry laugh. "Shut up, Vanessa! Fair is fair!" Summer replied. "And stop being mean,"

Sally cried. "We'll stop when we wanna stop!" another girl from their team said. "Enjoy it now, McFarty! We'll still win, anytime! You might as well quit, now. Wimp!" Mandy laughed, as the other girls laughed, and went their separate ways. Ginger only wanted to do better from being called a wimp. "It's okay, Ginger. Just ignore them!" Meredith told her. "I am. And thanks for telling them that, Summer. I didn't know she did that. Summer may have won us the championship," Ginger said, as the girls were getting excited all over again. "No problem. Now let's win! Woo!" Summer cried. All of the girls got in a huddle and wooed. Summer and some other girls took their seats as the last minute was about to begin. The girls were still in a huddle. Vanessa sat with Mandy and the other MMS girls. They just glared at the USMS team. How pathetic! "Wait, where's Coach Hector?" Jill asked, looking around panickly. "We can't worry about him, right now. We have to win! So, everyone, don't worry!" Ginger answered. "But whose gonna go play, then?" Jenny wondered. "Okay. If you think you can take on Mandy, go ahead. If not, you shouldn't play. Only if you can handle her, and the last minute! That minute that will decide who wins the championship!" Ginger announced. With that said, each girl, one by one, stepped up to the court, Ginger going first. When there were finally nine total, they had decided that they were ready. Ready to win. Mandy's team took the court. Still no sign of Coach Hector. Where could he have gone? "Ladies and gentleman, boys and girls! We ask you not to say any threatening words during these sixty seconds. And remember, no time outs, no shouting, and if the team loses, it doesn't make them a loser. All right! Since MMS performed an illegal move, it is USMS's ball. You may serve!" the announcer said. The ref blew the whistle. Everyone was so excited now, there was no silence. No, Coach Hector, no time-outs. Which meant Ginger was in charge for sixty seconds. "Do the P-1 Plan!" Ginger announced to her team. "The P-1 Plan! Do the P-1 Plan!" the girls said to each other, all agreeing. The ball was given to a girl on the team. She served it. The clock started. 00:59.18. She passed it to the opposing team. That team member had passed it back over to Ginger's side. 00:53.42. The P-1 Plan was in action. The girls took turns passing to one another. At 00:24.97, Ginger passed it over the net, right to Mandy. Mandy (not being smart), instead of keeping the ball on their side, shot it over to Ginger. Ginger caught it, and bumped it to a teammate. The P-1 Plan was back in action. 00:16.18. Everyone was ready to either throw confetti and ribbons all over the school or mourn greatly. 00:08.76. The girls were still passing. At 00:01.92, a girl passed it high right to Ginger. Ginger extended her arm and slammed the ball hard over the net. A girl tried defending, but missed the ball, and it hit the ground. 00:00.00. The buzzer beeped. USMS had won! "And USMS wins the Conference! USMS wins! USMS winsss!" the announcer screamed. Confetti and sprinkles of paper were thrown everywhere! Lots of yelling. Everyone in the audience (teachers, kids, parents) came crowding the circle of the volleyball girls. They were all happy. You'd hear: "No pushing! Be careful!" from time to time, but no one cared. Lots of celebrating. Ginger was lifted up, and USMS cheered: "We're number 1! We're number

1!" Mandy, Vanessa, their coach, and those girls just glared at all of them. They had taken their trophy. "Well, girls. The end is the end. We gave it our all. Let's go home!" the coach said. They gathered their belongings and silently left the gym. Vanessa followed. "That's right! The losers have left!" one kid announced, as they cheered even more, now! They were jumping on bleachers, having mosh pits, everything! Ginger and some other girls were being carried as if they were the stars of a live concert. The entire school fluttered with success and victory. Lanely, Uncle, Grammy, and Pappy decided not to get involved in that crazy stuff, for they could get hurt in the pushes, so they waited over toward the front exit of the gym, watching everyone else. They spotted Ginger easily. The school photography club was flashing away at everything, avoiding certain kids and trying not to bump into faculty members. Some volleyball girls stood next to the trophy, where the announcer and the two "judges" stood. The trophy was finally theirs! Ginger could hardly believe it. Ginger was finally let down, and she was receiving pats on the back, and "Good jobs!" Todd finally spotted her and quickly approached her. "I knew you could do it!" Todd said, taking his jacket he had given Ginger and putting it over her. Todd wrapped his arms around her. "I knew I could too! Thanks!" She said, trying to talk over the loudness. "No problem! Now we both officially have a lot in common! We're both captains of teams, and winning teams!" he bragged. "Hah, I know. I'm just glad it's finally over! We finally won!" Ginger cried. "Yea. You must feel awesome right now! I mean, you did something incredible out there!" Todd yelled.

"I know. I do! This is one of the happiest days of my life!" she screamed, "and I thank you for helping me." "No problem." She kissed him on the cheek, and they passed the crowd, making it to the trophy table.

CHAPTER 18

What Lies Beneath the Mind

Coach Hector was finally spotted. He was walking from the hall to the trophy table. Everyone was yelling, screaming, and cheering. All of the USMS volleyball girls were standing at the table with Coach Hector, the announcer, and the "judges." The photographers were busy flashing pictures here and there. The entire crowd was surrounding the table, the girls, the coach, "judges," and the announcer. As the crowd got quieter, and the photographers kept snapping pictures toward the girls and Coach Hector, the announcer was ready to make an announcement. "Congratulations, Upton Sinclair Middle School, for your wonderful success in winning the Sixty-sixth District. We are all proud of you. But you girls yourselves, should be proud of you and of one another. We congratulate you on achieving this wonderful trophy, because you deserve it. With further ado, I hand you the First Place Golden Trophy of your conference! Congratulations!

Here you are Coach Hector! How do you feel to accomplish this goal?" the announcer asked. Coach Hector wearily took the trophy. And then he smiled. The crowd just screamed. "I'm proud. I'm very proud. In fact, I am so speechless. USMS finally won after ten years of waiting!" Coach Hector yelled, as everyone yelled. For the first time, Coach Hector saw light in his own heart. It just took him to believe to achieve what was rightfully his. So after over a decade, he is finally holding the winning trophy. Not his trophy. Not the girl's trophy. The school's trophy. Their trophy. Victory does eventually pay off. Now Coach Hector was smiling as bright as he ever did, as the cameras were flashing in front of his face. The girls that he himself had coached were smiling and cheering and having a good time. They had achieved the gold. They were champions! All of the girls got a chance to hold trophy and take one big picture together. The principal, announcer, Coach Hector, assistant principal, and some viewing fans watched them put the picture of the team and the trophy in the trophy case in the hall. Photographers were still flashing away, and janitors were already on the move cleaning up the confetti and paper thrown everywhere, and mopping the court. Now, it was mostly people in large clumps talking in little groups (mainly parents, kids, and some faculty members). Others were leaving to go home. Ginger couldn't breathe from the publicity of all of the fans. It was to be expected; she had just won the finals, and she was captain of the team to begin with. Soon enough, she was able to spot her grandparents, uncle, and Lanely Tildon waiting for her when Todd got to her first. "Haha! We won! If you don't mind, do you wanna have a study hall tomorrow?" It was sudden of him to ask her that. Another date! "Sure, Todd. Where at?" she asked back. "My house, of course, after school. So do you want to?" "Okay. Only if we can walk there."

"Of course." Todd gave her an appealing grin.

"Well, my grandparents are waiting for me. My grandfather may get mad at me, again," Ginger laughed. So she was right. She took a glance at Pappy, who was ready to charge at Todd like a bull on medications. Uncle and Grammy had to hold him back before he did something incredibly dumb. "See ya later, Ginger," he called, as Ginger ran and caught up with her folks. "Ginger, you need to stay away from that guy! I hate him so much! Ain't no guy gonna get in da way of mah granddaughter!" Pappy yelled. So much for a good job. "Pappy, stop that! Good job, Ginger! We won!" Grammy cheered. "I know. I'm so happy! I know Coach Hector is too," Ginger cried. "Good job, Ginger. I am very proud. It must've been hard with all of that pressure on you," Lanely said. Lanely gave Ginger a big hug. "I'm sorry I couldn't come to the last game. But this game was the best! Too bad that other girl cheated, almost costing us the game," Uncle said. "It's a good thing that DIDN'T happen," Ginger reemphasized, "Well, let's go, already. I'm getting tired myself."

"Okay. See you Saturday, Miss Tildon. Take care now!" Grammy told her. "Sure thing, Marybeth. Good job, Ginger!" Lanely called, walking her way out of the school toward the parking lot. Ginger, her grandparents, and her uncle walked out as well. "You did great, Ginga. I'm proud of ya!" Pappy told her.

"Does this mean I get to go over Todd's house tomorrow?" Ginger asked. All of their eyes widened up. "What?" Pappy asked, hearing her already. "Please? It's for studying!" "Of c'urse not! Ginga, you know you're too young! Plus I can't trust you with that guy! No questions or comments!" Pappy concluded. Ginger pouted a little, trying to show no compassion. The ride home was quiet. Ginger wasn't given any freedom when it came to another guy. Pappy didn't care! And since he was the oldest, and the toughest, there was nothing they could do about it. But how could she tell Todd she couldn't go? He'd feel awful. When they got home, Todd called Ginger on her cell phone. "Hello?" Ginger greeted. "Hey, Ginger."

"Look, Ginger. About our study date?"

"What about it?"

"It has to be at the library. I'm sorry. My mom's being a total freak about it and doesn't let anyone come over on the weekday. I just wanted us to be alone."

"That's okay. I can't wait."

"Me either. Once again, congrats on winning the game."

"Thanks." "Yea, you guys deserved it."

"I can't wait. My grandfather hates company. Especially another guy. "No offense."

"None taken. So . . . I'll talk with you tomorrow. See ya later."

"Later." Hung. This meant that Ginger could go on the study date! She wouldn't have to go to Todd's house! She could say she was going to the library to study with some friends (which was almost true). That's exactly what she did. She said that the date was cancelled. Luckily for her, Pappy bought it. Ginger was receiving a bunch of texting from others about the volleyball game. Now, it was official: she is popular. Ginger had to work her fingers off to reply to all of those messages. It had taken a while, but it paid off. She had only seen the beginning. The next day would be even more chaotic. Before school started the next day, Coach Hector wanted to see all of the volleyball girls for some sort of conversation. "Girls. I would just like to say how proud I am of all of you. I know it must've been hard for you to come this far, but you never gave up, and now we finally won the Gold. This has been a great experience what you all have done, and I only wish the best for you, girls!" Coach Hector was actually smiling when he said that minispeech. "But, Coach, why did you walk out when the game was over before we had a minute left?" a girl asked. The others wondered about that too. "I had an emotional meltdown from certain problems. I really don't like to talk about that. Well, let's take our yearbook photos with the trophy!" Coach Hector cried. The girls were now investigating Coach Hector. What did he mean by "certain problems?" Was it because they had lost at first? Tough decision. The girls took their photos. Jill was holding the trophy, and Coach Hector was holding a certificate of excellence in a picture frame. They all looked wonderful together in the picture. Coach Hector did seem a bit drowsy. Terrible Tuesday, maybe. Or maybe it's something else. The problem was that the girls and photographers could see how Coach Hector was feeling. They couldn't understand why, though. They had just won an important game. Coach Hector had envisioned this practically most of his life. Now that they had won, he feels like this? There's no way! After the photos were taken, Coach Hector dismissed the girls to class. He had called Ginger to the gym office for a pass. Ginger waved to the girls who left and headed to the office. "Yes, Coach?" Ginger asked him. He was sitting in the chair, his face turned away. Luckily it was only them two. He slowly turned the chair around, with a mere look on his face. He looked distraught. "What's wrong?" she asked him, "you should be happy. We won the game! You've dreamed of this moment for years!" "I know. But there is something else." Coach Hector told her in a deep rather excruciating voice. "And why did you walk out before the end of the game?" Ginger wanted to know. "That locket you're wearing . . . ," he started again. Ginger became puzzled. Coach Hector was staring at the locket. Ginger was staring at him. "What about it . . . ?" She asked him. "Yesterday I stared in that window that those two mysterious teachers always look in . . . And I saw nothing at first. But then . . . I saw that locket of yours . . . And I saw it glowing . . ." Ginger was astonished beyond anything when she heard it. She felt her heart take a big thump. "What else did you see . . . ?" Ginger was actually amazed at this. "I then saw my dead relatives. And they were talking to me. Getting inside my head. They told me that a specific locket was the key between the life and death."

"You mean . . . . Reincarnation? . . ." Ginger asked. "Yes, that's it! They said that the evil souls upon the earth would take over, causing destruction, and for the restless to never be alive again.

They also mentioned that one girl with a specific locket, who was given the gift of a certain sport, held the locket between death and life. The locket that held goodness on this earth. I think they were talking about you. I believe your locket holds the good spirits from the bad ones. Without your locket, the evil souls would be released, and the world would be controlled by unclean souls and unrighteousness. Basically, without your locket, the world would end. All of the goodness would be cast out. We would all be dead. The evil souls would take over the world."

"How do you know it's me?" "There is more than just you. Ten, maybe. Here's what I suggest you do: keep your locket safe, and let it not get into the wrong hands. If it does, Reincarnation could never exist again, and the souls of evil or the devil's servants, would take over the world. Do you get what I'm saying? Reincarnation is at jeopardy! We may never see or communicate with the world again! The souls would be deadly! Everything is in the power of that locket. It is just a warning to you from the dead. Maybe that is why you were meant to change the world."

"Wait . . . So you communicated with the dead from a window . . . ? You're telling me this locket holds goodness to the world? And that I could change it and so-called 'Reincarnation?'" Ginger wouldn't believe it. Coach Hector nodded. "Hah! Yea right! All of that is a myth, Coach Hector. There's no way evil souls can take over the world. Plus Reincarnation has never happened before. I think the victory has gone to your head, Coach. Great story, though! Gotta go!" Ginger took the pass and zoomed out as the first bell rang. Coach Hector put his head down. He knew he was right. Only Ginger didn't believe. Now Reincarnation and the connection between the human flesh and soul really WAS at jeopardy! Ginger would believe soon enough, Coach Hector thought, *Just when the timing was right*. Loudness of cheers from the students and teachers roared as the volleyball girls walked to their classes. Todd was by Ginger's side all the way through first period. But Ginger couldn't help thinking: Was Coach Hector right? Did her locket really hold the secrets between life and death and the power of Reincarnation? Just the other day, Lanely Tildon was talking about the power of Reincarnation, and she even performed a Reincarnation Enchantment. Ginger was actually communicating with her parents that day. And now Coach Hector was talking about Reincarnation, the same thing Miss Tildon had been talking about. Was there some sort of connection? What is the Actual source? So many questions. Once again, no answer. Since there was a connection between what Lanely had been talking about, and from what Coach Hector had said about talking to his dead relatives through a window, Ginger knew he was telling the truth about that part. She wasn't so sure about the locket controlling goodness in this world. So she decided to go look in the window where the mysterious teachers always look. There was some sort of connection going on. When the halls were clear that morning, Ginger walked over to that little window where those teachers stand at. She saw nothing. Just the parking lot outside the school and the muddy field. After nearly a minute, she didn't see a field or a parking lot anymore. She saw an orange and light peach background, with winds the speed of a tornado hurling her way. Then from out of the ordinary, she saw a heart-shaped locket that was gold appear. That window DID symbolize something. It symbolized her own self in an unexpected way. Ginger heard footsteps from below, so she had to walk back to her class. As she was walking, the locket had glown. She couldn't believe it. The locket she saw in that picture WAS hers! How did the locket just glow like that, though? Incredible. That night there was a sign to Ginger. A sign that spirits would expose Ginger to the likelihood of the death. Her soul would have to face triumph to the one and only thing that keeps the soul separated from the world: fate. She would have to be immortal to her dignity. As time went by, she kept wondering why her locket glowed after she saw it in a window. Was that her locket? Or was it a fraud? It was hard to think when other kids bombarded her, wanting autographs and answers to dumb questions. Todd couldn't take his eyes off her the entire day. She was a little nervous about this date and about lying to her folks like that. They'd be pissed off to find out about what happened. All he was saying to Ginger was "Nice job!" or "You rocked the game last night." The study date would get even more interesting than ever before. Todd seemed like he wanted to talk about things or just talk in general. Ginger and Todd were on their way to the public library and they passed many high schoolers while trying to get there. "Whoa. Just seeing you strike the ball that day was amazing. I got to say, I'd be afraid to play you in volleyball. You have skills!" he assured her. "Haha! Very funny. I bet you have skills in kissing!" Ginger told him. "That I do. I've mastered that. Just for you!"

"Yea right!" Ginger teased. They held hands, and stepped inside the Main Branch Public Library. Books, books, and books. That's all there was. Except for a little children's sitting area and space for portable music. Ginger and Todd went in another section, one with desks and chairs. Luckily, there were no people or librarians around, so Ginger and Todd could have their own quiet time. "So are you loving the jacket?" Todd asked her. "Yea, of course! That was really sweet of you, Todd."

"Anytime. I'd do anything for you."

"You're just saying that . . . ," Ginger teased, as they both laughed. "Naah, not really. That's the point of boyfriend and girlfriend. They never let anyone down. Sorry that sounded gay, but . . . ," Todd laughed, "No, it didn't. It was . . . sweet. I don't see how others think you're a jerk. There's like this other side of you that no one knew about. To be honest I had the wrong impression," she admitted. "You did? I didn't know. Yea, it's weird. I guess it's because of my friends. They're the real jerks," Todd said, as they both giggled. Ginger flipped the book pages, as they began to study. Well, not study, but just talk. Ginger tucked her hair behind her, and Todd was just looking blissfully at her. All of a sudden, Todd's phone was ringing. A librarian was filing books and immediately saw them. "Shhhh!" she yelled, putting her finger to her mouth. "Sorry!" Todd whispered back, turning the sound off. He had gotten a text. Ginger just laughed at him. How clumsy could he be? "Forgot to turn it off . . . ," they both laughed when he said that. "Shhh!" the librarian urged. "Sorry!" They both just giggled. They were silent for about ten minutes trying to study and do some homework. It didn't take long to finish (she was giving him most of the answers, anyway!). They were almost finished when Todd tugged on her First Place Ribbon Award from the volleyball game. "You own at volleyball. I'm serious about that! You sent Mandy and the other team packin'! She'll never mess with you again!" he bragged. "Hah, I know we killed everyone! Now that Bitch of Bitcharia will never bother me!" Ginger cried. "Whoa. Language. Bad!"

"Don't care. Mandy makes me mad."

"All right, chill." He put his arms around her. They just laughed and sighed for a period of time then got back to work. "Where did you get that locket?" Todd asked. Ginger looked at him, not for using on the textbook. "I already told you. My great-great-great grandfather from Poland gave it to my mom, who gave it to me," Ginger told him. "Oh yea. You know, you're always talking about your grandparents, but never your parents." Ginger nearly choked when she heard that. "What happened to them?" he asked. Ginger sighed and turned toward him. "I don't like to talk about it, but when I was six years old, my father got in a car accident and died. When I was eight, my mother died of breast cancer. Now, I can never be the same again." A restless tear came down her face. "Is that why you're so shy? Because your parents died?" he asked her in a soft tone. "Yea," she shook her head. "I'm really sorry. I had no clue. Are you gonna be okay?" he asked her. "Yea. I'll be fine."

"Cool. I really am sorry, though. Having no parents must really suck." They both hugged each other. Todd was twiddling with her locket, and they hugged some more. "You've been through a lot. I don't wanna see you suffer."

"I'm not suffering."

"In your heart, you are. I can tell. There's nothing wrong with that." Todd cuddled her, making her feel a lot better. "How did you know I was feeling that way?"

"Because. Everyday I see you, I look in your eyes. And I see that you are hurt by a lot of things. Not to sound lame or anything . . ."

"No, it's not lame," Ginger took his hand, "It's the truth." Ginger kissed him on the cheek. There was that big red kissy mark on Todd's face. "I'm glad I met you, Todd. There's no one I can talk to. Until I saw you."

"I'm glad too, Ginger. You made me realize myself in a way I never knew about." He tucked her hair a little. "And that's what I love about you."

"Some people are just so scared to talk about things. Especially personal things. I never knew Stephanie's father had cancer (and survived) until we broke up. Don't tell her I said that. She'll freak!" Todd cried. "Wow. That's . . . sad," Ginger responded. "I know. I'm glad you told me something sad like that. Now I can trust you more." Ginger looked dead straight into his eyes. "I don't see how people can forgive and forget certain things. It's so hard to see not having parents, or having a grandmother surviving the Holocaust, or a grandfather surviving a war."

"Which war?" Todd was interested.

"Vietnam."

"Wow that's awesome! It's too bad he hates me! And your grandmother. I would've never guessed she survived the Holocaust. Your family is like historical!" he complimented. "Yea. Now I have to get my grandfather to trust you. He doesn't want me to suffer, which I feel is not true. He just doesn't believe me, which is just wrong." "Don't worry, Ginger. He hasn't met me either. He probably thinks I'm some stalker or something," Todd laughed. Ginger laughed as well. "I'll 'sweet talk' him. You know, I lied and told him I was coming here to study with friends."

"You would lie for me?"

"I had no choice. It's like he doesn't want me with you."

"That's understandable. He's just too cautious, that's all. Parents and grandparents are always like that. But now he'll just have to trust you. If we trust each other, he'll have to trust us," Todd cried, wrapping his arms around Ginger. "Well, this was really fun. Too bad you didn't get a lot of studying in," Ginger teased, as they both laughed. "I had a great time. Just the two of us. Wow. It's already four. Time does go by fast." Ginger was gathering her books and helping Todd gather his belongings. "You seem like you got over your parents. Moving on is hard, you know . . . ," Todd cried. "Not really. I still feel terrible, but you know . . . I have to move on."

"Exactly. It still has to be hard with no parents. Not to be subtle, but yea. It's too bad they can't come back."

"I know. But when a door closes, another one opens. Like when I met you." She kissed him on the lips, and took off her pink ribbon from her hair. Todd could only smile at her. Just talking about her parents did make her sad all over again. Especially thinking about her mother's first surgery half of a decade ago or so. She was lying down in tainted covers. The doctor had just come in. Ginger stood right next to her side. The side where she had almost no hair. Grammy and Pappy were sitting down. "We will proceed with the surgery. We will remove most of the tumor if we can, and then perform immunotherapy. Have you been taking your medicine?" the doctor asked. "Which ones?" Mother asked. "The chemotherapy medication." "Oh yes. It hasn't helped, though."

"It will take some time. Just be patient with us, please. I'll be back so we can start the procedure."

"How long will it take?" Pappy asked.

"About ten hours. This will be no easy task," the doctor explained. "That long? Oh gosh!" Pappy yelled. "I will be back soon. You will be fine." The doctor leaves. As if the doctor doesn't even get what's going to happen to her. Mother looked frustrated. "I don't wanna do it. I can't do this! First surgeries are always the worst!" Mother cried in draught. "Don't worry, darling. This will help you," Grammy reminded her. "I can't. I'm too weak. I'd rather die at home."

"Your home is about to be foreclosed! Yer lucky yer late husband's health insurance covered for the treatment!" Pappy reminded her. "Mom, Dad. I'm scared. I don't know what to do." Ginger only looked at her, and saw a fearful spirit that day. "Mommy."

"What is it, dear?" Mother asked. Ginger grabbed her hand in despair. "I know it's tough. But now you have to be strong. Like you always do when we play volleyball. Or when I race Shelby. We never give up, remember? You can do it." Mother started tearing up. She was just so proud of her daughter and what she had taught her. "You're gonna go through the treatment, and when you are better, we can play volleyball again. And we will stay here to support you."

"We will?" Pappy asked. "Yes, Pappy!" Grammy bellowed with anger. Ginger's Mother had the strength to hug her and Pappy and Grammy. "And tell your uncle he'd better come too," Mother joked, as they laughed. Then, the doctor returned with some other doctors perhaps. "Well, we are ready to begin. Let's strap her in and take her to the machine." The doctors were already strapping her in when she said. "What's gonna happen to my daughter?" The doctor gleamed at her, then at Ginger. "The St. Epiphany Hospital Team has nothing to do with that. I'd advice you call her doctor or talk to your parents, Madame. Now, let's begin." The strapping was complete. Mother had to take off her locket. She handed it to Ginger and said, "Take good care of this. If anything goes wrong, it will be in the right hands. Hold on to this locket. I will be back for it." That's when they wheeled her mother away. Right to her own death. Ginger took a look at her mother as she and the doctors have left the room. Ginger closed her eyes, and then they were gone. She'd never told her mother anything like that. Unfortunately, that would be the last time she ever said something so fragile to her mother which meant a lot. For all that remains is a locket untold . . . until today. Until Reincarnation has triumphed the evil spirit. For now, anyway . . . Todd helped Ginger pack her backpack with books. "So do you want me to walk you home, or is that a bad idea?" he asked. "You know, I don't care what my grandfather has to say. Of course you can walk me home."

"Cool. Wow, you don't even give a crap what your grandfather says," Todd laughed. Ginger didn't find it so funny. "I guess not. I wish he wasn't so cautious." Todd tickled her sides, startling her. "Maybe that's why," he joked. "Whatever! Come on, let's go before they get mad," Ginger cried. They gathered their things and left the library. She was glad to have a guy like Todd, though. Now she can open up and talk, instead of being so 'isolated.' You can insert your own definition of that here. How could Ginger tell Pappy about him, though? Last time he got so mad at her! He may forbid him and her from the house if she's not careful. There had to be some clear explanation. Is she too young? Does he want her to wait awhile? Or does he hate Todd Wyndelle for no apparent reason at all? Ginger thought this to herself as they walked all the way back to her house from the library. They were two blocks away from her home when Ginger stopped him and her own self. "Todd, maybe this is a bad idea. You know how my grandfather was last time. He probably has binoculars to 'spy' on me. Maybe we should stop here . . . ," Ginger cried anxiously. "Are you joking? Trust me, I can handle it," he insisted. "But I don't want you getting yelled at. Come on, Todd. I'll walk you home this time." Todd took her hands for relief, and looked down at her.

"Calm down. It's not that bad. If he has a problem with me, he should just tell me, instead of being a jerk about it. He's probably too cautious like everyone else." Todd started walking again. Ginger stopped him yet again. "Don't worry, Ginger. He'll get over it," he insisted, beckoning her to keep going. She doubtfully took his hand, and they kept walking to the house. Luckily they talked on their way, so that eased her anxiety. Time did not. In the meantime, Ginger checked her cell phone. 4:58 p.m. Yikes! She was supposed to be back half an hour ago! *Pappy's definitely gonna be pissed off now*, Ginger thought to herself. Pappy used his war-like binoculars device to spot anyone from the front window. Grammy approached him in an unpleasant mood. "What on earth are you doing?" she asked him. "What does it look like I'm doin'? That girl was supposed to be back over half an hour ago! It's time to scout out!" Pappy stared gruesome at the window, watching . . . waiting . . ."Pappy, you are NOT in the military anymore. Why don't you trust your granddaughter with another guy? He didn't seem bad to me," Grammy opposed. "Half an hour, Marybeth! I don't think so! She doesn't call, she doesn't talk? How we suppose to know anything? Exactly mah point! Who knows where she is! That girl gotta know her limits!"

"Pappy, she'll be fine. That's what teens do, hun!" Grammy cried. "I already lost a daughter!" Pappy croaked. "I'm NOT losin' another one! Not this one, dear. The curse is already nay!" Pappy explained. Ginger approached the house with Todd. They both took a deep breath. Ginger could already tell he was waiting at the door or window with his "Vietnam War Binoculars." "Now he was in the military, you know. He may go crazy, but oh well," Ginger cried. They grasped hands. Ready to face the truth and the humble. They rang the doorbell, waiting on the footstep. Then the door opened. Sure enough, it was Pappy. He started going ballistic. Todd could only watch. His face was red and angry. He was only doing this to himself. Grammy and Uncle came rushing down, thinking he had some heart attack or something. "You lied to me, Ginger McFraiddee! And you were supposed to be back thirty-five minutes ago! I was worried sick!" he yelled. "I knew you'd say no if I told you the truth," Ginger commented. "And this makes me even MORE furious!" Pappy yelled. "Wait. So you didn't go with friends?" Grammy asked. Ginger waved her head left and right very ashamed. "And what do you have to say about this?" Pappy asked when Uncle went back upstairs. Ginger and Todd were cuddled up, his arms around her shoulders and golden hair. "And why are ya touchin' mah granddaughter! Get'chor hands off her now!" he screamed at Todd. But they didn't budge. Pappy couldn't believe how disrespected he has been treated. He was so mad, he just didn't know what to do. "Why do you have a problem with me?" Todd asked. "Yea. Pappy, he hasn't done anything," Ginger budded in. "I'm sorry about making her late. I really am. You can trust me. I swear," Todd admitted. "It's not that. You lied to me, honey." Grammy went back in another room. "You would never listen. You never cared, either," she cried, and gave Todd a hug. "You won your Tournament. Of course 'ay care!"

"Then why don't you give me a chance?" Todd asked. Pappy couldn't even answer that question. It was just a slap in the face.

His wrath was the one that attacked him. Todd could only stare at the man, knowing that his girlfriend's grandfather had lost. He had won. Pappy sighed in relief. "If that's yur choice, fine. If yous wanna go with that scumbag, fine! That's wut he is, anyway!" Pappy yelled. "I'm the scumbag?" Todd was shocked. Pappy shouldn't be talking. But evilness always comes back in return Pappy felt it, and immediately ran upstairs. "Marybeth, get me mah medicin'!" he yelled, stomping away. "Todd, I'm so sorry about that, really I am," she confessed. "It's okay. No one can come between us." He grabbed her hand, and once again, slowly they kissed each other on the lips. Ginger's blue eyes glowed in the meadow, simmering through the light. Love transformed the shadow of the dawn. She had never in her life felt this way. Her misery had been lifted up and taken away. They kissed much longer than the first time. On that same footstep, they had stopped when Uncle approached from downstairs, "I still didn't see what his problem was," Ginger commented. "No clue, either. Well, I guess I better go, before he comes back," Todd laughed, kissing her on the cheek. "See ya. You can text me."

"I will." Ginger blew him a kiss, and closed the door as he left. Uncle approached her. "Oh, what did I do now?" Ginger mumbled. "Nothin'. You might have given Pappy a heart attack, but oh well!" he joked, as they both sat down in the living room. "I still don't know why Pappy doesn't like Todd. And he won't tell me anything. He calls him all those mean names and everything!" Ginger had no clue whatsoever. "It's not that he doesn't like the guy. He's just paranoid, that's all. He was the same way when your mother met your father. I'll never forget the day he told both of them to get out. He only wanted what was best for his only daughter. Since your mother passed, he couldn't relate to his 'little girl' having a boyfriend. It will just take time for him to adjust," Uncle explained. "I should've thought about that, huh? I feel terrible, now." "It's not just your fault. He shouldn't have taken all of his anger toward that guy. He knows he was wrong for doing that. Grammy and I are already telling him."

"Well that's good. I just want peace."

"Us too. Sometimes Pappy is 'too protective,'" Uncle laughed, Ginger laughing too, "but he is just scared. He doesn't know what the guy is."

"His name is Todd."

"Well he doesn't know who Todd is. Your Pappy will be fine. I've known him too long, now. Did you do your homework, dear?"

"Yea, I finished it all at the library."

"Good. Why don't you wash up? Dinner will be ready soon!"

"Okay!" Ginger and Uncle arose, walking their separate ways. In her room, she couldn't help thinking about if Pappy's actions were right, or if her own mind would set her free. What comes from the heart is a mind that will never develop. What could that possibly mean? Ginger too was trying to ponder that extravagant idea.

CHAPTER 19

Carnivorous and Carny Carnival

Ginger forgot all about Pappy's wrath yesterday afternoon. Cheers floated everywhere from the school. This eighth-grade class would be a living legacy. Ginger McFraiddee was proud to be the leader of this great legacy. Too bad Stephanie and her pitiful friends couldn't stop taking about it. "That amazing toss was awesome!" Nick yelled. "I know! And then the ball went bam! Right to the ground!" She responded. "You mean spike . . ." Melissa corrected Nick, as the girls laughed. "I'm just glad it's over," Ginger cried, as the girls, Nick, and Joe laughed. "But did you see the way Vanessa was cheering for MMS?" Rachael asked. "Yea. That girl is such a slut. She shouldn't have came here in the first place," Stephanie cried. "Remember the party?! Oh that was hilarious! High-five, Ginger!" Amy said, giving her a high five. "That was funny. Mandy and Vanessa were screaming their asses off!" Joe cried. "Too bad they left early," Nick added. "Those girls will never show their faces around here again!" Ginger cried, as they all gave each other a high five. Then Todd came to sit over. The party's over. Or has it just begun? The girls, except for Ginger, weren't too amused to see him. "Hey, Todd," Ginger greeted. "Hey, Ginger. Hey, guys."

"Hi, Todd," they greeted. Ginger made room for him to sit next to her. The only problem was that he was sitting next to his current girlfriend, and his ex-girlfriend Stephanie. "Geez. There's no space for you . . . ," Stephanie complained. "Yea there is. And that's what she said!" Todd cried. Nick and Joe thought it was funny and laughed their heads off. "Hah that's a good one!" Nick joked, giving him a high five. "You're lucky you're hot. Or else you'd have to leave . . . ," Stephanie cried. "Mmhmm," Amy agreed. "Amy . . . ," Rachael cried. "What . . . ?" she wondered. "El desperato much?" Rachael replied. "Hey, he is! Just admit it."

"Please . . . I'm not that desperate!" Melissa said. "You'd let me stay, anyway. You love me too much," Todd cried. "Hah, yea right. So, Ginger, how was the kiss . . . ?" Stephanie just had to know. The entire table "oooeeeuuued." Todd looked at her. "It was fine. It's just a kiss."

"JUST a kiss? Ginger, I thought you loved me," he told her. "Oh, I do. Nothin' serious, though." "I felt the same way, Ginger. No offense, Todd," Stephanie admitted. "Oh, none taken," he replied. "I would love to see you two kiss again," Joe joked. Too bad nobody saw that as a joke. Not even Nick. "Joe, he's my ex. And why would you say that in front of his girlfriend?" Stephanie asked. "Hey, it's just a question."

"A very terrible one . . . ," Melissa cried, munching on a half-ripe apple. "Let's see Ginger and Todd kiss, then! Since they already done it!" Nick said. *That dumb ass!* Ginger thought to herself. Next thing you know, the entire table and the table with Todd's friends went: "Yea!" Todd looked like he wanted to embrace at that very second. They leaned in, forgetting everything else, and kissed on the lips for a fair amount of time. For the first time in her life, Ginger actually felt a sense of love in her heart. She has never felt this from Bailey. There was something different about Todd; something that made them two right for each other, and that something is true love. Or so it could be. Everybody around them were being all immature, and whistling, and making crude remarks. Todd and Ginger didn't care, however. "You guys really ARE perfect for each other! The star volleyball player and the star football and basketball player. That is just so sweet!" Stephanie cried. Ginger and Todd just smiled in agreement. "I think I'm gonna cry!" Amy got all dramatic again. Everyone rolled their eyes at that, and then Luna came over to the table. "So what's all the commotion?" Luna just had to know. "Todd and Ginger, that's what. They just kissed each other. On the lips!" Rachael answered. Luna and the guys at Todd's table (his friends) gasped. "Oh, Luna, you don't have to be shocked," Todd told her. "I am, though! You guys make a great couple, to be honest!" Luna cried. "Thanks. Stephanie said that too," Ginger replied. "Great minds think alike!" Stephanie said, as her and Luna tapped their hands with their finger, pointing out her saying. "Great minds? Hah! No offense, but Stephanie's a dumb . . . ," Nick started. The girls gasped way too loud for him to even finish! "And Luna has the brain of a . . . ," Joe replied, the girls only gasping more making the guys chuckle. "That wasn't funny . . . ," Stephanie commented. "It was hilarious," Todd responded, high fiving Nick and Joe. "Joe, I can't believe you! I'll have you know I'm smarter than you! Right?" Luna begged to differ. All of the guys and girls at the table went "Naah" or "Uhh, umm, nooo," or just flat out shook their head no. Luna gasped and took a seat at the table, as if it already weren't congested enough. "Nick, I'm so mad at you, right now. Don't even talk to me!" Stephanie told him. She pouted. "Come on, Steph," he pleaded. "Are you serious? You just insulted her, and now you beg for her forgiveness? Get a brain!" Rachael commented. "Shut up, Rachael! And you can't talk about getting a brain either!" Todd said, as the others laughed. "Hey, don't talk to her like that! And since when was your dumbass smart in the first place?" Stephanie had a comeback. "Hey, hey, gentlemen. Break it up!" Malcolm came over to joke, as the others laughed. He gave Todd a high five too. "Seriously leave!" Melissa cried. "It was just a joke, Melissa. Calm down!" Joe warned her. "I don't care. I'm getting pissed right now."

"Chill . . . ," Nick warned. Stephanie, Luna, and the rest of the girls gave him a glare. "The smartest girl out of all of you is Ginger, to be honest. She Ace's like, every test," Joe cried. "Well, not every . . . how did you know that?" Ginger quickly asked him. "Because Joe is THE ultimate stalker in the school," Todd joked, cuddling Ginger. "So when's the big volleyball party?" Stephanie asked, popping chips in her mouth. "Coach

Hector didn't tell us, yet," Ginger replied. "It should be a lot of fun. Our cheerleading party was the best!" Amy said. "Except for when we had to turn in our uniforms. That was really sad," Luna admitted, as the girls moaned a little. "I can't wait for cheerleading to begin. Maybe we'll keep our uniforms (if we got to keep the pompoms)," Amy said. "I can't, either. Girls in short skirts . . . ," Joe began. "You perv!" Melissa said. "What? It's the truth!" "Those skirts aren't even that short. They come up to my knees. It's so stupid because the coach says we can't have them shorter because of 'Dress Code.' I mean who gives a damn . . . ," Stephanie complained. Stephanie was the leader of the cheerleading squad. Her friends were on the team as well (basically, cheerleading is the only sport those girls can play). "That sucks. Now we can't look at girl's . . . ," Nick started. Silence. "You bitch!" Rachael yelled, "Cheerleading isn't about that, retard! It's a sport . . ." "Whatever. Girls still look hot playing it," Todd budded in. "I'd love to see you do a back flip with pompoms, Todd," Rachael said. Everyone laughed at that. "I'd love to see you be QB in an all-guy tackle team," he defended, but only Nick and Joe laughed. Todd wrapped his arms around his girlfriend, and she cuddled in with him. Too bad there was hardly any space to move around, let alone space to eat. "Ginger, do you really like a guy like Todd . . . ? He's a jerk . . . ," Melissa cried. "Him, and his best friend Malcolm," Amy added. "Shut up!" everyone told Amy. "What the hell was that for? Some of you are still single, so I wouldn't be talking . . . And by the way, if you did NOT go out with the guy, don't say a word."

"Anyway . . . ," Luna commented. "Of course I like him. Why else would I be going out with him?" Ginger said. Yea, so back off," Todd kissed her on the forehead. "Hey, I'm just sayin'. Us girls need to stick together forever!" Melissa said. "Ignore her. She's just desperate," Todd cried. Ginger smiled and looked up at him to his shiny blue eyes. Todd smiled too, making Stephanie smile as well. She was probably smiling because Ginger was. "The best couple of the year definitely goes to them two," Luna admitted. "Are you kidding me? It goes to me and Shandi!" Malcolm budded in. "Really? Then where is she?" Melissa asked. "Absent?" he replied. "Stalker!" Amy yelled. "Okay, Amy . . . ," Malcolm cried, sitting back down at the other table. "It's definitely us two," Todd concluded, embracing with her. "Indeed. Now smile for the yearbook!" Luna cried, taking a pic of them two with her phone. "AKA her MySpace page . . . ," Rachael said. "Pssh. Yea right!" Luna protested. "You took the picture with your cell phone. Of course it's for MySpace! And since when were you in the Yearbook Club?" Rachael came back at her. "Since . . . today!" Luna answered, everyone laughing. Ginger kissed Todd on the cheek. You could even see the kissy mark on his face. Suddenly he knew: She was THE one he was looking for all along. After school that day, Todd had surprised Ginger with some sort of flier. "It's for the carnival this Saturday. My friends are comin'. Do you wanna come?" he asked her, showing her the flier. "Sure, I'll come," Ginger answered, tucking in her basketball jacket. "You didn't wash it yet, did you?" he asked her. "Nope. I sometimes spray it, though."

"Hah. That jacket means the world to me. Because the person who's wearing it does as well," Todd confessed. "Aww Todd that's so sweet. Knowing you actually mean it really does say a lot and mean a lot," Ginger smiled. "Of course I mean it. I couldn't lie," Todd cried. Or could he? "So I'll see ya at the carnival Saturday. I'll text ya. Later," Todd called, walking toward his friends. "Bye, Todd," his girlfriend yelled back. How could Ginger ever mention this to Pappy? He'd be so shunned to hear her tell him that. Grammy's heart would transform into melted snow. Uncle wouldn't bear to hear any of it. Their little girl ain't little anymore. But wait. That's what Ginger did on her way home. What would her parents say? Seeing their own child growing up would be too much of a train wreck for them. A train wreck, heading beyond the wall of life. What would her father say to his only daughter? He can't push her on the swing, or kiss her on the forehead multiple times now. And how would Mother feel? The day she lay on the couch with Shelby in her arms was when Ginger, only eight, knew her mother wasn't ready for her daughter to have a cervical cancer screening, to talk about the pill, or to not even think about a period, more so an orgasm. The cancer only worsened when she lay on the couch, Shelby barking all over the place. Ginger rushed in with a volleyball in her hands. "Mommy, Mommy! Let's play!" Ginger said, tossing it up and down, giving her mother a headache. "I'm sorry, Ginger. Mommy is just too tired," Mother cried. "Still thinking about Daddy?" Shelby barked after Ginger said that. "Of course, hun. But he's in a better place now. And he's watching over us."

"I miss him."

"Me too, sweetie."

"Mommy, when will I ever get my period?"

"When you're old enough and ready."

"But I'm ready now!"

"I know, darling. But like Pappy always says: 'It's good to stay young and die old.' Stay a child while you can. Good things will happen."

"Mommy, is your cancer getting better?"

"Yes it is. Everyday I view the imagery life's got to offer. I don't smoke. I don't drink. Honey, I know times may be tough, but you're strong. We're strong! And I know when you cross that stage completin' eighth grade, Ima be cryin' so hard, 'cause you're movin' on. No parent ever wants to see their child grow up. I know one of these days Ima have to. It may hurt, but . . . I ma have to deal with it . . ." Mother started crying. "Mommy, it's okay. I'll grow up when I'm ready."

"No, Ginger. The time is now. Everything is NOW!" She was wiping off tears on her face. "You gonna grow up to be a strong young lady, you hear me? Don't let no one tell you, you can't do somethin.' Yes, you can. You are way better than anyone, at anything you put your mind to. Growing up will come in time. But for me just to see you Graduate will mean the world to me. Knowing that my daughter accomplished a goal, and me being there to see it. When you make the volleyball team, I'll be in the stance, cheering you on. I am your number two fan."

"Who's my number-one fan then?"

"You are, Ginger," Mother cried, pointing at her. "You have to be a fan of yourself and cheer you on before anyone else can. Believe me, you will go in time. Time is only a burden by the human blood." Shelby licked both of their faces, making them laugh. "Thanks, Mommy!" Ginger gave her mother a hug, as she tugged her daughter's hair. "Let's get some food!" Ginger suggested. Her mother's voice was numb the entire time that day. It does pain Ginger that her mother or father aren't in the stance cheering her on, or will not be able to see her walk across the stage to get her diploma. Yet, they in fact ARE watching her, through their mind. Their souls can see Ginger from the stance, and they can see her graduating. Through the Spirit Transporter . . . Perhaps that is why Lanely Tildon wants her to fully understand the concept of Reincarnation. So then Ginger can read and see the lives of the living dead. Interesting, if you think about it. Very, very interesting . . . . Ginger arrived home, slouching as she dumped her schoolbag to the ground. It smelled like Grammy had already been started cooking. "So how was school, hun?" Grammy asked, with her cooking apron on. "It was good. Mmm something smells good."

"I'm glad you like it. It's a surprise," Grammy sounded excited. She went back into the kitchen. Ginger, tired and exhausted, decided not to tell Pappy about the big news. He had been in a bad mood all week because of the situation, and telling him wouldn't make it any better at all. Pappy staggered into the kitchen next to where Grammy was standing at. "Oh mah foot! It hurts!" he grunted. "I already gave you two baths and a foot massage.

What more could you possibly need?" Uncle complained. "My rubber ducky," Pappy smiled. Uncle rolled his eyes, and helped the old man to the bathroom. Ginger sat at the table, watching her Grandmother cook. "So how's life?" Grammy asked. "It's goin' great! Todd and I are really becomin' . . . well . . . great!" Ginger said. "Glad to hear. Any plans this weekend?" Grammy asked. "Nope, none at all," Ginger lied. "Oh good, I was hoping you'd say that. Some of our friends are comin' over to play bingo and have tea this Saturday night. It's gonna be fun, and I'm sure we'd love to have you there," Grammy offered. "Oh . . . well um' . . . that sounds . . ."

"You don't have to participate if you don't want to. Pappy and Uncle won't, it's only ladies."

"I'll see later on if I have anything planned," she suggested. "Good idea, hun! Dinner'll be ready in a jif!" Ginger quickly darted to her room, and pounced on the bed nearly crushing it, grabbing for her cell phone. "Hello?" Todd answered. "Hey, Todd." "'Sup, Ginger."

"My grandma's having some gathering that night. But I really wanna go." "That's all right. We can go during another time."

"It comes once a year, though. I wish you could sweet talk my family."

"Yea, me too."

"Wait! I can, though! She'll suck up to anything."

"Cool. As long as I don't have to deal with your grandfather." They both laughed. "Thanks, I'll see ya tomorrow."

"Later, cutie." Ginger tried as hard as she could to make her eyes watery. It's a good thing Grammy was gullible and could buy a sob story. Pappy was different, however. He and Uncle knew if you were lying. But maybe today would be different. Grammy was still chopping up vegetables and frying up a pot when Ginger arrived back in the kitchen. "So you can make it, right?" she immediately asks, almost forgetting about the cooking. Ginger made some what of a sad face, and then said, "No Grammy, I can't. My friends invited me for a sleepover. I'm really sorry." "That's all right, pumpkin. We can have it another time. I was really looking forward to it, but oh well." Ginger walked out, feeling "guilty." Then all of a sudden Ginger was happy, again. Now she would be going on yet another date (a group date in this case) with Todd Wyndelle, her charming boyfriend. And Pappy has no clue! Still, it was wrong of her to break her grandmother's heart like that, choose a guy over family, and to lie about it. Ginger didn't care. She wanted to be with Todd, she's growing up now; she is no longer a little girl with the young. The words "young" and "youth" do make but a huge difference. (Yes, it's very well the changing of two consonants). Ginger and Todd kept calling each other and were talking all the time through the phone. She tried everything she could not to let Pappy see her talking with him. It was like your normal "Romeo and Juliet." Only this time, the "evil" grandfather took the place of the father. When he did see Ginger on the phone with Todd, he immediately made her hang up the phone. He ordered Uncle to do the same, but Uncle was more lenient about it. Grammy really couldn't do anything, either. She could try to talk, but that would make things a little more complicated than it already is. None of that stopped their current relationship, however. They even met up Friday to even talk more. No friends, however. It was a blooming relationship. They were inseparable being together. Pappy was only getting madder and madder and madder. He couldn't see his own Granddaughter with another guy. It made him cry 'til he was blue in the face knowing he was the father in Romeo and Juliet. But he couldn't help it. That was just him. His only granddaughter was growing up into a young lady just like his late daughter. Maybe she has taught him a little lesson. A lesson about love, in a diverse manner. Saturday came, and Todd was waiting at his home. "Okay, I'm going to hang out with my friends. Bye!" Ginger cried, putting on a jacket, and adjusting a pink ribbon in her hair. "Okay, have fun, Ginga," Grammy cried, setting up saucers on the table of delight roses. She was dressed up well in a white dress with shiny church-like shoes. "Have fun at the tea party. Sorry, I couldn't make it. I'll try to come next time! Bye!" Ginger cried. "Thank you, and that is all right, dear. Have a great time!" Grammy waved as Ginger slammed the door behind her. Todd anxiously waited at his home. That's when Malcolm and Andy came approaching him. "'Sup dude," Malcolm cried, as they high-fived. "Wassup," Todd said. "Dude, this is gonna be sweet. I invited Shandi to come too," Malcolm started. "Why?" Andy asked. "'Cause she wanted to. And we're goin' out." "Malcolm's in love. Haha," Todd joked, giving Andy a high five as they laughed. "Hey, shut up! You love Ginger, and you know it, dude."

"She could be the one, though. I never actually met a girl like her. That's why I'm so attracted to her, man. I don't know how to explain it. I can just feel it," Todd admitted. So he *was* searching for the truth! "I say the same about Shandi. If only she didn't talk so much," Malcolm cried. "But dude Todd, are you serious? Do you think she's actually THE one?" Andy asked him. "I don't know, dude. I never felt this way before. Maybe she is." Personality. Does Todd actually like her for who she is? Or is it all a horrid scam? Having a true personality with one another does destroy the evil parts of love. Caring for someone genuinely really does matter. He has these feelings for her. Feelings he never had before. Whenever Todd even looks at her, all he keeps thinking about is what she liked, how she viewed herself, and how she carried herself with half of a full heart. Todd knows she has been through a lot. But isn't that what love is about? Developing that sense of character and just by talking. Getting to know that male or female, who could someday be your husband or wife. That's what life is all about. Loving a person has never been better. And it all starts by personality. Maybe Todd doesn't feel that way. He could be getting mixed signals. Or he is just being love struck, which is very normal at his age. Very hard to comprehend it also. The sun was reaching below the horizon. The carnival would begin any moment, now. "Man, where is she?" Malcolm asked. "She's coming. I just texted her," Todd answered, slipping his phone in his pocket. "Cool. Shandi's probably mad. I told her we'd meet her there," Malcolm said. "Why? She could've come here too," Andy cried. "Too late, now." Sunlight was beaming in his eye when she approached. Behold, she had arrived, and she was looking better than ever. Her jacket worn over her other one was the one she'd received from her own boyfriend. "Hey, Ginger," Todd greeted. She climbed the steps and laid in his arms. "Hey," she responded. Andy broke the hugging moment by saying: "No, heys for us?" he was offended. Ginger turned around as she and Todd laughed. "Hey, you guys," she smiled, hugging them. "You look beautiful," Todd cried, almost intimidated. Notice how he didn't say hot this time. "Aww, thank you. You look beautiful too," Ginger joked. They all chuckled. "Well, let's go! Some other guys are meeting us there," Malcolm cried, as they started heading off. Todd had his arms around Ginger the entire time. The carnival wasn't that far away. It was a good walk, especially on a calm night. "Man, I'm starvin'," Andy announced, texting away on his phone. "You always are, dude," Malcolm teased. "You're not nervous, are you?" Todd asked, trying to be a man. "No. It's just a carnival. When you're on my side, I'm never nervous," Ginger cried, as they took a pause to embrace the moment. "Guys, come on. The carnival's right there!" Andy pointed to the carnival sign. "Okay, we're comin'. Chill," Todd announced, as they darted for the carnival. Jason, Hillary, Luna, and Shandi were waiting at the front of the entrance. "Wassup, guys," Todd greeted. "'Sup," Jason cried, high fiving the guys. "Lookin' good, Ginger," he added, giving her a friendly hug. "You guys are late. I was worried sick!" Hillary cried.

"Calm down. Hillary," Luna said. "Hey, cutie," Malcolm said to Shandi. "No, you're cute," she budged. "No way, you are."

"No, you are." Then they embraced with each other. "So where's Steph and her friends?" Andy wondered. "Main Street. They didn't wanna come," Luna answered. "Ginger. I love your ribbon it's so cute!" Hillary cried. "Thanks. Your shoes are too," Ginger replied. For a while the girls talked with the girls, and the guys talked with the guys. By dusk, they were in the carnival walking around. There were many rides, tons of food, and lots of prizes to win. There were a bunch of people too. You could easily get lost. Luckily those eight were in a group. At this point, they were with their couple (Ginger with Todd, Malcolm with Shandi, and Jason with Hillary. Andy and Luna were the only two with no date). Ginger, Todd, Hillary, and Jason walked arm to arm with one another, and Andy, Luna, Malcolm, and Shandi were right behind them, walking together in arms. "What should we do first?" Todd asked. "I dunno. Let's get some food. I'm hungry," Shandi suggested, everyone agreeing with her. They all got cotton candy and some other sweet treats. Todd gave most of his to Ginger. There were many lights and lots of things to do. The guys played some of the games and won prizes for the girls. Todd won Ginger a white bear that was holding a heart that had the word 'love' on it, and he won her a teddy bear that was soft and fluffy. Hillary couldn't stop looking at Jason. Malcolm barely grasped his hands away from Shandi. This was the real feeling of dating: being with someone you can talk to. Being with someone you love. Finally, Ginger and Todd got some alone time when they stopped for more food. Not much (they were still with other people), but enough. "Here's a question: Why doesn't your grandfather want us to be together? Can't he accept the fact were goin' out now?" Todd wondered. "I guess not. I don't know, to be honest. He's just paranoid, that's all. I just hate hiding it," Ginger admitted. "I know. I know. He'll get over it, I promise."

"You think so?"

"Yea."

"He just doesn't want to see me hurt again. Like me and Bailey."

"You really hate Bailey, don't you?"

"Yea, I do. Well extremely dislike."

"Yea, I understand."

"Todd, thanks so much for the gifts. I love 'em."

"No problem." Ginger snuggled the gifts with him as they laughed. Todd immediately realized her blue eyes spark in the midst of everything. That's when Ginger saw something strange. The carnival was no longer a carnival. It was hell. There was fire everywhere and souls or ghosts or whatever were being shredded in the flames. The souls were flying, going one way and another. It's just like that image she saw while looking at that window back the school. Only this time there were souls flying around, burning their own kind. All she could hear were screams. And she couldn't see herself in any of the images he had. After about a minute, she finally snapped out of it and blinked many times. "Are you okay?" Todd asked. "Yea, I'm fine. Just a thought."

"Oh, I know what you mean. I daydream all the time. Once I thought I was a zombie, I literally lifted my parents from their beds and carried them down the stairs; it was weird!" Todd joked, as he and Ginger laughed while sharing a milkshake together. "Yea, me too. It makes me do weird stuff," Ginger teased. What Ginger saw WASN'T a joke, however. How could that image contract? Up in her head? Could it be some sort of message? Ginger had no clue, but today, she wanted to enjoy herself. She was with her boyfriend and her friends, and they were having a good time. "You guys, let's get on the Ferris wheel!" Luna suggested. "Wow, Luna . . . ," Malcolm responded. "I think it's pretty romantic," Shandi butted in. Shandi looked at him and grabbed his hand. "To the Ferris wheel then!" Malcolm yelled, as they got up from the table to start walking again. "At least we got some time to talk," Todd cried, making Ginger laugh. The line wasn't long and not many people were on the Ferris wheel compared to earlier. "Luna, why'd you choose the baby ride . . . ?" Hillary asked her. "Hillary, you were scared to get on the merry-go-round, so shut up!" Andy answered for Luna. "Hey, hey, dude. You shut up! Maybe she wanted to be with her guy instead of riding a silly ride," Jason replied, he putting his arms around her waste, "Yea, so back off!"

"Okay, dude," Andy cried. "Naah I'm jokin'," Jason said, as they both high-fived. The line was fairly a long time, however. "OMG, I'm so scared! Will you protect me?" Hillary asked Jason. "Of course. You have nothing to worry about," Jason answered, embracing with her a little. "Oh wow, Hillary," Shandi commented. "Who needs her when you got me, babe?" Malcolm told her. Shandi laughed, holding on to his chest. Andy rolled his eyes, and Luna looked the other way. They finally got on the Ferris wheel (four in a cart, four in another), and they could see the entire carnival. It was amazing. Beyond words. Ginger couldn't even believe the setup of the carnival. Malcolm and Shandi were talking to themselves when Todd came up with something interesting. "You wanna know how we're a real couple?"

"How?" Ginger asked. "If we stop at the top and kiss, we were meant to be. It's a joke, by the way." Ginger chuckled. The idea was funny to be honest. Their cart was still going up. "You think we'll stop at the top?" Ginger wondered. "Maybe. If we're a true couple," he answered, cuddling with her and the bears he had won for her. They went around for another round and finally slowed down almost at the very top. "Oh my God, what if we stop at the top?" Shandi worried. "Don't worry about it. Nothing can go wrong," Malcolm cheered her up, as they hugged. Hillary hid her head in Jason's left. Their cart was toward the bottom as it stopped. "You're gonna be fine. There's no need to worry. We're not at the top," Jason joked, as they laughed. Hillary budged, hugging her boyfriend with force. "You're fine."

"I know. I feel better with you," Hillary said, her face away from Luna and Andy. "Aww, how sweet," Luna admitted. "If you say so . . . ," Andy commented. They finally stopped. Ginger and Todd were at the very top. "I guess it is true," Ginger agreed. "I know it's true. With a girl like you, I knew ever since we met by the trash can that day," Todd admitted, "I guess this proved it. We actually didn't need a Ferris wheel to tell us, though."

"I'm glad it did. It showed us both what we already knew about each other. The truth." The karts were still paused. Ginger and Todd extended their lips and kissed. This kiss lasted even longer than ever. Todd even threw in tongue action while kissing. He must've been serious. When they opened their eyes, they hugged. "It is true. We *were* meant to be," Ginger had just realized it. "Yes, we were," Todd agreed. They had forgot Malcolm and Shandi were even in the cart with them. "Mal, we should've kissed!" Shandi cried. "You want to? We still can. I'm up for it," Malcolm responded. The Ferris wheel started moving again. "Aww, it's too late now," Shandi said. "You could ride again, Todd suggested. "That's okay, Shan-Shan. We can kiss anytime," Malcolm suggested. "Haha! Yea right!" Shandi joked. The ride ended, and all eight of them were reunited right beside the Ferris wheel. "Shandi, you freaked out the entire ride!" Malcolm cried. "Yea, I did! We could've fallen off or something!"

"But we didn't," Jason told her. "Shandi, I know what you mean. That's why I don't get on rides like those," Hillary stated. "Or ANY ride for the matter," Luna beckoned. It was getting mighty late when they all stopped just to socialize for a bit. Just then, more people were starting to leave. "Oh my God! I just realized the time, I got to go!" Hillary cried. "Want me to walk ya home?" Jason offered. "Of course, I can't walk in the dark alone! Later, guys!"

"Later!" Jason called back, as they went their separate way. "I came with you, Shandi, we're going, you guys! Later, Ginger! "Luna cried, giving all of them a hug. "I'll text you," Shandi told Malcolm. "All right. Later," he cried, as the two left. Todd immediately turned to Ginger. "Want me to walk you home?" he offered. "Hey, what about us?" Andy asked. "You know where I live, dude. Just ring the door bell."

"Are you sure?" Andy wondered. "Yea, I'll see you there!"

"All right, dude. See ya. See ya later, Ginger," Malcolm said, giving her a hug and high-fiving Todd. When those two were no longer in sight, Todd and Ginger were all alone in the moonlight. "Todd, you know how my family is. Are you sure you wanna do this?" she asked him. "Of course I am. They can never take away our relationship. No one can. Are you sure you wanna do this?" he asked her. "Absolutely." And they walked off. Crickets were wide awake as they left the carnival into the town. "This night is gorgeous," Todd noticed. He has never used an adjective such as "gorgeous."

"Yes, it is," Ginger agreed. She could hardly see anything, but that was just fine. She had someone next to her side that would always be on her side. "You know, you didn't have to ditch your friends for me," Ginger said. "I know. But I wanted to. I can't let you go by yourself. I would be like the worst guy ever for doing that. No guy should ever leave his girl hanging," Todd told her. "That's very nice of you. I love the way you express yourself. It's very chivalrous."

"I can say the same for you too. That's what makes me crazy for you," he cried, squeezing her and the bunnies she had into his arms. "Oh, was that too tight?" he asked. "No, not at all."

"Oh, cool. No pun, by the way," he joked, making them both chuckle. "You should be in a circus. You'd be hilarious," Ginger suggested. "Only if you'd come to see me."

"Of course I would." "Good." They continued walking, ignoring sounds and other people nearby. "Your parents are okay with me and ya, right?" Ginger asked. "Yea. They really don't care who I'm with. As long as I'm out of the house, they're fine," he replied, making Ginger laugh. Ginger played around with her bears. "I'm gonna keep these some place safe. It's very special."

"Like the jacket?"

"Heck yes!" They continued walking, almost approaching her house. "Do you think you can handle my grandfather?"

"Of course I can. We can together. Don't worry. He'll get over it. I promise," Todd was for sure of it. "I hope so. Oh yea, I told them I was hanging with my friends! They'll know I lied!" Ginger said. "You still can't help hiding it, can you?"

"Well, no, I can't. It's just . . ." Todd stopped her by putting his finger over her mouth. "It's okay. I'd do the same thing."

"You would?" "I wouldn't have a choice, so hell yea." They were now one house away from Ginger's house. "So I guess this is where I stop," Todd said. "Yep. For now, though."

"Yea. I better go before Andy and Mal get mad at me," Todd laughed. "All right, then. Later." Before Todd could leave, he noticed Ginger was a little sad. "You seem a little worried."

"I'm not. I had a good time."

"Come on. Smile, then!" Todd told her, but she wouldn't. Just to test him. Todd put his fingers on her lips, making her to smile. "Aww, how cute," he joked. "Haha! Very funny," Ginger said, both of them laughing at one another. "Okay, I better go! I'll text ya! See ya!" he said, kissing her cheek. "Bye, Todd," Ginger responded, as Todd started running the other way. Ginger could only laugh. As she began to walk to the house, she wondered, Maybe Todd was the guy for her. Maybe she was even starting to fall in love all over again.

CHAPTER 20

Lanely Tildon's Message

Grammy was dressed up in a white shiny dress with saucers in her hands and teapots. "Where have you been, sweetheart?" she wondered, clearing up the living room table. "Oh. Just out with my friends. What time is it?" Ginger asked. "Only 11:30," Grammy said sarcastically, "the tea party ended nearly two hours ago. What were you doing?" "Just talking and stuff on Main Street like I always do."

"You weren't with that guy, were you?" she immediately asked. "His name is Todd, and no, I was not," Ginger lied. "Good. And what's this?"

"Gifts my friends gave me for winning the volleyball tournament."

"Oh, how lovely. Well, you better get ready for bed, hun. It's awfully late. Next time, please let us know when you are coming home."

"Okay, Grammy. Good night!" Ginger replied, running up the stairs and racing to her room, slamming the door behind her. She set her gifts on her dresser beside the picture of her and Shelby she found. It did mean the world to her. It came from someone she truly adored. She quickly opened up her diary and wrote about all she did today. She also wrote a love poem, and it went like this:

> Today I wait, for the guy of my dreams. He sends me away, to a place of happiness, to where my tears have meaning, and my eyes are pure. I'm in a distant meadow, forecasting my soul, seeing the light that was once a black hole. He has opened my Heart, he and I are not apart. We are one: And only one. I *know* he's the one. When I look at him, I see a man who will do me no harm but will be there to protect me. We were meant to be. Oh how I see, the life that has become of me. Maybe it is love, or maybe it is the world above. For he does have a name: His name is Todd.

The word that seems to pop up everywhere is "Maybe." "Maybe I love Todd, maybe I don't. I want to be with him, but then again, maybe I don't." It sounds like Ginger is curious for grace, but her own fate could mess up her own self. She looked at the poem with gratitude, and she thought to herself, *Anything I write about is true. This poem is true.* Not only is it true to her heart, it is also true to Todd's heart. Sure he may not write poetry, but he feels the same way. It also sounds like Ginger is being very predictable in that poem. The future hasn't happened yet, but to her, it sounds well. At least it seems well. Love and the future are two things that can't go together and probably never will. We all want them to, but reality says otherwise. Sometime it's best to be unpredictable, because then you can be able to predict the unpredicted, knowing that what you predicted is unpredictable. Monday morning came. This morning was a teacher's conference and Mr. Daniels was not pleased with the "mysterious teachers" at all. He watches nervously as teachers conversed themselves with others, drinking coffee while in a conversation, or sitting down at the table eating a donut and waiting for the conference to start. Mrs. Robbin and Mrs. Duffy were in a corner, staring at yet another window. Mr. Daniels went over to the two teachers dressed in their lab coats. "What could you possibly be staring at?" he asked them. "Why does it matter? In fact, why does anyone even care what we do?" Mrs. Robbin implied. "Because what you're doing is plain weird!" Mrs. Maalone answered, some of the teachers laughing. The two ladies now turned around, facing the others for the very first time today. "We don't tell you what to wear, what to eat, which television show is best for your children, or any of that crap. I suggest you don't with us," Mrs. Duffy has beyond lost her patience. "But why? That's all we wanna know?" Mrs. Daniels insisted. "Why do you wear that shirt? Why are we having this meeting?" Mrs. Duffy wondered. "To discuss the past few months of course. Report cards come out next week. Now answer the question!" he was getting mad as well. "Don't push us too far," Mrs. Robbin whispered to him, "You know damn well we would quit in a heartbeat. You wouldn't want that knowing you don't have a replacement. Now you answer this before I pack my bags and leave for good: Are our paychecks in cash this time . . . ?"

"Well . . . uh . . . not that I know of . . . ," he answered. "Well, fix it!" Mrs. Duffy demanded, "If not, we can very well got a court day. I don't have a problem calling my lawyer. Is that what you want, sir?"

"No. It is not," Mr. Daniels was helpless and hopeless. "Then I suggest you treat us with respect. You know darn well the school would tumble without us. If you want to see the next year, you had better give us the same respect like we do to those children! Understood?" Mrs. Robbin cried. "Like you respect them," Mr. Ukaktchi joked. "Don't play with us. Today is not a good day. We are not in the mood . . . ," Mrs. Robbin commented. "Are we understood, Mr. Daniels?" Mrs. Duffy warned again. Finally after a good while, he responded. "Yes, we are, ladies. Sorry for the confusion."

"Good. Oh, by the way, that child you grabbed the other day DID have a disability like we had already known. Don't tell us how to do our job EVER again. We don't tell you how to do yours . . . ," Mrs. Robbin cried. "The teachers' conference will begin in two minutes. The teachers' conference will begin in two minutes!" the announcement was made. Mrs. Robbin and Mrs. Duffy took their seats and waited for the conference to start. This conference was an important one. The principal would be at this one, and he'd be discussing ways to improve the school. The "mysterious teachers" knew that everyone wanted them kicked out of the meeting. However, they are the only two in the area that worked as an elementary psychologist, who has a master's degree in that career, and who worked at schools for more than ten years. Principal McNally only saw those ladies like mutated children. They were just asking for way too much, and they barely did any work during the day. Circumstances allowed these ladies to stay, but their own personality just wanted people to kick them out from anywhere. The rest of the teachers quietly took their seats, and all eyes were on Principal McNally. "Good morning, staff and faculty. As you can know, we have been called here for a reason. Money is the big issue here. But before I talk about that, I just want you all know that as we progress throughout the year, we will be making changes. Like that new band program next year, as well as more teachers, and more support for our community."

"Oh, thank goodness! Finally! About time!" Some of the teachers said in relief. "Wait! A new band program? We don't need a new program! Honest to God, we don't. The program is already doing great. Well, with the exception of a few annoying students . . . ," Mrs. Alvarez commented. "Well, when you become principal of Upton Sinclair Middle School, you may decide, Mrs. Alvarez," the principal commented. "Principal McNally, may I suggest something?" Mrs. Smith asked. "And what might that be?" Principal McNally asked. "Mrs. Alvarez does have a point. There are just way too many children who think they can come into the classroom, make a mess, disrespect us teachers, and do whatever the heck they want. We should enforce more rules. I'm tired of stupid nonsense these children are doing. They are too old for nonsense like that. Gum under the seats, pulling of the hair, pushing and shoving in the halls. It's ridiculous!" Mrs. Smith said. "She's right. There's constant bullying and fights almost every day now. We teachers must keep the school a safe environment for all. The bullying needs to stop now!" Mrs. Divine agreed. "We will take care of that. Also, to prevent that, there must be more teachers in the hallway during the passing periods at all times. When I'm walking during lunch periods, I see almost no teachers at all. Because of that, students think they CAN do anything they want! Starting today, you will be working on guard so that it won't happen. Thank you, Mrs. Smith," Mr. Daniels commented. "Also, we will be having our Fun Fair soon. I've already talked to our administrative district, so we are good for that. Also, we are providing for the disability of our children. This can help them get around better at our school, and they can get more educational support with the help of their parents," Mr. McNally testified. "Well, what about the children in Social Work Care? It treats them and not anybody else," Mrs. Robbin replied. "Then that would mean every child would have to get supported. Think before you speak, darlin'," Mrs. Alvarez was being smart. Some of the teachers laughed at that. "It's important that children who ACTUALLY need to get the help, *get* the help! They need to see the outside world just like children with a disability. We shouldn't be laughing at that either. There's nothing funny about that, in my opinion . . . ," Mrs. Duffy agreed. "If you say so. You may take your seat, Mrs. Duffy," Principal McNally told her. "You know what? That's it!" Mrs. Duffy cried. "Mrs. Duffy, just sit down . . . ," Coach Hector told her. "No! All right, we have been treated like crap every day, and we're tired of it! You better include the social work students. You'd be sorry if you didn't," Mrs. Robbin also stood. "You ladies need to get a reality check quick, or else you'll be out that door without a paycheck. I would like to see you both in my office during homeroom. And about your offer, we will see about it. We're only doing what's best for the school," Mr. McNally told them. The two ladies sat back down, a bit intimidated. The meeting kept going on and on, and it seemed like it would never end. It only got more boring and more stressful to Mrs. Robbin and Mrs. Duffy. They got tired of the biased criticism their peers kept giving them. When the conference was finished, school had begun, and that's when the two mysterious teachers waited outside of Principal McNally's office. He finally called them in his room after a good twenty minutes, and they sat down wearily. "Okay, ladies. First of all, the reason you two are here is because of disrespect to your fellow staff members. Secondly, you are here for miscommunications and contradicting authority. Now before I request a referral to the superintendent, is there anything you'd like to say?" The two teachers looked at each other hopelessly and then back at Mr. McNally. "Well, what *can* we say or do when you've just threatened us?" Mrs. Robbin asked. "I suppose nothing, but to do your job and get along with your staff members. Until then, that's all I can say," he responded. "We are doing our job! You don't know

a damn thing about psychology so I'd suggest you shut the . . . ,"
Mrs. Duffy started . . ."Front door! "Mrs. Robbin finished for
her. "You know we could quit in two seconds, and gosh, damn we
will if you keep treating us like bullcrap. You may be my boss, but
you, I, and Mrs. Robbin know about our contract agreement with
the district. If you abuse us, you're abusing the contract. Don't
bother us anymore with this, and let US do OUR JOB! I'm so
sick and tired of going through this mess every day, and I'm sure
Mrs. Robbin is too."

"I'm very tired of it," Mrs. Robbin agreed. "Now let us be, or we
will be walking out that door and ripping up that agreement we've
had since the beginning of the year. Have I made myself clear?"
Mrs. Duffy warned. "Yes, you have," Principal McNally agreed,
shocked about the entire conversation. He then started sorting
papers thoroughly in an unorganized pile. "And you can submit
that appeal if you'd like. But lemme warn you: It'll be the biggest
mistake of your life. Have a great morning, Principal McNally,"
Mrs. Robbin cried, which was the signal for the ladies to get up
and leave. "Bye-bye, ladies," he called, the door slamming behind.
Those teachers were lucky that they were the only teachers in
the district who taught psychology for elementary and middle
schools. If they weren't, Principal McNally would fire those two in
a second and no longer. But as he stared at the appeal papers for
wanting a teacher fired, he couldn't help thinking to himself, *Am
I making a good decision?* The answer came when a speck of wind
knocked those papers he was holding into the trash bin beside
him. Was it the wind that did that? Or was it something else?

Principal McNally had no time to even imagine it, so he forgot about the papers in the trash bin and moved on with his day.

Saturday came just that fast, and once again, it was time to see Lanely Tildon at the antique shop. Ginger couldn't wait to tell her about her new relationship with Todd and how she feels about him. But she also wanted to tell her about what Coach Hector told her and about the window. Was the locket really hers? Did she actually control the power of Reincarnation? Could her mother come back to life in a new body? Perhaps. Maybe Coach Hector was right after all. He had to tell her about the secrets past, one that Ginger never knew about. But how could you hide something that important from a person who is literally holding the key between life and death? You can't do that: it could be a matter of if you'll ever see a today or a tomorrow. Maybe it was manifestation. Manifesting evil that is (not to sound cliché). So there she was, walking up the stairs, not knowing what to expect but what to turn for. It was thundering outside, and Grammy forgot to bring her umbrella with her. Luckily Ginger and Grammy didn't get that wet. "Hello, you two!" Marie greeted. "Hello, Mrs. Tildon," Grammy cried. "Buying something today?" she asked. "Oh, not today. We will come back next week. Thank you, anyway!" Grammy answered, as the two headed for the back of the store. They walked very slowly, and then pulled back the curtain covering the room. Sure enough, Miss Tildon was sitting where she normally sits, but this time there was a crystal ball on the table. She had on a wizard's hat, with blue color and yellow stars. The glowing ball looked like it was spinning round and round, and it wouldn't stop. Maybe it was a hallucination, but who's to say? There were also some artifacts that were set on the table next to the crystal ball. "Hello, ladies," Miss Tildon greeted. It appeared that her eyes were closed. "Hi, Lanely," both of them said, as they eerily sat down. After about a minute, Lanely finally opened up her eyes. "So how is life?" she asked. "It's goin' good. How about you?" Grammy responded to her. "Oh, well, great if I must say." Lanely coughed after she said that and kept coughing for another couple of seconds. "Lanely, are you okay?" Ginger asked. "Oh yes, dear. I just have a bad cough," she answered, continuing to cough violently. Next to her was a used ashtray with many cigarettes piled on top of each other. "Oh, Lanely. Drugs are never good," Grammy cried. "Yes, yes, I agree. Sorry about the constant coughing," she took some kind of servin' from the shelf and drank it at a steady pace, "Now let's begin." Finally, she had stopped coughing. Ginger and Grammy looked over at each other in disappointment. "So tell me, Ginger: How are you? How have you been?"

"Well, I guess a little bit of good and bad. My relationship with Todd is going great, but Pappy doesn't like him one bit, and he has not told me why. It hurts really bad knowing my family does NOT like a guy that I could be . . . ," she staggered a bit. "That I could be . . . in LOVE with." This was the first time ever that Ginger has quoted the word "love" in the relationship. "In love with?" Grammy was shocked. She had to gasp for air, and Lanely Tildon nearly fainted. "Well . . . yes! He's sweet, cute, funny, and he understands my heart. My heart has been broken for so long now, and there he is, waiting to repair it. We've only been together for a few months, but I can just feel this change, you know . . . The . . . , the sigh of anger lifted above me. He completes the heart that was once mine. I believe he could be the one. In fact, he IS the one." Grammy was in tears, and Lanely tried to hold back from sobbing. "Ginga, I never knew you felt this strongly about another man. I saw you crying on your bed when you told me the news about Bailey. I didn't want to see you like that ever! You have suffered through enough. I should've believed," Grammy apologized. "Yes, Marybeth. Trust is the key. The key of everything! If Ginger McFraiddee is happy with another man, Marybeth should be happy too! Love can be a burden to those who deny. Us adults don't want to see our grandchildren and their children grow up to be a young male or female that they will be. But we must remember. They will someday. They will HAVE to. It may not be an easy task, but we know we CAN. Now, Ginger, ball to make it glow. "Now how have you been, Lanely?" Grammy asked her. "Good and bad, I guess. My England trip has been moved to sometime next year," she stuttered, coughing in between, "and I guess I haven't had enough time for me of my family. It's starting to get cold, and I fear the worse may come: foreclosure."

"Why was the trip moved, Lanely?" Ginger asked. "Money issues, darling. Ever since we bought this shop, we had to pay it off in full and not a minute late. It's good to have your own business, but only to a certain extent. Work is getting more 'frustrating,' if I must add. The government won't pay for our food stamps anymore or other benefits, and this means I won't be able to retire for another five years." When Lanely said that, Grammy's mouth dropped wide. "But nonetheless, our shop is getting more customers, and newspapers are being rolled in. I'm excited that we've doubled in customers from the past two years. Making new perfumes is a career in its own. In my heart, I feel and believe that this shop will last a lifetime. After the day I die, this shop will still stay here, and it will be great. Legacies are *always* fulfilled: Even when the person dies. I just had a vision to start this shop, and now look what we have accomplished so far. We can only continue to grow and grow until we reach beyond the top. As I grow older, I soon perish, and I move on to see the other souls and Reincarnation takes way in an immoral sense, NOT the sense we know: which is being born in a new body. That is why it is so important. New souls will take over, and if they are evil, this world will be come evil with it."

"Is that why we're in the signs of times?" Ginger asked. "I believe it is. The Bible says that the world we live in will end. We do not know when, but we know it will happen soon. But that is what I think. There has to be a source to evil. The only source is the source that always starts from the beginning. I search for the truth, and the light, but it will only happen from *death*. Stories have been told by the dead; that only Reincarnation can save them. Only Reincarnation can help this world become better. Life and death has to come together to tell us the psalms we've been waiting for. Secrets *must* be revealed. Only secrets can set us free. Every human was meant to know. As you can see, life, is an untold dream."

"Untold dream? Who was meant to tell it?" Grammy asked. "Good question. We were all meant to tell our own story. We all have different points of view of life. Neither is wrong. You may have your say, and I may have mine. Fact and opinion are two different things. Could it symbolize life and death? If it did, which would we select? Many choices. Neither is wrong."

"Lanely, there's something important I have to tell you," Ginger said. "What is it?" Lanely asked, coughing while she did. "My coach told me some weird story a couple of weeks ago that when he looked at a window of our school, he saw my locket in the background . . ."

"Mmhmm." Cough. "Very, very interesting . . ." Lanely herself had to think for a minute. "Who usually stares into that window?" She was interested. "Two ladies named Mrs. Robbin and Mrs. Duffy. They're teachers at our school, and they're always looking at that window. Nobody knows why, but they just do it until somebody talks to them." Total pause. Utter silence. "I know those two ladies. They used to come here, but now, I rarely see them. Can you keep a little secret?" Lanely explained, almost choking up blood. "Sure."

"Well . . . ," Lanely started, her voice all creaky, "those two ladies have the same locket as you do . . . Theirs has a blue glow however. Yours is red. They try to keep it a secret from us."

"Where'd they get the locket from . . . ? The one Ginga has is the one her great-great-great-grandfather had," Grammy was puzzled. "The lockets come from more than one place, hun. They could've gotten it from anywhere. With lockets like those, they loosen your mind. *They* let you communicate with the dead. Like I said before, the locket holds the truths within the untold death. How does it do that, you may ask? Because of the central power of the dead. The only place that is located is . . . hell. Souls are too evil. Reincarnation cannot work with evilness. Until this world becomes clean, the central powers can be sent to heaven, where life was meant to be." So why does it need the locket?" Ginger asked. "The locket holds truth to life itself. When you look at something with the locket on, you immediately look at the past and how effective it may be, and you try to understand that. When those two ladies look at something, they are immediately drawn in by the souls that have lived there. That could be why those ladies seem a bit strange to the naked eye." *So that's why* . . . , Ginger thought. "The sad part is that no one understands it. No one ever *will*. Once the central powers of souls are exposed to the world, we can *all* see what they see. We will *all* be able to know our loved ones, and the life ahead us. It takes a gift to get there. Having not knowing the good and bad souls will be a burden for Reincarnation, and the shadows it long belongs for. But do not worry, those ladies are only communicating with souls to try and make them good again. Evilness has always been king. It takes rituals and rituals and spells and spells to make them good again."

"But wait. How did evilness even take over?" Ginger asked. "Battles. Souls were always good. The central powers belonged to us for so long. Then evilness fulfilled this world. Violence and killing. Anger and hatred. That is what made the world evil. Whatever happens on the earth is the result in happening to the 'afterlife' and the effect on Reincarnation. Souls won't be able to get whole again and come back to life (if they wanted to). Madness will reign! Humans are souls. Your spirit is in your body. Whatever happens to it WILL affect your spirit! Always remember that! It is very important. Now that this world is full of evil, souls become evil. They try to kill more people on the earth so people can become like them. It is our job to stop that from happening. The Spirit Transporter can. How? It can transform good things from the earth to the central power and bad things. Whatever happens on earth *will* happen to the souls. If you can see the dead, or even talk to them, you could be one step closer to making the world a better place. Enchantments help. Ginger, you could've saved lives from the Enchantment of Reincarnation, and the Identity Enchantment performed a while ago (little do you know). If you use love, passion, and proudness in any enchantment, ritual, spell, or whatever you choose, salvation will occur at any point, at any time. Good and evil are alike in ways that can't be classified, but good can stop evil once and for all. We humans have to let them happen. God gave man the authority over the world. All we have to do is make peace on the world, and Reincarnation can be alive."

"Wait, so nobody can reincarnate?" Ginger asked. "Not like before. You were able to be cleanseth and then go into a body to help another soul or to help a human become whole. The laws and principles are changing nowadays. Evil is now the unworthy dictator of not only the spirits present, but our spirit as well . . . They could destroy our earth in a blink of an eye if they wanted to. This is no joke. Your locket holds Immortality to the entire world. Eternal life. Man will finally see their doings, and see that it is the WRONG DOING. The three powers (love, passion, proudness) can set us free from the world. Cherish the memories, live today . . . visualize tomorrow, conquer the evil that stays . . ."

"I think I should leave for a minute. I don't want to be in the way," Grammy cried. "Sure. If you say so, Marybeth. Ginger McFraiddee must hear this herself," Lanely cried. "Okay then. Thank you, Miss Tildon."

"Be seeing you, dear. Bye-bye, Ginga."

"Bye, Grammy," Ginger waved, as Grammy stepped out of the room. "So what else did he tell you?" Lanely asked. "He said that not only did he saw my locket, he saw dead relatives of his talking to him."

"And what did they tell him?"

"They told him that evil souls or something were taking over and how Reincarnation couldn't exist. He also mentioned that the dead couldn't be alive again," Ginger explained. "That the dead couldn't be alive again . . ." Lanely pondered, "Does that make sense to you?"

"No. No, it doesn't. Well, not until I got enchanted. I thought that once you were dead, you were dead!"

"You and the entire world thought that. Do you see where I am coming from? It may not make sense at first, but believe me it will when you start meditating it more. Ginger for your own good or bad, what he told you is RIGHT. I hope you were listening to him, and didn't think he was joking . . ."

"Oh, of course not! Not at all!" Ginger lied. "Good, good. The devil is a lie. I can't promise you that he and I are saying are two the same thing. You *cannot* be made whole again from the wicked. If you are, you have become an evil soul, and once that happens, they will try to promote evil around the world and expose the good to the bad and make good souls evil. Good and evil are alike in so many ways. I say that all the time because if you are a good soul, you promote the good, and let Reincarnation happen for all. If you are bad, then evil things will happen, and death will take over. The law is simple really; yet hard to obey. Treat others the way you want to be treated. The Bible does NOT lie. It is a guide for all humans and how we should live on the world. Signs of the times are already here. More natural disasters, more wars, more destruction. It only means it will get worse, until heaven reaches earth. Until then, our job is to save others from hell. That's why you see pastors ministering and evangelists on the street. The type of religion does not matter, what does is this: there is a good in every religion. You must be saved and be good to nature. Reincarnation can happen, and the dead will be delivered."

"I have a question: Can you as a person talk to your own soul, or is it just the dead?" Ginger asked. "That is a very, very good question. You see, your spirit is in your own self. When you have days where you are talking to yourself, or gaining self-confidence, your spirit speaks upon you. You can speak to your own spirit. Your spirit can't speak to other spirits, however. Well, perhaps it can. Through prayer, speaking in tongues, spirits do get cleaned that kind of way. So yes, you can, Miss McFraiddee, but it's on how you look at it. Hinduism, Judaism, Christianity, Catholic, and other religions let you. If you have no religion at all (atheist), or you just do not care, then no, it won't. It all goes back to believing. Knowing who you are is also important. The identity Enchantment was an eye opener to what it is like in the real world. Hate to say it, but the world will only get worse by the day. That is why we must take back the goodness and let the spirits live on for an eternity. The only way that can happen is if Reincarnation occurs. We are our own destiny, and only we can choose to make it last a full lifetime. When I say we, I mean *all* the people of the world."

"I saw something odd at the carnival the past Saturday or so. I was just gazing at Todd, and then a fire was all over the place, and there were souls flying all over the place! They were lined up, too, and the sky was dark purple! You have to believe me, Lanely, you have to!" Ginger explained. "I do, sweetheart. Now some quick questions: were the souls flying one way?"

"Yes. A line of them flown toward the fire, and the other line away. I think that's how I pictured it. The fire was everywhere."

"And you say the sky was purple that night?" Lanely asked. "Yes. It was dark purple. You could barely see it or anything because of the fire."

"Mhmm. That must be a sign that THEY ARE COMING. If you can visualize that type of moment, it must mean that something very important could happen soon. Did your locket glow after you had that illusion?"

"No. I also did see some souls burning, others fighting each other: It was a disturbing scene. I couldn't bear to even watch it!" Ginger cried. "Were there tears in their eyes?" she asked Ginger. "There was." Lanely paused for a moment and then said, "You have been chosen." Ginger gasped in shock. "If anyone could see such an illusion like that, it is purely coming from the souls themselves. They are warning us. Death is upon us. Evilness is here! The only bad thing is that from your illusion, it does not tell us when it will happen, or IF it will happen. It could've already happened, and we just do not know it. As more come, they send a message. A message of what is to become of the world. Take in those images; it may save all of us in the end."

"But the end has just arrived . . . ," Ginger commented. "Child, let me tell you about the curse. Years ago, a prophecy was made. It was made, that every spirit of the dead goes through Reincarnation not only to be whole, but to be cleanseth from all evilness and to ever sin again. Years went by, and the more that died were still evil, or had become evil. Not because of Satan (all blame is NOT on him), but because of the choices for immortality and bad decisions made in one's life. Soon enough, evil reigned over the good, and all of the good souls could not have their chance of reincarnating, making everlasting life, or resting in peace in huge jeopardy. There is a fable told that some spirits created seven lockets. These lockets were given to those whom they could trust, and the lockets allowed the person who was wearing it to communicate with the living dead and to foreshadow the wicked demons among us. Unfortunately, whoever in this locket would have a life of sadness *only* if the family did not accept the locket. Most people on the earth do not believe this is such a thing. They take it for granted, so the spirits have nowhere or no one to turn to. Then there are people like you and me, whom they *can* trust, and whom they may even want to communicate with. There are only seven lockets, however. Seven represents the number of completion. It took six days for God to create this world, and on the Sabbath day, he rested. Seven in the entire world, scattered about. Some have been washed away on shores. Some have been brutally burned. Nature has led the lockets where they are today. The person who wears it has the ability of letting goodness reign upon the earth. You just have to believe that it can and will happen. However, the family who has the locket will endure (in quotes): 'Serious, if not deadly illusions from our kind, loss of reality, harming of the body and skin, and the ability of talking to us, or hearing to what we have to say.' That is true. None of us knows who actually said that, or what it may mean. But the curse isn't an actual curse, it is just side effects of 'spirit talking.' I can show you more of what I am talking about on my crystal ball."

"Please do," Ginger insisted. "Okay then." Lanely Tildon rubbed the crystal ball, transforming it into different colors. One minute, it was light blue, then next minute, it turned bright red. "This is NOT the Enchantment. We will perform the last one after I show you this. It will only take a few seconds," Lanely warned. "All right. I can handle it." Glowing yellow stars filtered the entire crystal ball, and it nearly shattered Ginger's eyes. "Get used to the symptoms, which may include a sudden change in eyesight, dear," Lanely cried, taking Ginger's hand and squeezing it. Let the orientation begin. Lanely Tildon opened her eyes, deep in the intense moment. It signaled Miss McFraiddee to do the same. "View the light! Embrace the faith! See unto what you were called to see! For the memory . . ." The crystal ball showed numerous amounts of pictures: Pictures that Ginger could comprehend. It showed one of her and Shelby, sitting near a swing set, as they were laughing and playing. The only thing that was odd about it was that the picture was black and white, and the others were in color. Could that actually mean something? "Of the just . . . ," Lanely continued. All pictures were formed into a circle, and they circled the crystal ball, as if it was a globe. Ginger's eyes turned the same color as the crystal ball did. It was strange, because nothing happened to Lanely Tildon. "Is BLESSED." Blackout! The crystal ball stopped its bright light, and Ginger's eyes were back to normal. Ginger took enormous deep breaths, and Lanely touched the crystal ball with her filthy and unsanitized fingers. This would make things a little bit more interesting, because during all the other times and enchantments, Lanely Tildon made sure her hands were clean and not dirty. Then again, this was *not* an enchantment . . . "Is it over with?" Ginger wondered. Lanely gasped in agony. "Miss McFraiddee! We have only just begun. The images you saw were the ones of your mind. Now, close your eyes, and when I say 'OPEN' in the next few minutes, open your eyes. This is a mind test. If you see what you have seen before, your mind is ready for anything. Your mind is ready, but are you ready?"

"Yes. I am."

"Good. You may close your eyes, now." She closed her eyes, awaiting the moment Lanely would say the magic word. Ginger heard that sounds of humming and the sounds of wind. She could visualize the entire room, her mind letting her see within another. She also heard a sound that she thought she would never hear. The sound of her locket shining. She also understood a prophecy, or a speech Lanely had been quoting. It went something like this: "Sounds of the tormented, times like this. Reincarnation exists. In the eyes of the living one. One, meaning you. Let the spirits reign, let the Lord deliver us *all* from darkness. For we walk by faith and not by sight. Come now, into my own eyes and soul. Let everything that has breath, praise the Lord. Let the Spirit Transporter ... arrive." ... Complete silence for a few moments ... Some hums and sighs here and there ..."Open!" Her locket had stopped glowing. Ginger opened both her eyes at the same time, as though nothing happened. "Look into the crystal ball." Ginger did what she was told. Lanely looked into the crystal ball, and saw vigorous amounts of color. Ginger however, saw something different. At first, there was nothing. In an instant, she saw her own locket that was glowing inside the crystal ball, and then she saw that peach background. Above it is where she eyed the window: the same one Mrs. Robbin and Mrs. Duffy glare at every day. Then came the fire. She saw the fire and the souls. They were wandering, wondering which way to go. Behind them there was a white light, where most of them were at. They were staring at something quite odd: The purple sky. However, a girl appeared to be different than the rest. She wasn't flying like the rest of the souls; she had on a locket, and she was looking straight into the distant flames. Just like Ginger had pictured at the carnival. That disturbing image had gone away. Another one approached from the crystal ball: one that was unexpected. Flashes were made from this one, so she couldn't quite understand it. The picture then stood still. Out came a girl dressed in patterns of modern day clothing. She was light-skinned, yellowish natural made, and she wore a locket similar to Ginger's. Hers, however, had been green, with a touch of grand flora. One of her eyes appeared red, as if it was beaten. Then, there were those scars on her neck and face. One was easily seen on the side of her neck, and toward as the tip of her nose. These were no light scars either. The most shocking part was that she was riding on an elephant. The elephant had been dressed up in all sorts of beads and elegant artefacts, and it was in the middle of the street, as others were surrounding it. The image slowly faded away, and the crystal ball was dark again. Lanely quickly turned on the lights, as Ginger snapped back into reality. Lanely sat back down, adjusting her eyes to normal light. She sprinkled the crystal ball with some sprinkles (it must have been a way of cleaning it), and rubbed them all over the crystal ball. "Okay. That was good. Now let me tell you one thing. This is NOT magic, or sorcery, or any of that stuff. Magic is said to only worsen the weak who were destined to be strong. I am just putting that out there." Lanely coughed a little more. "Before we begin the very last Enchantment, is there anything you would like to tell me?" Ginger could've said *no*, but then she'd be lying to herself. "I saw the exact thing I saw at that carnival. This is unreal. I also saw the locket, that window, and it was all in a peach background. It was no different than before."

"It is unbelievable. But it is IN FACT REAL. Like I said, it may have already happened, and it may have not. With the locket, you have the power to see the past and present. You can see all that you may want to see. Believe me, those images were there for a living purpose, and guess what, you can only see it if your mind is ready for it, and if you are wearing that locket."

"Like those teachers do . . . ?" Ginger asked. "I believe so." Cough and sneeze. "Sorry, pardon me." Now it's all starting to make sense. "Is that all you've pictured, or was there more?" Lanely wondered. "There was, actually. I saw this girl, and she was on an elephant, and she had dark red eyes with scars all over. Both the elephant and her were wearing tons of beads and jewelry, and her clothes were like robes you'd see in the Middle Ages."

"Was she light-skinned with dark spots on her face?" Lanely stopped Ginger. "Yes, she was. She looked maybe Mexican, or even . . ."

"Arabic . . . ," Lanely answered, coughing. "Exactly. How did you know?" "Guesstimation, really. Tell me more about the image, dear."

"That was it, I guess. That, and she was wearing a locket that looked just like mine. Only hers was green. I think it may have been glowing. I saw that, and then some other people dressed like her with jewelry and necklaces and high-heeled shoes that were walking around. The most amusing part was that the elephant was walking around in the streets, and there may have been other elephants too! It was amazing!" Ginger had never seen anything like it, before. Lanely had been wide awake when she heard that part about the necklace. "A . . . a . . . a necklace . . . you say?" she asked. "Yep. Or at least that's what I thought I saw," Ginger responded. "Really? Very, very interesting," Lanely replied, thinking to herself a bit. "How?" Ginger wanted to know. Total silence . . . In a low and calming voice, Lanely answered, "Can you keep a secret?"

"Of course I can!"

"Well, then . . . Marie Tildon is my daughter. What people don't know is that I have two daughters, her and one that hasn't spoken to our family in ages. I cannot tell you her name, but what I can say is that at around the age of eighteen, with no warning, she was going to marry a guy that she met online. He's an evil man. I've seen his online picture years ago. Anyway, the man was Arabic, so she decided to go to Saudi Arabia to wed that man. The only other thing I've heard is that she gave birth to a baby girl a few years later. I do not know what happened after that day, and that's all I DO know." "So you think that girl in the image could be your granddaughter?" Ginger wondered. "I do. Only because of that locket. Her eye showed a sign of the curse, but that does not mean it is her. I had a feeling it maybe was her, but I am not sure. That is all I can think to tell you, and please let's keep this between you and me. Our family sort of forgot about my second daughter. That's why I do not tell it to them, or even to my own daughter Marie Tildon."

"I won't tell. But do you think it could be the curse?"

"You can't blame that for everything in life. This meaning of a 'Curse' is way more transversal than the dictionary meaning. But in away, yes. In some ways, no. It all depends on the situation."

"And . . . I can communicate with the living dead . . . ?" Ginger asked. "When you are wearing that locket, yes. Why your family did not mention this to you, I have no clue. Your grandparents knew WAY before your parents ever had a clue. I will speak to them about that." "What . . . ? They knew the entire time? I can't believe this . . . All three of them were too selfish to tell me what was actually happening. All of our lives could be in jeopardy now. And it was all because of some locket! This whole secret could be null and void!" Ginger was paranoid. "I know it may seem tough, but at least now your secret is revealed. You have the power to talk to the dead, and you have the power to make things that are dead back to life through Reincarnation COMPLETELY."

"But anyone can bring someone back from the wicked praying, and being saved is a good example of that. Am I right?"

"Yes, definitely. Getting souls saved themselves that are or will soon be dead is a rewarding thing to do. After the last Enchantment, you yourself will see the difference, and see how affective it can be. The whole point of this is to go ye into the world and preach the gospel. Anyone can do that, and when it comes to renewing your spirit, only seven on the earth has the power to renew for good. But guess what, those seven people have seven billion people to back them up, because the world will believe of what can be done. It sounds impossible, but it can be done. Heck, it WILL be done. The spirit has a life of its own. You think about that. Your spirit will live on forever and ever, but will it be good, or will it be evil? We get one chance in life. To succeed, to achieve, or to be a crack, drugs, and stayin' in the streets. Reality hit us all in the face at a time. Just because your flesh can no longer be seen doesn't mean YOU shouldn't be seen. All of us are equal in one special way. The only thing I want to do is to see my mother again and to know that she is all right. I know she's in this world. I walk by faith and not by sight. I know she's here with us. What must I do to know? I have to claim it. Living like the world is the last thing I ever want to do. I've seen so many of those who have been hurt and unloved. I never want to see people that way, but I know I'm going to, because it's the way of the world. Fact and opinion do hurt, and it is up to us to decide which is a choice." "So that's my secret? I can talk to the dead?"

"Not the dead. Reincarnated and unreincarnated souls. Your mind allows you to see those images. Images that our ancestors left behind. But you must not tell anyone. No one probably would believe you if you did. It has to be kept within the family, or else . . . the curse could become deadly." This scared Ginger, because she knew she would tell someone (she wasn't good with keeping secrets), and then she'd end up in trouble. She was smart however, and she'd do anything to not tell anyone, even if it meant forgetting about it. "Okay, Lanely. I won't tell. I am just amazed that there are only seven of these lockets that are out there. I just thought it was an artefact. How much do you think it's worth?"

"I wouldn't know. It is not an artefact, it's a gift from our dead ancestors. They are warning us of what is to come. If I could guess, I would guess $10,000. That does not mean you should sell it, though. That locket is sacred to all. Now, with furthers and ye, let's perform the Final Enchantment. Shall we?" Lanely asked. "We shall," Ginger replied.

CHAPTER 21

The Enchantment: Part 3—Final Glory

Ginger was very happy, yet nervous to have another Enchantment upon her life. What did these Enchantments mean? What *COULD* they mean? They are obviously used for good and not the bad, but is that all? This is no folktale Enchantment or a Cinderella story; this is real life. A happily-ever-after Enchantment would be great: just not the one Lanely and Ginger does. Try not to interpret this as those types of Enchantments, because these Enchantments were meant for leaders. This was serious business, and the more Miss Tildon kept thinking about it, the more it troubled her. She couldn't help to think if Ginger was utilizing these tools, or if she was just wasting her own time. Telling a young teen a topic such as Reincarnation and performing it for that matter is a very hard thing to achieve. Lanely knew in her heart from the first Enchantment if Ginger would be ready for this or not. The answer is this: she WAS ready! If she wasn't, she would've stopped seeing Ginger a long time ago. They could've just talked on the phone and gone to the antique shop on a monthly basis. Lanely saw more in Ginger. She saw greatness. She saw the light that she long waited for to see. Greatness does take work. Remember that when you're going for your next job interview. Ginger got out her diary and her locket. "Now what are the three keys to Reincarnation?" Lanely asked. "Um . . . hopefully I can remember! One is love . . . the other is passion . . . , and . . . , oh right! Proudness."

"Good job remembering. It's very substantial that you know and learn those three words. It can't come over night either. Love. Love is a verb. It is something you can feel on the inside, but it is special to all of us in our own way. When a man looks at you, what do you personally love about him the most, Ginger?"

"My definition is that I love his smile, his eyes, his personality, the way he talks to me . . . , the way he laughs . . . , his cuteness . . ." Ginger was drooling on the table at that point. "You must be in love with someone."

"No! No way, Lanely. What makes you think that?" Lanely got a bath towel and wiped up her drool from the table. "Because you're in denial. But never mind about that. Your answers are what I'm concerned about most. You and I both know that love is something very, very special. It tells us the truth between one another. As souls become evil, retribution is made. That means they die off, creating more destruction for all (as if there was not enough). Love can make Reincarnation occur all over again, and it can let the spirits reign upon all humanity. The only problem is that the souls are so reactive and not proactive. They can't think for themselves. They do not want to be anything great. They forgot the meaning of love. Once they see it and know the true meaning of it, they can be renewed through cleanseth."

"But why are they like that?"

"Because it's the way of the world . . . ," Lanely answered. "The world transformed the meaning of love. Man made it so that the wicked wins over the wise. Nowadays, love to a man is a girl's body appearance, the way she dresses, her jewelry, makeup, etc. All of the physical traits make a man attracted to a woman. They quickly forget about the traits that really matter—the traits inside of her heart. I can tell you now: those people are going nowhere in life. That's why you see fourteen-year-olds who are pregnant. They got caught up, they forgot about who: themselves. You have to start with yourself in order to make love real. It's the same way vice versa. When a woman only likes a man because of his muscle, the way he tries to be cool, it will go nowhere. It may sound lame and cheesy, but it's what comes from the heart and mind. The world can't see that however. They are too busy trying to look cool and do what they want, and the only place it will lead them to is hell. I am only speaking the truth."

"But it's the world's way of doing it. It has to lead somewhere," Ginger insisted. "It leads to the same place it always has been: hell. That's why so many souls are evil. Not souls per se, but the person. A spirit can only be its own self before it is a spirit. Remember that. Love is a verb that can be an action upon your heart forever. You may be a little confused right now, and that is perfectly normal. To save those that really need saving, it is up to us to help them understand the true meaning of love and the values they share. It's all about values. Choosing the *right* decision. The good words to use. We cannot be judgmental to others. Love was meant to be good, not to be about pornography, stripping, any of that stuff. It was meant to get to know someone of the opposite gender and to learn more about him or her for the rest of their days. I may not be a matchmaker, but that is what it's all about. Happiness, purity, tranquility. Pardon me if I sound a bit dry, but it can set our loved ones free. If you truly loved someone, you'd be next to them forever, and you would never leave them through the hard times. Spirits will learn how important love is. How it brings them together as a whole. How evilness cannot get through, because if you're evil, you cannot love. It will help them understand their own heart and how things would've been in their lives if they loved one another. That is why love is an important element, and why it is used in these Enchantments. It's now time for the procedure. I have told you a little what love is, but now you will see for yourself how it can save the souls. These three principles can and will set us free. We will get a glimpse of the world of souls right now. Maybe you can save one or two. Come along, please."

"Wait. We're actually going to see spirits?" Ginger was astonished. "Mhm. Well, you will because you have on your locket. It allows you to. Okay. Take off your locket, and open up your diary." Ginger did what she was told. Miss Tildon was preparing. She took a bottle from a shelf and the crystal ball, and she sat next to Ginger. Ginger flipped open the diary and put her locket next to the diary. "What I want you to do is to say a little sonnet from your heart. I want you to say it about a certain someone whom you love to be around. Look closely at the crystal ball. Ignore everything else around you please. Let us begin." Ginger looked into the crystal ball. Lanely poured the material from the bottle on the crystal ball, and the ball started spinning and spinning. The color of the crystal ball was rainbow colored, with white spots seen. Next to her, light was coming from her diary and from the locket. "Listen to me carefully. When you are inside, listen to me only. You will be able to hear my voice inside. Do not worry about anything you encounter. This is part of the last Enchantment. Now, say your poem, or your feeling toward love. It could be about a guy you now like."

"I'll have to read it from my diary. I wrote plenty of stuff about Todd there," Ginger cried. "Okay, then." Ginger took her diary and skimmed through the pages until she found something that stuck out. The poem is called 'You.'

My last tear, my only chance.
I cry for you, I search the truth.
You could be mine, who I divine.
My soul has spoke, my dreams awoke.
Don't fade away, you are my hope.
You open my heart, you fill in the gap:
You're in my life to close that trap.

Love is who I want to be, but you are more than a
prince I see:

You are you.

Suddenly, her diary closed. Her locket arose. Light and power glowed from the crystal ball. She glanced over, and saw Lanely's eyes brighten wide. "Remember . . . only listen to me . . . Souls will be . . . SAVED TODAY!" Those were the last words Ginger heard. A black background vigorously came her way. It seemed as if she was hallucinating, but she wasn't in reality. A small voice told her to blink her eyes, and she did. When she was finally "awoke," she was sitting on the ground. Surrounding her was a pure black and cold sky without a cloud to be seen. She glanced all over. Cold winds shuffled through her body, making her shiver. Looking, she eyed a gravestone next to her. In fact, she saw many of them. Flowers, bouquets, and memorials all were around her. She slowly stood, removing her hair that the wind blew in her face. Sounds of owls and bats bellowed where she was. Lanely was not with her, and now fear was on her mind. Ginger heard a sound of something that fell. It was her locket. She quickly put it on wiping dirt off the heart-shaped item. "Do not panic, Miss McFraiddee. You will be fine," a voice from above told her. "Where am I? Who is that!" Ginger yelled out, walking in circles, freaking out a bit. "It's me, Lanely Tildon. You are now a part of the spirits. You can see what they see, feel what they feel. You have the power to communicate with them when you have that locket on. Take it off, and you will be able to see the souls.

You are in your flesh, however. The spirits will be able to ONLY SEE YOUR SOUL."

"So now what?" Ginger asked, still wandering around the area. "You wait. And remember, always listen to my voice. You will do well in this Enchantment, Ginger McFraiddee." Lanely's voice sounded like a king's voice from where she was at. Ginger didn't know if she should run and scream, or if she should ask to get out somehow. Ginger quickly took some deep breaths and slowly began to catch herself. Moments later, she heard whispers. She also heard buzzing and whirling noises. She looked round. Nothing. Her shoelaces were untied. She bent down to tie them. Before she stood back up, she saw something peculiar about a gravestone. It was her mother's. Right next to it was her father's gravestone. Ginger got on her knees and sobbed a little. Then she looked at both her mother and father's gravestones and blew a kiss to them. "I will never ever forget you both. Thank you for teaching me how to love." She rose up and took a huge sigh. "Ginger, always remember your true destiny," that was her father's voice. "For it will lead you to great things and the extraordinary," that was her mother's voice. Ginger could only look up, smile, and say yes. At that point, the whispers became louder. "Love is in your heart. Hate not those who hate you. Love the broken-spirited. Your mind is the government of love. Your heart is bigger than you." These were whispers Ginger was hearing. She glanced ahead and saw flames and smoke. She also saw people like figures who were not flying in air, but walking. There were two lines of them. One line extended all the way back from where

Ginger was standing. That line was headed toward the fire. The other line was the spirits coming out of the fire. Their feet weren't touching the ground. That line as much shorter however. The fire extended everywhere from what Ginger saw. When she turned around, there was no fire. This was her exact image. Coach Hector had never been wrong. "Ginger, you're doing a good deed," she had heard her mother say. "Now save the evil souls," her father replied. "Okay," Ginger cried. "Come along, Ginger." That was Lanely's voice. She led her to basically the center of that fire in the midst of darkness. The question is how could it be dark at the gravestones that's near the city Ginger lives in when it's morning in the town? Very weird. She looked right at all of the souls (at least that's what she thought they were). Most turned around to stare at not just her soul through her flesh but also her locket. These spirits were clear, and they did not want to say anything. They knew she could save them from the roaring flames. She was the Mother Nature in this world. "Love can save them. They need it. They are not evil, but the world has made them who they are. Now vision the light even in the center of darkness. Shine upon everyone here! You can do it, Miss McFraiddee. I know you can. Go out there and show the love! Do not worry about anything either," that was Lanely Tildon's voice. Was she dreaming? Was this some sort of fantasy? That's all Ginger wanted to know. The souls were emancipated to see her. The minute they saw that locket, they knew she could be their savior. Relentlessly, she looked above and saw a flashing light spark on not only her, but her necklace. "Do you yourself love, Miss McFraiddee? And what does it mean to love?" Lanely's voice was saying, "Show them your heart. Show them that there's goodness while even being dead." The spark was coming from the dark sky. Ginger gazed around. So much destruction. Fires growing, souls drowning in the pit of shame, and nothing seems to be getting better. A new soul enters the world of darkness every five seconds or so. It only gets worse and worse. She noticed all of the souls burning. The ones that were walking away from the fire were the survivors. The ones who knew *some* sort of love in their restless lives. These spirits have an unfinished story to tell. It is their turn to tell the story that was never finished. Only this time, they will tell a story of good. "I do love. It means so much to me. I would be here if I did not. Love is important to all. It demonstrates a happy and wonderful life." Right when Ginger spoke the word "light," the fire grew more. The spirits were now screaming. Flames were everywhere. Ginger could not do anything about it either. She was hoping that the fire couldn't touch her. "How could this happen? I thought this would make it better? I know my heart's in the right place. I KNOW it is!" Ginger cried to herself in her mind, hoping that Lanely could hear it. Everyone was running around and running right through Ginger. They could see her, but they could not feel her. How could that be? Was it a spell? Maybe flesh wasn't allowed here (wherever "here" was). "They don't understand their own selves. Remember the first Enchantment: Identity. Show them the love. They need it. Look up and say the verse." Ginger looked up, and saw a reflection upon the spirits. "They all looked sad. They just needed some hope, some caring, someone to talk to. Their story isn't over with yet, and someday the world will hear it."

"You cannot take love away. You all are loved. Don't ever think for a second that you are not. It is a gift. So please, use it wisely. In my heart, I have seen the dead. You all will come back and tell the world how different you can become. How optimistic you are. How you mean something to the face of the earth. You are more than just a soul. You are the ancestors of our world." With that said, Ginger could see the souls smile. When she looked around, some had a light upon their heart. "Now, repeat what I say: Love, passion, and proudness will make you whole," Lanely cried from above. "Love, passion, and proudness will make you whole." From the soul's heart, a white light shone from it through the darkness and above the darkened sky. It seemed as if they had created a sun from their heart. Some souls shone; some did not. All of the souls were wearing an exact replica of Ginger's locket. It was not the same however; it was crystal clear, made to represent freedom and completion of one's mind. So light came from some spirits' necklaces, and for those who were becoming whole, Lanely's voice from out of nowhere began speaking, "Delivered from the dark. Saved by love. Ginger McFraiddee; you have created a new legacy—one that will be fulfilled by greatness. You go along your journey; you will find more challenges, more obstacles. Do not worry. Seek your identity, and YOU shall be the mirror of the world, an image we *all* have longed for. An object that is closer than it appears. Now, it's time for the Spirit Transporter to deliver the souls. Reincarnation MUST happen in this Enchantment. Now, I will snap my finger; and you, Miss McFraiddee, will have some spirits delivered." As Lanely was saying that, more spirits appeared, and of course they were evil (ones that had the light on their locket were the good souls). Some souls that had the light faded it away, and it wasn't seen again. More evilness surrounded Ginger. They were laughing at her; making ugly faces too. A sheet of paper fell on her head, and she caught it. She read the words aloud, "For the good do you believe? Do you love those to believe? Are you truely good on the inside? Believe in love, envision your mind. You were meant for something in the world. Your life meant for something in the world. Your life is not over. Your story is NOT over with yet. Believe in yourself. Start with who you want to be, even before you were born. If you believe, you will be delivered, and your story can be told." It took a second, but soon enough, some of the souls that had the light had risen up and were engulfed inside of the giant sunny light that has created by them. Some of the spirits that were created with the light went back to being evil. They simply didn't believe. For the majority, most souls were delivered and were going to be reincarnated. Ginger only saw the fire grow and grow, as if it were going to burn her up to shreds any minute. Before she turned around, sparks were around her, and she too was sucked in by the light. After she left, the light no longer shone, and the fire and evil souls remained there. Soon enough, she was sitting back down at the seat where Lanely was, her necklace already on her neck. Her diary pages were still waving, and right when she glanced at it, the diary closed. Ginger looked up, and everything was back to normal. Ginger could not stop breathing, and Lanely could not stop starring at her bright, bulgy eyes that were down to the ground. Ginger caught reality and looked up. "What happened?" Ginger wondered. "A miracle. That is what happened, my dear. You went and saved some souls. They will now be reincarnated and will never be the same again. Their lives, (new lives I should say) will be transformed because of you. I knew you had a gift within you, Miss McFraiddee. Now I want you to think about your identity, and if you realize your own self. Before you do that, is there anything you'd like to ask me?" Lanely wanted to know. "Lanely . . . I saw my parents' gravestone. Old memories came all over again. Sometimes I forget to love, you know. Sometimes I lose hope. It gets hard, you know. Stressful too. I just want my heart to be opened. I'm so tired of everything. I want my parents back, but I know they'll never come back. What I fear the most is that if Todd Wyndelle is the one, will he be the one? Bailey obviously wasn't. I just want someone to open my heart all over again."

"So this is relationship issues, isn't it?"

"Not really. I just want a full heart, that's all. A positive one. You know: One that can fulfill my own spirit and my true self."

"Too bad not all people are like that. You can see that in our next and last part of the Enchantment. About you seeing their gravestone, it's part of the dead. I'm sorry you had to see that. We are pressed for time today. I'm seeing a customer today in a half hour, which gives us just enough time for the last part. (Your Grammy is probably getting worried too). For this last part, we will incorporate passion and proudness together. I feel they work together in many ways."

"Will I have to go back at that place?"

"No. You already saved enough souls for one day. More will be saved because of the light you started." Who would've thought a light could be shined in such a deadly place? A place of nothing. Nothing but harshness remains. It just goes to show you that one person can make that much of a difference. One person can make that change and change the world. Are you that one person? "Okay, okay, no worries: just we're out of time! Ginger, see those two potions over there?" Lanely pointed, "Grab the yellow and the blue one." She removed the potions from the shelf and placed them next to Lanely's cauldron. She mixed the two, adding another liquid to it from the bottle called "Herbal Scent." It smelled foul and of rotten vegetables at first. Soon enough, the aroma was of a crisp cinnamon with fresh-sprinkled olive on the top. Simply cashing. "Do you care for others, Ginger McFraiddee? Do you want them to know your accomplishments? Passion and proudness are ways of showing that. To have passion is to show that you care for another person. You must also care for yourself and have self-respect. Respect in yourself comes before respect in others or anything else in life. Passion and proudness (the two Ps I call it) only symbolizes that the evil spirits never have heard in their lives. They are good on the inside, but all of them have that one thing in common: they were hurt in some kind of way. They didn't have what we have, Miss McFraiddee. Foundation. Tranquility. When you leave this earth, you make sure you know your place before anyone else. You did something I never could do before, and that something is to actually speak to your own ancestors. Do you know how many of us wish we could do that? Where would we go after we die? What are we destined to do in the biased world we live in? Think about that for a minute. I know you're still young and only a girl. I thank you for doing this. You were the chosen one, Ginger. You have the power to communicate not only with your own ancestors, but also with spirits ! Your locket holds so much power to it; the material is unknown only to substance."

"Where'd it come from?"

"Your ancestors, Ginger. Didn't your Grandmother tell you that?"

"She said my great-great-great-grandfather, but I'm not sure."

"She was telling the truth. That locket is so rare, it could be worth tons." Ginger's eyes brightened when she heard that. "But who's gonna take care of it? Will your Pappy want it sold for a new house, a new car, better settlement? Or will your family trust you with it? They understand what it does and how it affects others. Like I say, that locket is important. There are only a few in this world. Oh, by the way, tell your grandfather to wash up and clean face before he comes. My scents and natural spices get harmed from outside smells, as known as BO . . ."

"I will, Lanely."

"Great. On to the Enchantment. Look inside the cauldron. You will visualize something deeper than before. Always remember, these Enchantments are performed to understand and expand the mind and reveal our heart of what is to come later on. So look, and just look for a few minutes. Sorry, Ginger, I know my constant talking holds us up, but this is very essential for someone like you. Look and blink once after a few seconds. I will tell you when to stop." Ginger felt timid at first, but after a moment, she leaned over and looked into the cauldron. The odor was everlasting, and the color was oh so beautiful, and worth seeing. She could see the yellow and the blue color creating more colors (red, green, pink, silver, black, etc.), and it made the shape of a heart. Ginger's heart. Then came the herbal scent Lanely sprinkled around, and crystal was created around the heart. Surrounding the heart was a pool of tan-colored sand-like substance. The heart began to glow, reaching up to Ginger's heart. Ginger blinked quickly, and the substance was gone. Only the glowing heart was shown. How could you only see a heart-shaped liquid like substance with nothing surrounding it in a bowl? The liquid, or whatever the stuff was, *should* fill the *entire* bowl! Ginger didn't understand that part. Within the heart, she saw her own self. Ginger looked so worried in that image and saw something greater than her fear: the feeling to be proud. The Ginger inside of the heart smiled, her hair waving in the midst of it. Through all the dark colors, she realized her passion to others was null and void. The two loser kids showed her that. She knew she could've been more concerned for them. She felt bad for them, especially when her boyfriend and his friends made them yell even worse. Or when she noticed the kid who was mentally ill that day. She remembers how Mr. Daniels didn't care for neither the child nor the mysterious teachers. What a selfish man. It was all coming back to her. She now understood from just those two memories that popped in her head and on the heart inside the cauldron. "RECOMPENSE! Take back everything that has been stolen! The world's system can no longer prevail. The believers are now taking over." As Lanely was talking, the heart started rising up, almost reaching Ginger's own heart. "Reach out! Love, passion, and proudness can set the world free, but they have to see. Recompense is to pay back and get whatever that was stolen. Your parents wanted this for you, Ginger. Their secret is apart of your own body. Now, the last question: Do you believe? Are you ready to overcome, and become the soul seeker of spirits? To save them from the wicked. Are you ready, Ginger McFraiddee?"

"I am ready, Lanely Tildon. I now realize my mind and the minds of others. I want to be an example. I am who I am. I'm not what the world say so, 'bout me. I am more than that. I am Ginger McFraiddee, and I am queen of the world!" Ginger wasn't saying that, but the Ginger within the heart that was risen said it. Both Gingers smiled and laughed, as a teardrop from Ginger fell on the heart. The heart was then absorbed into Ginger's own body, and the cauldron was empty. Ginger felt a sudden change within that, a change of happiness. She had become a young woman. "Enchantment complete. Congratulations, Ginger McFraiddee. You have now completed these Enchantments. You can visualize your mind to the impossible, see what souls can see, and be where they are now. Today, you can do what no others could do. You listened clearly, you weren't afraid, and now, you are ready to take on the earth. Today begins of what is to come. Today is a day of vengeance and recompense (vengeance, meaning 'to love justice')," Lanely explained. "Wow, I feel better and better every time we have these Enchantments. All I can say is . . . thank you. Thank you very much. I never knew so much could happen at such a time like this. I love you so much, Lanely. I don't have my parents around to tell me that or to even show me, but I do have you. So thank you. I never knew my own self, and so much potential I had until now." Lanely tries to teach Ginger something, when Ginger has taught Lanely something too. She taught Lanely to never give up and always have a kind and an open mind. "I thank you for that, Ginger. Really, I do. I love you with all of my heart." The two hugged tightly, each learning something from one another on this day. They hugged for maybe two minutes, and that's when Lanely turned on the lights. "Wow! That was only fifteen minutes. We made good timing today. I bet you're exhausted from all of this," Lanely joked, as they both chuckled, "Let's go get your Grammy so she won't be worried sick." Lanely gathered all of the empty vials and scents and tossed it all on the shelf. "Luckily, it won't break. I use special medicines to keep all of this stuff eternal. Let me find Marybeth real quick." With not another word, Lanely darted out the room, only making the sounds coming from the beads that covered the exit. Ginger had so much on her mind. She couldn't stop thinking of all the great things that just happened to her and the souls she possibly saved.

Marie and Grammy were sitting at a table with two wooden chairs near the register when Lanely glanced at them. "Style is always the best, especially when it comes to houseware and many types of furniture," Grammy said. "It is. Why settle for all of the fancy junk? That's why I buy antiques and collections of styles of fabric and clothing," Marie agreed. "Marybeth. I am happy to tell you that your granddaughter has been fully enchanted and can now perform great wonders," Lanely explained, grabbing a chair herself. "Well, that is wonderful! I'm so happy for her! Wait a minute; where is she?" Grammy wondered, searching and scanning the shop. "She is fine, my dear. What I wanted to tell you about is the Curse . . ." That's when Lanely's voice got really deep and cold-blooded. "Not the curse of all curses . . . ," Marie cried. "YES . . . That one . . . ," Lanely responded. "The curse? Lanely, I thought we agreed upon to never talk about that!" Grammy was puzzled by it. "Why didn't you tell Ginger? How could you not tell her that locket isn't powerful?" Lanely's voice was rising. "Because she was too young. She'd never understand, and I bet she still doesn't understand the truth!" Grammy emphasized on, her voice rising too. "How would you know! Do you not believe in her? You knew darn well about this a long time ago, and you just ignored it!"

"Don't blame it all entirely on me! Not to be rude, Miss Tildon, but that is completely obscure. I didn't want to tell her something that would scare her! She has enough going on right now!"

"Bullshit! What's important is important! You wonder why her life is so sad: you and Pappy and your son do not believe!"

"Believe in what? Some silly little ritual that is only correct according to you? Give me a break!"

"You both need to settle down! Mama, you know the curse is none of your business! You should not talk about it ever! Miss McFraiddee, you WILL have to tell Ginger McFraiddee about the curse," Marie resolved. "I already did! I just can't believe you didn't tell her," Lanely commented. "That's because I'm tired! Okay! I never wanted to mention it when her mother died, EVER do you hear me? My husband had to deal with it for so long! I don't want Ginger to know about something so treacherous. She's been through enough. I don't want her to be heartbroken by it again," Grammy was tearing up. "It's okay, Marybeth. Lanely Tildon already told your granddaughter about it. You will not need to worry ever again," Marie added, handing her a box of tissues, as she wiped her face and cleaned her nose with them. "If you say so," Grammy sobbed. "I know so, my dear," Lanely corrected her. "Then tell me why my daughter and stepson died? They believed in it too! You said the exact thing in that exact seat! I wasn't born yesterday, sweetheart!" Grammy debated. "Your granddaughter is different, however. She WILL become something. She has age on her side and talent. Not to dispute anything, but trust me: Good things will happen if you have wisdom."

"I'm sure they will . . . ," Grammy contradicted. "As long as she and you all are in good health. That's all that matters," Marie agreed. "Pappy's getting kind of ill."

"He will be fine. He's just going through a period of old age," Marie replied. "Listen, Lanely: Do not tell Ginger anymore about the curse. It's just too much right now at once," Grammy said. "If you want, Marybeth," Lanely answered. The ladies turned around and saw Ginger waiting next to the cash register. It seems as if she heard the entire conversation. "What's going on?" Ginger asked with her diary in her hands. She slowly walked to the table. "Were we really *that* loud?" Marie whispered. "I'm afraid so," Lanely answered. "Afraid of what? I heard about some curse. You all were talking about me, weren't you?" Ginger wondered. The three women were all in shame. "Ginga, I was telling you about the curse earlier today. It is no joke, either. Honey, I know you can withstand the power of it. You proved that when you were enchanted. Now it's time for your Grammy and Pappy and Uncle to handle it too. I know times are tough. They are for all of us. You all can do it. You all can handle the curse upon you. Like I said, don't take it as the curse that is defined today. Take it. Take it as a life lesson."

"If it's a life lesson, maybe it doesn't need to be called a curse," Ginger cried. "Maybe that's the point of this. See how I take a physical problem and make it heal mentally? It's all in your mind. Whoever came up with the curse is playing with our minds: getting inside our head. All I'm saying is to not trust it. Don't worry about anything."

"Okay," Grammy and Ginger said at the same time. "Very good," Marie said, getting up to help a customer at the cash register. Grammy and Lanely both stood up as them two and Ginger walked to the door. "You did a very great job today,

Ginger. You should be proud of yourself," Lanely cried. "I am. Thank you so much," Ginger smiled, as all three hugged each other. "Let's go, hun. Uncle has brunch waiting for us at home," Grammy laughed.

CHAPTER 22

Answers to the Real Truth

Ginger still didn't understand, nor could she comprehend Miss Tildon's voice. What was *her* purpose of life? What were her goals in the world that she wanted to accomplish? How did Lanely's daughter know more about the curse than her own mother? You'd think by now most questions would be answered. It seems like when you answer a question, it becomes the question of your own answer. Some weeks went by, and it was the middle of winter once Ginger got into cheerleading. She decided to try it out after all. Todd became the star player of the basketball team, same with most of his friends. This made the spotlight shine on Todd, not so much Ginger anymore. The cheerleading squad. It consisted of Ginger, Brianna, Stephanie, Hillary, Stacy, Amy, Melissa, Rachael, Jill, Shandi, and some other girls. Joel was also on the team, and he was the only guy on the team. Stephanie and Hillary were the captain and co-captain of the team, so he gives Hillary a very hard time. "Hillary, you'll never be a good cheerleader as me. You may be my love, but let's just face it, I'm still better than you," he emphasized, right before a home game began. The squad was on the side of the court, and the basketball team was on the court, practicing for the team to come. "Shut up, Joel. You're not better than her. You shouldn't even be on the team; a team for girls!" Stacy laughed, as they all laughed. "I still don't know how you fell for that Jason Kid. How could you like him over me? Seriously . . . ," he nagged. "She never liked you . . . ," Amy commented. "Plus I like Jason. He's soo cute!" Hillary cried out loud. He was on the court, shooting around. She blew him a kiss. He blew her one too. "Seems like a perfect couple to me!" Brianna said. "Now help us cheerlead, faggot!" Melissa told Joel, as he pouted when the girls laughed more. "Sluts . . . ," he replied. "I'll take that as a compliment," Stephanie answered (as if she wasn't already one). When the game was over, USMS won 42-36. Everyone cheered. Ginger went in the crowd with everyone else to find her boyfriend. What she couldn't believe was that Mandy was sitting in the stance with Vanessa and some other MMS girls with them. Ginger gasped. "Why are THEY here?"

"Calm down, Ginger. We won! That's all that matters," Todd told her, as they held hands. Ginger had on her cheerleading outfit with her basketball jacket on. She was holding pom-poms, and all cheerleaders had on miniskirts. The guys had orange-and-blue-colored basketball uniforms and red socks for good luck. "Great job, Todd," Ginger told him. "Thanks for cheerin' me on, babe!" he told her, as more loudness and cheers were made. Later that evening, Ginger goes home only to discover Pappy, Uncle, and Grammy, particularly Uncle, disappointed. "Where've you been?" Uncle asked. "The game I had to cheerlead today."

"And why are you wearin' that jacket? I told yer no more contact with that guy!" Pappy screamed. "So you'll let me go out with Bailey but not Todd?" Ginger cried. "I wasn't a fan of him either," Uncle said. "When will you realize that I'm growing up? I'm graduating in a few months! When will the curse not bother you? In fact, don't even believe in the curse!" This made the three adults think. "Pappy, why didn't you tell me about this? Why'd you wait!" Ginger yelled. "I didn't want yer to get hurt," he answered. "It can't hurt me. I believe in the good. When will you?" She then ran up the stairs and locked herself in her room. "The curse? How would she know about it? I thought it was a family secret never to be told to children," Uncle said. "It is. Marybeth, how'd she find out? Did you and that ole gypsy Tildon tell 'er?" Pappy asked. "Well, yes. We can't keep hiding it. You know that as much as I do. We have to let her grow up a little. It's already winter. She'll be graduating soon. She *needs* to *know* things! What's important is important," Grammy explained. "I guess your right on that aspect," Uncle agreed. "Your mutter is always right, hun," Grammy told him, as they all laughed. It is a shame to know Ginger has been hidden from a secret within her own family for years. It is a shame to know that no one could tell her, not even the people that supposedly "loved" her. She had to find out for herself. How couldn't Pappy open his eyes to see what has become of the lies? Why didn't Grammy anticipate this long ago? And where was

Uncle when Ginger needed him the most? Was he in the spirit world, trying to decipher the clues? Maybe he was lurking through the woods yonder valley. Whatever the matter was, he knew he could've been more supportive to someone he was close with and someone he loved dearly. She didn't come out of her room the rest of the day. Pappy and Uncle felt ashamed and hurt by it. They only want to help Ginger, not make her feel uncomfortable in the home. It's hard for them to take their current role to Ginger and to be a father she scarcely had. The first six years of her life will always be the most important years of her entire life. What will happen to her if she didn't have her grandparents?

School had to have been a heartbreaker the next day. Ginger's walking to the lunchroom when Bailey approaches her. "Hey, Ginger . . . ," he greeted. "Hi," she responded, passing him up, walking to the lunchroom still. Todd and his friends caught up with Ginger. "Sup," Todd told her. "Hey," she cried, giving him a hug. "We'll save y'all a seat. Later," Malcolm cried, leaving the two alone. Jeff and Billy approached Bailey, and the three went over to Ginger and Todd. "What do you guys want?" Todd asked. "I want mah girlfriend back, that's what! You can't just steal her like you did!" Bailey yelled. "Dude, get over it. She doesn't like you anymore," he replied. "Yes, she does! You think you're so cool when you're just a load of nothin'!" Bailey was mad. "Bailey, can I talk to you for a minute?" Ginger asked. "Um, sure . . . ," he cried. "What?" Todd asked. "One sec," she told him. That was Billy and Jeff's cue to leave. "Why do you want to go out with me again? Why'd you think I'd say yes, anyway?" Ginger immediately asked.

"Ginga, I want you. Look at'cha. That guy isn't right for ya! You've changed ever since he came into you." "You can't tell me who's right for me. After what you said to me, I can never forget. I can forgive but not forget. I'm sorry, Bailey."

"But what about us? I'm sorry about that day, all right! I was mad. I didn't know! Give me another chance, please!" Ginger sighed. "I'm sorry, Bailey. I can't do that. Todd has stolen my heart. He could be the one. I'm sorry. I really am. The truth is: I've found someone else. We can still be friends, though."

"I guess this is good-bye, then."

"As boyfriend and girlfriend, it's *official* closure." Bailey looked as if he was going to cry. The bell had rung. "Well, there's the bell! See ya, Bailey!" Ginger told him, running to Todd. Todd literally caught Ginger in his hands. "Wait, so what happened?" he asked. "I want you and only you. Bailey wanted us to get back together, but I said no. I just want you, Todd! Nobody else! My heart feels just right when you're around. Thank you so much for understanding." She then kissed his cheek. "No problem. You know I'd never try to harm you in any way. I could never let you fall. I only want you too. By the way, you're hot when you're cheerleading," Todd commented. "You're hot all over!" Ginger cried, feeling for his chest. "You seem high," he joked. "I'm *completely* over Bailey, that's why," Ginger told him. "Oh, okay. Come on, let's get some food," he offered. The two went inside the lunchroom, leaving Bailey where Ginger left him at. Bailey felt himself cry on the inside. Tears filled his heart. He just couldn't find the right words to say. Love can handle a man: but can a man handle love? What Bailey couldn't understand the most is why she actually said yes to Todd Wyndelle. He was nothin' but a full load of BS to Bailey. But it didn't matter, Ginger has made up her mind. Relationships don't work like that. He can't just come up to her begging her for grace or another opportunity. No one should ever do that. It just means he is the wrong man or is just seeking fame (which Bailey is trying to do within the school). Ginger finally realized it. She finally took the time to say, "What is right for me and who I need to be with." And she'll never have to look the other way again. Everyone was going to Main Street Friday night. All of the middle schoolers and some high schoolers were there, crowding the streets and roaming the walkway. Main Street was teeming with teenagers either on a bike or skateboard or with jackets (it wasn't a warm night, even in the winter). This, of course was a problem, causing tons of traffic. Ginger and Meredith were shivering, as they were surrounded by most of Todd's friends, and some other kids he knew. "Meredith, I'm sooo cold," Ginger muttered. "Me too. Why are we on Main Street in the winter anyway?" Meredith was puzzled herself. "Chillax. It's like fifty-five degrees right now. It's not that bad," Mack commented. "Uh, yah it is," Jenny overheard. "Girls can't handle the cold," Jason joked, as the guys laughed. Hillary approached her boyfriend and stood next to Ginger. "Oh shut up! You guys are wearing jackets . . . ," she commented. "Hillary, so are you," Meredith cried. "Meredith, I love your red hair," a guy told her. "Um, thanks?" she answered. Todd gave Ginger a hug to make her feel warmer. "Is that better?"

"Oh yes!" she replied. "Meredith, your hair is the best. Red with a mixture of brunette is just the best!" Hillary told Meredith. "Says the girl who changes hair colors every day. It's still hot, though," Rockstar Kid said. "Very funny," she said. "So when's your wedding with Joel?" a big, buff guy joked, as they all giggled. "Hey! Shut up! She's with me. She wouldn't marry that homo," Jason said, giving her a shoulder rub. Hillary couldn't help but to laugh. "At least it doesn't snow here that often," Jose mentioned, as they all sighed in relief. "USMS girls are hot!" another guy said. This just made the girls sigh or say "I know!"

"I'm the hottest, though," Stephanie called out. "No, me!" Jill added. "Me!" Melissa also commented. "I'm hotter than ALL of you, so shut up!" Amy said. "NO!" everyone answered, making Amy feel left out. The night was young and beautiful. Things changed when Mandy, Vanessa, and other MMS girls arrived. They couldn't believe their eyes. It wasn't that Ginger was there, it was something else. "What is this?" Mandy started. Everyone literally stopped talking just to stare at Mandy's posse. "I have one question: Why are all the MMS kids even here? We're all partying at Starbucks! You guys are lame!" Mandy continued. "Mandy, it's not MMS vs. USMS, all right. We can do whatever we want. Plus, the USMS kids are pretty cool," a girl commented on, as everyone agreed. "Wow! I told all of you about this. How could you just ditch us like that? Fine! Just remember one thing: I own Midway Middle School. If you try to come in between that, your ass WILL be sorry."

"Excuse me, Miss 'I'm so cool, I know everything.' You don't 'own' the school . . . ," another girl cried. "Uh, yah, she does. If you don't know what you're saying, don't say it!" one of Mandy's friends mentioned. A chunk of MMS kids came to where most of the USMS kids were. They all got back to talking and being normal teens. Ginger was talking to a group of girls with Todd by her side when Mandy, Vanessa, and the rest of their clique decided to join in on the conversation. "I didn't forget what you did, Ginger McFraiddee. I'm sooo freakin' tired of you stealing my spotlight. You think just because you have a boyfriend who's the coolest guy at your school means your queen of all the middle schools. Well, guess what, I AM. You need to know your place quick before I put it there, do you hear me!" Mandy screamed. "Oh, give it a rest, Mandy . . . ," Luna was annoyed. "Wow. You seriously have a problem, Mandy," Todd told her. "Shut up! No one was talking to you . . . ," Vanessa butted in. "No one was talking to you either!" Todd responded. "Remember this, Mandy: I'm still number one in volleyball. You may be popular everywhere else, and better than me at everything, but you're not better than me at volleyball," Ginger told her. Everybody 'oooed.' Mandy's friends gave her the middle finger. "Oh, now it's personal. We won that game. The stupid announcer was on YOUR side. But I didn't come here for that crap! I came here to get EVEN!"

"We are even. What have I ever done to you?"

"You stole my man!"

"I would never go out with a bitch like you!" Todd said. Everybody was yelling and screaming at that. "Mandy got burned!" Meredith yelled, high-fiving Ginger. Vanessa smacked Meredith in the face. Everyone's mouth dropped. She was bleeding in the nose. "That'll teach you not to laugh at Mandy Liverstone!" Vanessa yelled. Meredith fell to the floor in tears. "How could you do that to her?" Ginger yelled at Vanessa. Stephanie and her friends, Luna, Jill, Jenny, and some others girls helped Meredith up, cheering her up, and saying kind words like, "Meredith, are you okay? You'll feel better. Come on, let's get help. Vanessa's a whore."

"Thanks, I am a whore," Vanessa snarly answered. "You are! I never wanna see you again!" Meredith screamed, smacking her face. "Meredith, come on. Let's go somewhere so you'll feel better. I hope you're happy . . . ," Jenny cried. Practically all the girls and a few of the guys went with her. Ginger was about to go, when Mandy said, "We're still not done, Ginger! We have some unfinished business to take care of!" So Ginger stayed while the rest went. "You can't go with your best friend until we're all done . . . ," Vanessa added. "I'll handle it," Todd whispered to Ginger. Before she could speak, he immediately shouted to the posse, "Just shut up! No one likes you! Your freakin' sad, you know that! Leave Ginger alone, she did nothing to you. Vanessa, you're the biggest asshole I've ever seen. How could you hit Meredith like that? Meredith's like the nicest girl ever. It's impossible to make her mad. You did though. For the sake of everyone, just go home!" Mostly all the guys and some of the girls there on Main

Street agreed with him. "I don't care! They're lucky Summer isn't here. She ruined the game for us," Vanessa replied. "You go to USMS, stupid!"

"All right, that's it! Ginger, you, me, fight, right now! I'm sick of this bullshit! This'll settle it of who'll be the best girl in the eighth grade!" Mandy yelled. All the guys eruptly screamed: "Fight! Fight! Fight!"

"Just say no," Todd whispered. "No way! I've been waiting for this for a long time. I'll prove to her that I'm better once and for all!" Ginger whispered back. Todd had no choice but to step back. Same with Vanessa and the rest of Mandy's friends. Everyone made a circle between the two. "Two hot girls who rule at sports, which one will win?" a guy joked. Everyone then screamed, "Fight! fight! fight!" again. Mandy pimp-slapped Ginger on the cheek. "I'm number one, McFarty! You need to let me control everything, like it's always been!" She then pushed her to the ground. Ginger stood, and boy was she mad! She kept slapping Mandy, until Mandy couldn't take anymore. Mandy grabbed Ginger's arm and punched anywhere she could. Ginger dodged and started kicking. The girls kicked, scratched, yelled, and screamed. Mandy was cursing the entire time, Vanessa and their posse were cheering for Mandy, while the others just yelled. They were pumped up. Ginger then remembered the evil marks Mandy had said to her. She remembered the evil smirk and that evil laugh Mandy has. That's when Ginger punched her in the face three times in the row. Right in the nose! Mandy was on the ground. The biggest of the girls carried Mandy to a nearby store. She was unconscious.

Before Vanessa ran off, she told Ginger: "This isn't the last of it, Ginger McFraiddee!"

"Yah, it is, Vanessa Timmington!" Ginger yelled. Everyone yelled, cheering more for Ginger. Nobody but maybe a few MMS kids followed Mandy. They didn't care about her. "You're okay, right?" Todd asked her, grabbing her bruised up hand. "Yea, I'm fine. A few scratches here and there but nothing serious!" Ginger answered. "Cool. I gotta admit, you were hot out there. I knew you were tough."

"Aww, thank you so much." He kissed her bruised cheek, and the two went to find Meredith and the others. "Meredith, are you okay?" Ginger asked her later on when they were all back outside. "I'm fine. Look at you! What happened?"

"I got in a fight with Mandy, that's what."

"Oh! Thanks for covering me. I really appreciated it. You too, Todd. They told me what you said to Vanessa." "No problem, Meredith," Todd answered. "What are best friends for?" Ginger replied. The three smiled, and Todd gave Meredith a friendly hug. "Am I really the nicest girl at our school?" Meredith asked. "Yeah. You and Summer," Todd answered. "Oh, that deserves an extra hug!" Then they hugged some more. Ginger and Meredith then hugged for quite some time. Soon after, everyone was having a good time, and the best part was that neither Mandy nor Vanessa showed up after the fight. Ginger remembered Lanely's message back in school on Monday. It was to try and talk to the mysterious teachers, for they too knew who Lanely Tildon was. Ginger decided to stop by their room after school that day. They weren't in the classroom, so Ginger thought she'd check out some stuff inside the room. This classroom was totally weird! There were five skeletons that were hung up everywhere. She had to dodge three of them just to reach the front desk. The students' desks were facing the chalkboard (which was right behind Ginger). There was tons of wall posters, many about the human mind, therapy and its importance, lifestyle fitness with nutrition included, and the work of some psychologists from then to now. The front desk was piled with papers and packets and other files of work. Ginger glanced at the clock. Not a lot of time left. Wherever those teachers were, they'd best hurry up; Ginger needed to speak with them. The room she was in was airless, and it seemed like no space was available. She was beginning to become claustrophobic (even though no one was in the room but herself!). She waited ten more minutes, and nobody was in sight. 'Where else could they be?' That's when the lightbulb turned on in her head. The window! Ginger grasped for her backpack and darted to where the mysterious teachers were always at. On her way there, she was stopped by Coach Hector. Ginger hadn't seen him around that much. He seemed hidden after the volleyball season. It was like he had disappeared from immorality. "Hi, Coach Hector," she greeted him. "Hello, Ginger."

"Listen, you weren't lying after all. I'm sorry for not listening. The souls *are* evil. They're coming for us! Coming for ME! Oh gosh, I'm all of a sudden so scared!"

"I'm glad you believed. You won't have to worry anymore. The curse may be upon us, but listen to me carefully; it won't matter anymore. It is just a sign of the times. A nice woman named Lanely Tildon . . ." that's all Ginger needed to hear. "I know her! You know her too?"

"Indeed I do! I get most of my air fresheners from her!"

"Oh my gosh! What are the odds! What ARE the odds of that . . . Anyway, she told me about Reincarnation a year ago, and she told me about you. She said one day to tell you what I told you a few months ago. It is no joke, sorry to say. The world has to be cleanseth of all evil, to be good, so Reincarnation can happen, immorality will be transformed to spirits, the Spirit Transporter will become the source of all human life and the spirits. Everlasting life could occur if we can succeed. If not, evilness shall take over!"

"We?"

"The believers."

"So that's why I got enchanted."

"Yes, darling. You were chosen to be the believer. To lead the pack. I know tough times occurred throughout your life, but I believe it was to show you things you didn't think you had that you DO have. I'm glad you realized it. It is never too late to perform wonderful miracles within the grounds of the earth."

"Thank you, Coach Hector. By the way, what days do you see or talk to Lanely?"

"I call her on Sundays."

"Oh, okay. I'm not sure why she didn't say anything about this." Ginger sees her provisions and understands her values. The people in her life are here for one reason: to see her make a change for the better. She cannot be in bondage anymore. Can she figure out her own identity? What is her exact reason for being anywhere at anytime? You should ask yourself those two questions every day, wherever you go. It can answer if you're making a good decision, and maybe if you'll ever see a morning again. Ginger said good-bye to Coach Hector, and she went over to the window. There they were. The ladies were staring at the window: as if no one was around. "What are you looking at?" she asked them. The two ladies ignored her for a second, so Ginger asked them again. They then looked at her. The moment they did was the moment they saw the imagery of what was theirs all along. "Um, hello." The two ladies were shy all of a sudden. "So what are you looking at?" The two teachers saw the necklace on her neck and were immediately exasperated by the feeling of it. "Look for yourself," Mrs. Robbin said. Ginger slowly went up to the middle of the window. Mrs. Robbin and Mrs. Duffy looked at each other in confusion. Who was this girl? How'd she get that locket? Why did she want to look at the window so bad? "That locket . . . ," Mrs. Duffy muttered. "I'm sorry?" Ginger replied. "Nothing, never mind." Ginger turned back around, and the two ladies looked at the window. This is what she saw: Winds of dust filled the air. The school building was gone. In the window, she glanced up and saw two gravestones. It was her parents' gravestone. There she was in the picture. She was crying. It was dark in the scene, so she could barely see herself. A wind passed, and flowers appeared in the girl's hands. A tear from her fell on the dirt. The girl dug a hole in the ground and placed the flowers in the dirt.

Her own tears filled the flowers with water and enough soil to grow. The girl then smiled and looked above her. The background went from black to blue. It represented life, in the times of death. The girl then pointed to the three girls, and her finger shone. A yellow sun appeared behind the girl. Ginger actually heard birds chirping, animals singing, and sunshine mourning to heaven. She smiled brighter, and more darkness was ever seen. The scene blackened out, but another picture was approaching. This time, it was something familiar Ginger looked at: it was her dream. She saw a bunny walking through a meadow, and a brown-haired girl was running. The bunny reminded Ginger of Mr. Chippers. There were two adults toward the bunny and the girl. The four of them hugged, and then they all looked down. Down below, it led to a fire. Souls were rushing to it. But one soul was risen up, and it shone and sparked brighter than the fire. She tilted her head, and a locket was seen. It shone over the land, and the souls were going above the ground, and they were flying. They flew up upon the land, and they were going to a better place. That's all that was allowed to be seen in the window. The locket was the last thing seen, and it was in a peach background. It all went away, and the thing Ginger saw was the parking lot of the school. Ginger turned to her left and to her right. Mrs. Robbin and Mrs. Duffy were trying to meditate on what they had just seen. They didn't speak for five whole minutes. "What was that?" Ginger asked. They didn't answer for a few minutes. Finally, Mrs. Robbin answered, "I believe those girls were an image of you, Ginger."

"How do you know my name?"

"We know all the names of the children in the school," Mrs. Duffy said. "Why would it be an image of me? Why does all of this have to do with just me?" That's when Ginger's locket shone. The two teachers couldn't believe their eyes. It was the deliverance. Mrs. Robbin and Mrs. Duffy were silent. They didn't know what to say anymore. That locket already spoke the words itself. That's when the two knew: she had been an outsider herself. She wasn't part of the world. It's amazing how one person can be this inspiring to even ones that needed it. The teachers understood the works of Reincarnation, but what they didn't understand is how it happened and who can really show the world something so powerful. The teachers learned something today. They now know that they're not the only ones that are in the world but not of it. Now they won't have to feel bad if they are condemned by others, and it was all because of one girl, of the X generation. "Wow! Those were some fascinating scenes!" Ginger cried. "Yes, they were. Well, we must be going home now. Nice seeing you, Ginger," Mrs. Duffy said, the two walking off. "Wait! I have to tell you something!"

"Sure! Follow us to our classroom," Mrs. Robbin offered. So she did. "Do you know a woman named Lanely Tildon?"

"The woman who owns the antique shop?" Mrs. Duffy wondered.

"Yes, her!"

"Oh yes, we know her! Her antiques are one of the best and the oldest!" Mrs. Robbin answered, "What about her?"

"You believe in Reincarnation, don't you?"

"I don't actually prefer it over my religion, but I do try to understand and study it. Reincarnation is important to the world these days. Immorality will determine our own fate. The souls' story is not finished. Some stories have not even begun yet. It will be their turn to tell a story to the world and clean the world forever. Nobody knows about Reincarnation that much, but I can tell you this: The entire world will know about it soon," Mrs. Duffy said. They arrived to the psychology room when Ginger stood around. "Oh gosh, I forgot to turn on the air-conditioner! Sorry about that," Mrs. Robbin cried, turning it on. "She's a good friend of ours actually. Really, really hard to understand sometimes. She's probably the only one that accepts us as people in this neighborhood. The staff definitely doesn't . . . ," Mrs. Duffy commented. "She's also very nice. Miss Tildon is a wonder to this earth. She taught me things in a way I never could have thought of. I'm glad I decided to accept her too. I'm also glad I met Mrs. Duffy. Great minds think alike, ya know: but similar minds ARE alike," Mrs. Robbin added. "I agree 100 percent. Wow. You all aren't even as bad as everyone thinks you are. No offense," Ginger said. "Oh, none taken! I'm just glad that there is a student out there who really does care about us. I thought no one would ever talk to us. People only look at us in the weird aspect, when they can't see the aspect of themselves," Mrs. Duffy cried. "You're absolutely right. If people took the time to actually ask of those who seek it most, then they'd reap of their own possessions," Ginger confirmed, the two ladies agreeing with her. Ginger was shocked herself. She didn't think out of all people, these two women would even bother to speak with her. The rumors and the false stories about them had been wrong. The mysterious window was basically an insight of the spirit world and what the Spirit Transporter has to say to humans. Mrs. Robbin and Mrs. Duffy were just normal people to Ginger. If she could get in a little conversation with both of them, then anyone could if they had the willing to be nice and to want to try and understand the ladies better. People are people. They come in every shape, size, color, gender, etc. What they also come with is emotions. You cannot change the emotion of a person based on how you feel about them. If someone doesn't like you for a certain dispute, it can affect you in many ways. Some just brush it off their feet and keep going. Others absorb it like a sponge and can never be resilient to squeeze the liquid out of the sponge. Words are powerful. They affect people every single day. Words can make a wrestler cry or can make a day perfect. Sometimes, we get so caught up in the stress and the condemnation and the sides of weakness, hurt, doubt, and shame we forget what's really important. The mirror shatters when we think we're ugly, when we're really an example from above. It's hard to actually see those things because it cannot pass by the brain in time for us to realize the unforgotten when a situation is brought up. Never give up. Don't let your emotions, evil souls, or anything get in the way of your happiness. You were made to do something great. There will always be a block in the way of the road. Take another road, and that block will still be there. You can overcome it, though. Knowing you instead of your emotions can help you succeed through life. Imagine you, and the happiness you want, and the peace you've always wanted out. Words are emotions themselves. "Well, Miss McFraiddee, it has been a pleasure meeting you, and we hope you have a wonderful school year," Mrs. Robbin cried. "Oh, thank you! I'm glad I had the privilege to talk to you both about such an off-topic subject. I wish you both well with Lanely Tildon, and who knows, maybe we'll run into each other there sometimes!" Ginger was excited. "I agree. I'm glad we found someone so special, with tons of talent, someone who really DOES care," Mrs. Duffy said. "Me too. And remember, you didn't find me; I found you!" Ginger joked, as the three laughed. "Well, it's best we be gettin' home now," Mrs. Robbin said, gathering her bags and walking to the door, Mrs. Duffy and Ginger following. "Oops! Forgot my backpack!" Ginger said, grabbing it next to the front desk. "She does have something special. The locket is the key to all," Mrs. Robbin whispered to Mrs. Duffy. "It does. Without it, I don't think it could ever reverse the universal curse . . . ," Mrs. Duffy started. "The what?" Ginger gasped in fear. The two teachers looked at each other in agony. They didn't know what to say. "Oh, never mind, Ginger! Ignore that part! Well, we must be going! Turn off the lights and the air-conditioning vent when you leave!" Mrs. Duffy managed to say, as the two raced out of the room, leaving winds of breeze behind. Ginger was puzzled. What were those two talking about . . . ? The answer appeared when a jacket on the chair behind where the front desk was fell to the ground. Ginger picked it up, but on the chair, she saw a heart-shaped locket that was golden. This locket appeared to have a green glow to it. Lanely Tildon had been right after all: there was more than one of her own kind in the universe.

EPILOGUE

Months passed, and it was all the same in the land. It did change on a spring May morning when Todd was going to his locker one day after school. Inside, he found a folded-up letter with a heart on it. He laughed to himself; it had to have been Ginger. He was correct! Inside the letter was a note. It read, "Todd, meet me at the park where Pharaoh's Creek is. I wanna show you something special. Go there today at 5:15 p.m. See you there. Love you!—Ginger M." Todd folded the note and darted to his house. He didn't even realize his locker had been open still. He arrived home and slammed the door shut. He had never been this excited in his life ever before: Probably because she wanted to be alone at the park. Just them two. No one else. It's been a few months since they actually had quality time together. With basketball for Todd and track for Ginger with cheerleading from the winter, they rarely had any alone time (except on the weekends). On the weekends, both their friends wanted to hang out with each other, so that gave them no time either. School would be over in a month, so things started to wind down a little. The only thing Todd was glad about was graduation and to soon start high school. He was also glad about summer approaching and the vacation packages that came with it. It's been almost half a year since Ginger and Todd have been going out. He just can't seem to find another girl that's right for him. Ginger *is* right for him. Ever since that day they met near the trashcan, to their first date, to the fun they had at the carnival, Todd Wyndelle's life has been greatly influenced, and he too has been changed. No other girl could handle Todd. Not even Stephanie, and she could handle any guy there is (when it comes to personality). Todd, however, sees something greater within his girlfriend. Just that little something, that gave that extra "umph" to it. What was that something? Could the opportunity happen? He decided to wait for all of it at 5:15 p.m. Ginger had the door closed. She was writing a few poems in her diary she would share with Todd at Pharaoh's Creek. Nothing's really changed in Ginger McFraiddee's life. Lanely was the same; she never will change. Ginger hasn't gotten enchanted since that day back then. Lanely and Ginger only talk about modern-day things now. Sometimes she would bring up Reincarnation, but it wasn't often. Why was that? Ginger hasn't found the guts to tell her about discovering the locket on the chair in the mysterious teachers. She will someday—just not today—or the day after that, or the day after that. Speaking of those two women, they didn't say another word to Ginger. She'd ask about the locket, but the ladies ignored it. In fact, nowadays, they didn't talk to *ANYONE*. They used to talk to some students, but they won't talk to them either. These women were very antisocial. The family, of course, will never change. Pappy still has that attitude toward Todd, but now Ginger is starting to ignore it. Today would be a different day however. Ginger gave Todd a "love letter" and told him to meet at a specific place at 5:15 p.m. While she was writing down poetry and jotting down some notes, she couldn't stop thinking about where they would be going today. She wanted Todd to view a glimpse of her own world. She wanted him to get away from reality and just imagine a place where her childhood and her stories became dreams for the future. She and him had been going out for a long time. They were only getting closer and closer together as a couple. By now, Ginger knew Todd was more than ready for what she was going to show him today at 5:15 p.m. "Grammy, I'm going to the swing set today," Ginger said, running down the stairs. She was wearing a palm yellow skirt with a cute white blouse with a golden jacket. To match it up, she had two yellow ribbons in her hair with her hair in two long braids. "Oh my gosh! You look like a barbarian's wife in the Middle Ages!" Grammy was shocked. "Thanks . . . I guess."

"It's very beautiful. Did you say the swing set?" Grammy was shocked. "Yes." "You haven't been there in ages!"

"It's part of my childhood. I just hope the swing is still there. I want to show a very special person something so amazing, it will blow away his brain socket." Ginger gazed at the clock. "Oh no! It's 5:00 p.m. already! I better go! Bye, Grammy!"

"Bye, Ginger. Oh, Ginger, wait! You almost forgot this," Grammy smiled, handing her diary to her. "Thanks, Grammy!

Love ya, bye!" Ginger said, dashing out the door and closing it. "Have fun, sweetheart!" Grammy called. Ginger ran for the park. The sun was at a perfect spot, the birds were singing, the clouds making a scorching fade of blue in the sky. The roses were dancing to the everlasting sound of peace. Nature was having a good day today. Just what Ginger wanted. So she arrived at the park, where the green grass faded into blue. Children were flying kites, families were at picnics, tag and racing and sport games were going on. The benches were reserved for the men who played dominoes there, and the benches next to a birdhouse was where bird feeders and bird watchers came to sit at. Ginger ran over to Pharaoh's Creek. It was a bridge, and there she stood, waiting for her prince. Water streamed down the creek. The sounds of laughter and simplicity made Ginger want to rejoice. The sky was literally yellowish-blue from the clouds. Light was everywhere, shadowing a figure that was approaching Ginger. It was him. Ginger looked the other way, pretending not to see him. She scanned around, wondering what would happen next. Then he tapped her shoulder. And she turned around. Todd saw a sadness that creeped upon her face. A sadness that couldn't be taken lightly. Todd was wearing his cap on backward, with shorts, and a plain shirt. His hair had grown a little, and Ginger liked that the most. "Hi," Ginger said. "Hey," he greeted. The two of them. Alone. At a waterfall. She stared at him for a minute. He had tons of grease on his face. "You smell really good," Ginger cried. "Thanks." Silence for a minute. Ginger had to think for a second. "So . . . what did you want to show me?" Pause. Air of breath. "I want to show you a place so special, it's a place I showed no other person. Not my grandma, not my grandpa, not my uncle, not Bailey. A person who has done so much for me he deserves to see it."

"Aww. You're the cutest," he smiled at her, pinching her cheeks tightly. "Thanks, you too. Now come on! The place isn't too far from here!"

"Want me to walk you there?"

"Of course." They held hands, and Ginger led the way. They talked, and after a couple of minutes, they passed some trees and arrived in some sort of field. It looked like a wheat field, but it was an assortment of grass. Everywhere around was this field of greenish-blue grass. In the distance was a tall tree, with ivy and white leaves on it. The tree was tall, and it was the only tall tree around. Attached to the tree was an old wooden swing set, which was not yet broken. Winds were howling their guts out. Ginger looked around, and she brightened up. "What is this place?" Todd asked. "It's my childhood. Come on. Let's get on the swing set. I used to when I was a little girl." Ginger pranced around and jumped on the swing. "Come on, Todd. Push me!"

"Sure," he said, starting to push her on the swing. "Aren't you afraid it'll fall off?"

"Not at all!" They laughed and talked all during that time. "My daddy hooked up this swing with rope to the tree. It's been here ever since. All my life, I would come here to just relax, see the beautiful sunset, play with nature, ya know. Shelby and I were unstoppable out here. We'd play for hours! If it rained, hailed, stormed, or flooded, he and I were always here. This is my life. Right where you're standing is the exact same spot my father and mother once stood. I'll never forget the day Shelby ran away. In the rain. I sat here for five hours that next day. I could only wonder what happened to him. Thanks for coming, Todd. You don't know how much I appreciate it. I will never forget this moment ever in my life."

"Anytime, Ginger," Todd cried. He had stopped pushing her. She was sitting on the swing set, looking at him. "You know I'd do anything for you. Anything." He kissed her forehead. "Come on! This used to be my favorite spot! It still is!" Ginger and Todd sat beneath the tree, on the tall and thick branch. Some leaves surrounded the tree (even if it was spring). "This is awesome, Ginger. I know you've been through a lot and everything, and I just want to tell you that I've never met someone in my life who's brave, strong, and wonderful as you. When I see you, I see that part of me wants to hug and kiss you, and the other part that wants me to just talk with you. The dates we went on were so awesome and so cool. I just wanna talk with you more. I could never look at and see the inside of me and my mind. You made me realize that there's more to just a girl than looks. There's personality, strength, and of course, romance. Whenever our eyes meet, I know you were the one."

"I'm glad you feel that way. Here. I want to read you a few poems I've written. It's basically about as and how I really feel. Okay. Here's how it goes:

Saved

The summer and the winter; the nights and the days.

Beyond the roasted glaze of dark, a man lays.

A psalm I've yet sung, under the bird's wing.

He knows my troubles, he feels my pain,

He suffers with me, through sun and rain.

Love gave me an opportunity; he gave me grace.

He saved me, from a falling vase.

He knew my heart, he saw my light, and vanished

the shooting dart.

Mystic colors is my sweet integrity;

I want variety: he's given me no pity.

Todd Wyndelle is who I have; I won't let him go,

he grasped my soul and let it flow.

"What'd ya think?" she asked. "Wow. That was so good. I knew you felt that way about me, but, man, that was deep." Ginger reached closer for him. "Todd, you saved me. From my own self. I was hurt when Bailey broke up with me. I only want to be with someone who cares about me. One last poem. It's shorter.

Choice

Searching the nothing, seeing the locket.

Wanting to know if he is the one.

My flesh says yes, my body says no:

Todd found my way, and treated me greatly.

No one can replace him, or ever steal him away.

Shyness can no longer hold me,

I am free, for it is the world,

I wish to see.

She closed her diary.

"My choice is yes. You will never leave my heart. You're always number one to me. Yeah, Mandy tried to come in, and steal me away from you, but I didn't let her. I just . . . I just wanna follow my path with you. When you're in pain, I'm in pain too. Seeing your laugh and smile blows me away. You've been sad. I'm here, baby. I'm here." Ginger lay on top of him, and for a few minutes, the two enjoyed the view of the sun, and the sound of the animals and felines making music. "Todd."

"Yeah?" She leaned on him, grabbing for his hands as they embraced. "I think you're the one for me. Nobody else but you. When I say you saved me, I truly mean it. From my grandfather being mean, you were there to help me. I can't get away from you. I *gotta* be with you. Todd, you fully complete me and my diary. You were the person missing all of this time. I'm glad I found you." Ginger's crystal blue eyes were lightning up. "I never would've made it without you. I need you. You put that smile on my face every single day. I may be in love."

"I know I'm the one for you. You're perfect for me. Your happiness completes me." They smiled at each other and laughed.

Life would never again be complicated for the two of them. Things calmed down, and after an hour of playing around the tree and talking, it was almost time to go. They were sitting and were both hugging each other. "Are you serious when you say I'm everything to you?" Todd asked Ginger. "You are, Todd. It's hard to not have what you had. I now have what I had, which I thought I didn't have. I could be in love all over again." Ginger felt for his hair. "Same here. It's like I know I'm in love. It's just I don't know if I'm in love now."

"Oh my gosh, we both do feel the same!" Ginger was glad for that. "Promise me that you won't get hurt or anything. I hate to see you down or tortured. And don't be intimidated by me. I don't wanna see you fall. I hope you feel the same for me."

"I do. Trust me, I do. I feel that I want to be with you forever. Maybe it's just me."

"Naah, I feel it too. I'm glad we came here today. I love you, Ginger."

"I love you too, Todd. With ALL my heart." The two stood, Todd helping Ginger up to her feet, and they kissed mouth-to-mouth. Their tongues were moving while they were kissing, also referred to as lip action. They hugged and kissed for some time, then they sat for some more beneath the large tree. "Today was amazing. You've given me so much. I just want to thank you. For everything," Ginger said. "No problem, Ginger. You're the best!" They laughed and played some more in the fields and on the swing. Love happens for a reason. We just have to search for ours. It'll come to us. We just have to show passion and proudness. They both were starting to walk off holding hands when they heard a sound. It was a familiar sound to Ginger, yet a new one to Todd. Ginger and Todd saw a creature in the shadow. It was running toward them. Ginger laughed. So did Todd. Lanely Tildon had been wrong about a certain death. The creature came to the two, and Ginger and Todd could not be sad at that moment. The familiar sound was the sound of a barking dog.

Edwards Brothers,Inc!
Thorofare, NJ 08086
19 January, 2011
BA2011019